MONETARY POLICY AND CREDIT CONTROL

MONETARY POLICY AND CREDIT CONTROL

THE UK EXPERIENCE

DAVID GOWLAND

CROOM HELM LONDON

© 1978 David Gowland
Croom Helm Ltd, 2–10 St John's Road, London SW11

British Library Cataloguing in Publication Data

Gowland, David
   Monetary policy and credit control.
   1. Monetary policy – Great Britain – History –
   20th century 2. Great Britain – Economic
   policy – 1945–
   I. Title
   332.4'941   HG939.5

ISBN 0–85664–327–0

Printed in Great Britain by offset lithography by
Billing & Sons Ltd, Guildford, London and Worcester

CONTENTS

TO MY PARENTS

INTRODUCTION

This book has two purposes. The first is to provide an analysis of recent British monetary policy. The second is to consider what techniques of monetary control are most appropriate in the context of the UK in the late 1970s and 1980s. It is thus a study in the theory and practice of monetary policy (and in particular techniques of control) rather than (yet another) book on monetary theory.

I would argue that conclusions about monetary policy making have to be specific to their context. This may seem trite yet there is a tendency to 'export' conclusions based on the US to all other economies without consideration of their applicability. This is surprising given that no one would deny that all disputes in monetary economics are empirical, even if agreement cannot be reached on a suitable test. Furthermore, lip service is paid to the notion of the importance of the structure of the economy and financial institutions in providing the background to monetary policy. However, this never translates itself into discussions of, say, the relevance of the distinctive nature of the UK bond market to monetary policy. Equally, however, it is not very desirable to abandon rigorous analysis of monetary policy on the grounds that institutions explain everything. There is and must be a great deal to be learned from both the theoretical and comparative analysis of monetary systems.

As a contribution towards the analysis of monetary policy, this work has at its core the analysis of *competition and credit control*: the authorities' bold experiment in monetary policy in 1971–3. This hastily abandoned experiment provides us with the unique experience of an economy operating under three different régimes of monetary management within four years. Furthermore in contrast to the pragmatic traditions of European Central banking the 'new approach' to *competition and credit control* was based on a coherent, intellectual analysis of what was wrong with the previous system, of direct controls on bank lending. Thus it is possible to analyse the official rationale of the scheme and see how far the problems which led to its abandonment were predictable, or if the authorities were unlucky. The replacement scheme, the new 'new approach' can then be examined to shed further light on the problem of what is an optimal control scheme for the UK as an example of the general problem of how control mechanisms should be chosen so as to facilitate the best possible integration of monetary policy into overall economic management in pursuit of the chimerical goal of rational decision making.

During the period, however, it is the case that monetary policy was of crucial importance in overall economic management, and was increasingly recognised to be so. Thus it is hoped that this book is a contribution towards answering the crucial questions of economic management in this period: was the rapid monetary expansion in 1972–3 the cause of the acceleration of UK inflation? Were the large Public Sector Borrowing Requirements in the period 1974–6 harmful or beneficial in their impact on the economy?

It is hoped that light will also be shed on the issue of how well official policy was made during this period, since it is possible that official policy was the best possible response to the situation with the information then available, but disastrous with the benefits of hindsight or vice versa.

This book then is intended for any serious student of monetary policy or recent British economic history. The rather heterogeneous nature of this group is responsible for the structure of the book. In particular the appendices to Chapters 1 and 5 are provided for readers without a specialist knowledge of monetary theory and try to explain simply what is involved in the theoretical issues referrred to in the text — 'Monetarism', 'Keynesianism', Tobin's model, the flow-of-funds approach, the monetary theory of the balance of payments etc. — and how they relate to policy. Those familiar with these issues or not interested can happily skip these appendices. The Appendices to Chapters 2 and 9 are similarly dispensable, being technical analyses of the overseas impact on the money supply and two-tier exchange rates respectively.

Part of Chapter 7 is more formally restated in the appendix to the Chapter. The text includes two chronological sections (Chapters 3 and Chapter 8, Sections (iii)–(vi) which can be read independently of the rest of the book for those interested only in the historical aspects of the study, or, ignored entirely by those prepared to take the author's analysis on trust.

Chapter 1, after sketching the earthquake-like impact of the 'new approach' on the British economy, considers what monetary policy is, and why it is regarded as a complex abstruse subject. To study monetary policy is to study proximate targets and indicators so as to be able to measure the effects of official actions and the behaviour of financial intermediaries. In turn this enables one to make judgements about the appropriate use of official instruments which influence financial flows (with their final objective being to bring about the optimal constellation of output, employment and inflation).

The old approach is then analysed. This policy, the offspring of the first new monetarism of the late 1940s, consisted of a 'credit' policy based on direct controls on bank lending and hire purchase. It was abandoned after 20 years because of the authorities' belief that it was no longer effective, but, in fact counter-productive. The reasons for and validity of this view are considered. The chapter concludes by studying the inter-relationship between political and economic forces in determining the prevailing monetary orthodoxy.

Chapter 2 discusses the 'new approach'. This was a classic answer to the problem of ineffective direct controls: the market mechanism of allocation by price. However, the authorities chose to use the 'supply side' mechanism of control. This is analysed and it is shown how the scheme depended on the interest elasticity of credit. All aggregates would be controlled by the impact of higher/lower interest rates on bank lending to the private sector. Thus the new approach was supported by those seeking to control money, DCE, credit, liquidity and nothing respectively. The impact of the 'new approach' on the gilt-edged market, banks, discount-houses, day to day operations and competition is also considered.

Chapter 3 analyses the history of the 'new approach'. It is divided into four sections — the 'era of easy credit' (May 1971 – June 1972), the 'reappraisal' (June – October 1972), 'willing the end but fearing the means' (October 1972–July 1973) and 'competition and credit control in action' (July–December 1973). By December 1973, it was clear to all that it was necessary to control money and credit for both economic and political reasons. Yet the authorities were unwilling to let interest rates rise, as implied by their scheme, so they abandoned it as a failure.

Chapter 4 analyses the reasons for their 'failure'. This was because of the authorities' unwillingness to accept its implications, reinforced by lack of control over (or adequate statistics on the behaviour of) banks. The 'merry-go-round' and CD tax loophole are analysed in their context to assess how large was 'genuine', as distinct from apparent, monetary growth. Having considered various measures of this true growth, and various official alibis, it is argued that the true growth must have been excessive on any view of the workings of the financial system — Keynesian, monetarist, Tobinesque or whatever.

Chapter 5 considers the effects of this excess monetary growth on the residential and commercial property markets, on the stock market, on inflationary psychology, on the exchange rate and on inflation. The author concludes that the monetary policy pursued would have caused the inflation rate to rise to 20 per cent even without the Arab–Israeli War and the 1974 miners' strike. These, however, may have been responsible for the realised peak of 27 per cent.

Chapter 6 considers the problems in combining prudential oversight of banks with efficiency. The failings of UK policy are considered, for example, the secondary banking crash of 1974, and alternatives considered. More recent UK government policy is then analysed.

Chapter 7 considers all the available techniques of monetary control both theoretically and drawing on US, German and French experience. The conclusion is that any system of control can work given sufficient ruthlessness and political will on the part of the authorities.

Chapter 8 analyses the new 'new approach' — an amalgam of a much more aggressive policy in the gilt-edged market and ceilings on bank liabilities. The theoretical rationale and apparent success of the scheme are analysed. It is concluded that the success of the scheme is unlikely to be permanent as it depends on a favourable conjunction of short-term phenomena.

The book concludes by considering what are the appropriate policy targets and instruments for the UK in the context of the late 1970s and 1980s in the light of a number of conjunctural and theoretical considerations.

1 THE 'OLD APPROACH'

(i) Introduction

In May 1971 the Bank of England announced a 'new approach' to competition and credit control[1] which was proclaimed as a major advance towards more effective monetary management and a more efficient banking system. Within three years, this had been tacitly abandoned and the competition and credit control régime was almost universally condemned as a total failure. The reason is not hard to find, as Table 1.1 shows: the rate of growth of the money supply had exploded. Even non-monetarist commentators agreed that this was not unconnected with the equally rapid acceleration in inflation. Furthermore, the period had seen an equally rapid rise in the amount of bank credit extended, especially to property companies. This was widely held to be responsible for the rapid rise in commercial property prices in 1972–3 and, indirectly, for the 100 per cent rise in house prices in the period. In this book, the origins, intellectual rationale, history and consequences of this 'new approach' are analysed to see both how justified the criticisms of the régime are, and what lessons can be drawn for the appropriate conduct of monetary policy in the UK and to a lesser extent in other modern economies with highly sophisticated financial systems. Consideration is also given to the 'new "new Approach" ' which replaced it in 1973 and to experience in other countries.

Monetary policy tends to be regarded as a rather abstruse and technical subject for various reasons. First, it tends to be swathed in the mystique of generations of central bankers and commentators. Political sociologists[2] may be over-cynical in suggesting that this is a deliberate ploy to minimise rational analysis of central bank decisions and so maximise central bank autonomy and power. Nevertheless, the mystique has served to reduce academic analysis and journalistic criticism of central banks, at least in Europe, for the last century.

Next, many students of monetary economics, both formal academic students and informal ones in the City and official worlds, regard it as a form of conjuring trick when millions of pounds are created apparently out of thin air or are equally mysteriously destroyed. So long as a financial institution's assets and liabilities change by the same amount, thus observing the accounting identities, this can happen.[3]

The final and most fundamental reason for the obscurity surrounding

Table 1.1: Growth in M_3 (Annual Averages) Per Cent p.a.

1965	1966	1967	1968	1969	1970	1971	1972	1973
6.4	6.9	5.6	9.5	4.6	6.1	11.2	21.8	27.1

monetary policy is that, on the one hand, the authorities manipulate a limited range of tools — discount rates, reserve ratios, open market operations and similar technical manipulations, and seek to influence output, incomes, employment, prices and the balance of payments on the other. Yet analysis tends to focus on intermediate links in the chain, and on what is and is not an appropriate transmission mechanism, that is, how the instruments affect the ultimate targets. Ultimate cause and effect often become lost in a mire of technical detail on the one hand and intermediate analysis on the other.

The analysis of monetary policy is thus essentially the study of proximate targets and indicators to try to measure the effect of policy decisions (and the decisions of financial intermediaries) on the ultimate targets (the price level, output, etc.). Unfortunately, the distinction between a proximate target and an indicator is frequently not made and when it is it tends to be the subject of bitter controversy.[4] A proximate target is a variable through which a change of causality runs from instrument to final target. This relationship should not be affected by an attempt to use it as a policy tool. 'Monetarists' and 'Keynesians',[5] for example, would both agree that, without official intervention, a whole range of aggregates such as currency, the 'money supply', the 'volume of credit' would indicate developments in the economy reasonably accurately. However, they disagree about which are proximate targets; in particular if you try to use these relationships for control of the economy, will they break down? The analogy with a thermometer is often cited. A thermometer is a very good measure of the temperature of a room (i.e. it is a good indicator) but plunging a thermometer into a bucket of ice will not reduce the temperature of the room. 'Keynesians' argue that the money supply is an indicator but deny the monetarist proposition that it is a proximate target. The issue is complicated at an operational level by having to define theoretical concepts such as the 'money supply', which become either metaphysical constructs (rather like Plato's ideal objects) or statistical artefacts. Monetary policy is, then, the appropriate use of official instruments so as to influence financial flows with the aim of ensuring an optimal constellation of output, employment and inflation. The monetarist would argue that one flow, the money supply, was of paramount importance. The Tobinesque analyst would argue that all flows mattered. An extreme Keynesian directly constrained real expenditure – e.g. denying credit to private individuals may restrict expenditure on consumer durables. Any monetary policy must implicitly, if not explicitly, depend on a theory of how and which financial flows influence the economy. The appendix to this chapter sets out the various economic theories of how such flows influence the economy. The appendix to Chapter 7 considers the way in which various instruments influence the aggregates concerned, and the interrelationships between them.

(ii) History of the 'Old Approach'

Contrary to the view presented in the Press at the time, the 'new approach' was neither the result of the conversion of the Bank to monetarism nor the result of 'Selsdon man' applying his nostrum to monetary policy. Rather it represented an attempt to apply the lessons of history so as to produce a scheme of monetary control which was both operationally feasible and as immune to criticism as possible. Thus to understand the 'new approach' we must start by analysing the history of the 'old approach' to see what the authorities thought they should and could do.

The relevant starting point of this history is in the late 1940s, when informed commentators on both sides of the Atlantic gave an ever-increasing role to monetary and financial policy in their analysis of economic developments – the first 'new monetarism'. Criticism focused on Dalton's cheap money policy and, in the US, on the 'Fed-Treasury Accord'. Both these policies consisted of (largely successful) attempts to peg interest rates at an artificially low level by unlimited support operations. One likely consequence of such operations was massive monetary expansion (since the authorities were, in effect, committed to carrying out expansionary open market operations irrespective of their monetary effects). In any case they meant that the whole of the public-sector debt was a very liquid asset (irrespective of its notional maturity structure) since holders knew they could always sell at a price equivalent to that then prevailing. For these reasons, it was argued that this policy was inflationary and a prime cause of the then unprecedented 'great inflation'.

In 1951, these criticisms were heeded – in the US the 'Accord' was ended and in the UK Bank Rate was raised for the first time since 1932 (except for a quickly reversed increase on the outbreak of war). This was part of the incoming Conservative government's policy of 'setting the people free' by replacing rationing and other direct controls by a less *dirigiste* system of demand management. The raising of Bank Rate was of both symbolic (of a new active financial policy) and practical significance (by raising interest rates) in its effects. It was quickly followed on 29 January 1952 (a full chronology appears on pp. 177–96) by the imposition of hire purchase controls, which introduced a minimum deposit and maximum repayment period on instalment buying.[6] This was symptomatic of financial policy for the next twenty years (monetary policy is an inappropriate term). It combined direct controls on credit, by either HP regulations or restraining bank advances, with variable interest rates. With a half exception in 1957, interest rates were normally raised for overseas rather than domestic reasons – the idea being to induce a capital inflow by the higher interest rate; this policy was theoretically justified by Mundell[7] and has been analysed by Hutton,[8] whose results cast doubt on its effectiveness. It was thus a 'credit policy' rather than a 'monetary policy', though it obviously had effects on the money supply through the downward operation of the 'credit multiplier'.

In 1955, this policy was put to its first serious test, when the authorities pursued a bizarre combination of an easy fiscal policy (notably by cutting income tax by 6*d* in April) and a tight credit policy (directives to banks to restrict lending and HP controls) designed to offset the effects of the easy fiscal policy. As one commentator put it, 'having only recently rediscovered monetary policy, the Bank of England and Treasury officials overestimated the extent to which this could cancel out the effects of a budget hand-out'.[9] Nevertheless, the cynic could not fail to observe the juxtaposition of the tax cuts (19 April) and the general election (26 May). In any case, the official policy led to massive overheating of the economy and so in the autumn the authorities were forced to reverse their April budget, no doubt taking comfort in their newly tripled majority in the House of Commons. For whatever reason the policy had, and was seen to have, failed and irrespective of the authorities' reasons the effect was to damage the image of 'the resources of a flexible monetary policy' (to quote Butler's Budget speech in April 1955).

This distaste for and dislike of 'monetary policy' (really credit policy) was reinforced by the unpopularity of the 1956–8 credit squeeze, especially in business circles. This led the authorities to set up the 'Committee on the Workings of the Monetary System', whose report[10] (known after its Chairman as the Radcliffe Report) appeared in 1959.

This and the events described above led to much less emphasis being placed on monetary policy for nearly ten years — despite the presence of a self-avowed monetarist (Mr Thorneycroft) at the Exchequer for part of the period. The Radcliffe Report took a generally 'Tobinesque' approach to monetary policy stressing a very chimerical concept called 'liquidity'. In so far as this was defined it was a weighted average of all assets in the economy with weights declining as assets became less liquid. However, this aggregate should in turn be multiplied by a variable representing market sentiment.[11] This and the consequent stress on portfolio movements is very 'Tobinesque'. The means of control advocated were interest rates and — *so long as capital markets remained imperfect* — direct controls on bank lending and hire purchase. The authorities could exploit the imperfections so as to have small but significant impacts on the economy. More important, they would be fast-acting, whereas fiscal policy was rather ponderous. Special deposits were also recommended. These (introduced in 1961) were deposits lodged — at Treasury Bill rate — with the Bank of England by the banks and calculated as a percentage of eligible liabilities. Although bearing some superficial similarity to a variable reserve ratio, they were intended to speed up the movement of assets and/or to restrict 'liquidity' rather than to operate as a reserve ratio scheme. This objective was in fact ruled out in the report.[12]

In the 1960s, the authorities reverted to the pre-Radcliffe policy of direct control over credit. Hire purchase finance companies were asked to exercise restraint in December 1964 and the familiar controls on repayment periods and minimum deposits were actively used in 1965 as the government slithered towards the deflationary policy stance, ultimately reached in the July 1966 measures. There was a new development in the control over bank credit — explicit ceilings were imposed rather than guidance or moral coercion. Nevertheless, it was very much the mixture as before, even after the adoption of a DCE target in 1968 and a gesture towards monetarism with the IMF 'Letter of Intent'.[13] Thus the late 1960s saw a battery of 'ceilings', 'requests' and similar restrictions placed on bank lending. In 1971, this policy was abandoned because the authorities believed it could no longer work, if it had ever worked, and was replaced by the 'new approach' to competition and credit control. The authorities had become 'increasingly unhappy about the effects of operating monetary policy in this way over a prolonged period of time', as the Governor of the Bank of England expressed it in May 1971.[14] The reasons for this volte-face will be examined.

(iii) The Effects and Effectiveness of the 'Old Approach'

There were several reasons why the authorities dropped the 'old approach'. One was the classic free market argument that any system of rationing or direct control leads to a misallocation of resources and encourages inefficiency. Like the Governor,

> I do not need to labour the ill effects. It is obvious that physical rationing of this kind can lead to a serious misallocation of resources, both in the economy and in the financial system and that inhibiting competition between banks can do much damage to the vigour and vitality of the entire banking system.[14]

Hence the 'competition' of competition and credit control. More important than this theoretical consideration was the 'credit control' — the authorities, rightly or wrongly, believed that the old approach was ineffective, in fact more than ineffective, in that it prevented the optimal use of other instruments.

This, in terms of control methodology, represented an abandonment of control by rationing and reflected the emergence in the financial sphere of the textbook argument against rationing — 'black markets'. This was described as the problem of 'squeezing the balloon', that is any attempt to squeeze it merely pushed air into a different part of the balloon, as new financial markets and mechanisms arose to replace those which were controlled. There was the successive growth of 'parallel markets' which duplicated banking transactions outside the controls. These included money brokers, the inter-corporate loan market and various near banks and banks in the secondary, tertiary and fringe banking areas. Some of the controls attempted to allocate funds as well as control the total flow and these led to a special problem — that assets could be reshuffled so as to meet the authorities' requirements without any economic effect. (The 'privileged' sector of lending was to comprise the public sector, exporters and loans for shipbuilding, 'non-privileged' (or 'restricted') the personal sector. Industrial borrowing was sometimes privileged, sometimes not.) The stylised example in Table 1.2 shows how this might work.

The authorities order the bank to cut non-privileged lending to 20 (in reality they restricted its growth, but the point of the example remains). The bank exchanges 30 of non-privileged lending for 30 of the other financial institution's privileged lending. The result is shown in Table 1.3. All economically relevant magnitudes are unchanged — total of borrowing by the privileged sector (90), of borrowing by the

Table 1.2

	Bank		Uncontrolled Financial Intermediary	
	Assets	Liabilities	Assets	Liabilities
Privileged lending	50		40	
Non-privileged lending	50		10	
	100	100	50	50

Table 1.3

	Bank		Uncontrolled Financial Intermediary	
	Assets	Liabilities	Assets	Liabilities
Privileged lending	80		10	
Non-privileged lending	20		40	
	100	100	50	50

non-privileged sector (60), of bank liabilities (100) and of the other financial institution's liability (50). Yet the form of the control is satisfied. The result could — and probably did — happen as a result of normal market response rather than collusion as the bank seeks alternative assets and the displaced lenders alternative sources of funds. The insurance companies, for example, found property companies an ever more attractive home for funds and the banks increased their holdings of government securities.

It should be stressed that there was nothing illegal in any evasive techniques. Indeed one might argue that duty to clients and shareholders demanded such action.

Evasive actions were also known as 'disintermediation' as a bank ceased to act as an intermediary between borrower and lender. Strictly 'parallel market' normally implies that a new intermediary has replaced the original one and 'disintermediation' that the transaction now occurs without a middleman. However, the terms tended to be used interchangeably.

Thus the terms 'parallel market' and 'disintermediation' were also used to cover the inter-corporate money market and the general use of trade credit whereby companies lent money to each other so as to evade the controls. Furthermore — and this worried the authorities still more — as new institutions continually sprang up to perform the functions of controlled ones the area of controls, and the number of institutions covered, had to grow continually. This problem was perhaps exaggerated by the authorities, but a desire to control the whole balloon (to use their metaphor) nevertheless grew as the experience of operating controls became more and more frustrating.

This experience, of course, is a classic example of how black markets develop when non-price rationing is used without adequate powers of enforcement. Equally, the attempts to allocate credit between sectors **was, or seemed to be, as ineffective as simple microeconomic theory would suggest. The authorities had very clear ideas about who should get credit and who should not (exporters being the most favoured and property** companies and consumers vying for the least favoured position). However, the general evasion slurred these distinctions. An exporter who obtained credit could, and often did, also extend credit to retailers in other parts of the company's operations. Who could say whether the borrowing which was nominally to finance exports was in fact used to extend additional credit to retailers who in turn, of course, might extend additional credit to their customers, i.e. consumers. Thus the selective credit control had been evaded. This example is relatively simple — what if Company A obtained a bank loan, and extended credit to company B who lent via the inter-corporate money market to company C who extended credit to a retailer. . . ? The possible ramifications are endless and lead to the other weakness of the system — the authorities were no longer able to monitor the size or distribution of credit. Thus being unable to control something whose size you didn't know was the unenviable position of the authorities in the late 1960s. Hence the search for an alternative, which led to 'competition and credit control'.

Whether the authorities were in fact so hamstrung is a moot point. The impact of hire purchase controls has been analysed by Allard,[15] who found that they had a significant if small impact on spending. His work also confirmed the 'front-loaded' effect of the policy. His results included (by *a priori* reasoning confirmed by econometric results):

(a) the long-run effect of HP controls is zero;

(b) changing the maximum period of repayment has no effect; all effects are from varying the minimum deposit;

(c) the effect of lowering the minimum deposit on cars from 40 to

20 per cent is to increase expenditure on new cars by £30m in the first quarter. However, consumers' cash flow increases by a further £30m and it is reasonable to assume most of this is spent. Hence the effect on consumers' expenditure is about £50m.

The only serious study of the impact of inter-corporate flows on monetary policy is by Brechling and Lipsey [16] who found that in the 1950s about 60 per cent of the quantity impact of squeezes was offset by movements in trade credit.

If one believes that the evasive devices were both more widely used and better developed in the sixties, as common sense would suggest, then indeed the controls were close to useless. Nevertheless, the huge explosion in credit after the removal of controls in 1971 led many observers to conclude that they *must* have been effective.[17] This, of course, begs the question of whether the credit explosion in the period when competition and credit control was operational was a genuine phenomenon or not, and whether it was inflationary. Several views are possible:

(1) that controls worked (and their removal was inflationary);

(2) controls 'worked' (but their removal had only minor effects, especially on the commercial property market);

(3) controls never worked (and the apparent expansion reflected in the growth of bank lending (see Appendix C) merely reflected the re-emergence in the official statistics of 'black market' transactions);

(4) controls were initially effective (but became less so over time and were virtually totally ineffective by 1971).

The important point here is that the authorities believed either (3) or (4) when they dropped the controls. The underlying issue is considered below.

(iv) The Politics of Monetary Control

In both the 1940s and 1960s there seems to be some connection between political swings to the right and a greater emphasis in the media and by politicians on monetary policy in both the UK and the US. This is to some extent logical in the 1940s when monetary policy was being considered as an alternative to price controls and rationing. Thus the end of the 'Accord' in the US was one of a number of related measures forced on President Truman by sweeping Republican gains in the mid-term elections of 1950 (and to Senator Taft's triumphant re-election). In the 1960s this relationship continued, although why fiscal and interest rate policy were regarded as 'left wing' is not clear. The Republican administration headed by President Nixon was responsible for a re-emphasis on monetary policy. It is idle to speculate on whether the upsurge in the popularity of monetarism owes more to Friedman or to political developments, but both were important.

In the UK right-wing economic commentators similarly plugged the importance of monetary policy in the 1940s.[18] In the UK there was also some interrelationship between 'monetary policy' and 'setting the people free'; the campaign slogan of the Conservative Party in the 1951 election. Ironically the credit controls that were the centrepiece of Butler's swing to economic liberalism were seen as a victim of a similar policy under Heath, the era of the famous 'Selsdon man'. It is clear that the 'new approach' was not conceived as an offspring of Selsdon man as the planning had started before the Conservative victory and in any case the initiative came from officials, not politicians. However, the connection between market mechanisms in industrial policy (the lame duck era) and in monetary policy no doubt helped to win the support of Ministers for the 'new approach'.

It is always difficult to assess the impact of ideology and party politics on monetary policy but it should never be forgotten when assessing events.

APPENDIX: Monetary Theory: a Summary

The text — and the media — frequently refer to 'Keynesian' and 'monetarist' positions and, therefore, a summary of the distinctions between them is presented here for the non-specialist reader. Like most disputes, this one includes many caricatures and straw men and most economists, certainly most specialising in the field, take intermediate positions.

The pure monetarist position comprises two propositions:

(1) a 1 per cent increase in the money stock is both sufficient and necessary for a 1 per cent increase in the price level (or in nominal income);

(2) the only way open to the authorities to regulate the economy is by monetary policy. Tax changes or increased government spending are ineffectual except in so far as they have monetary effects.

A. The Quantity Theory

The monetarist position is derived from the 'Quantity Theory of Money':[1] $MV = TP$ where

    the number of transactions = T;
    the average money value of each transaction = P;
    the medium of exchange used in each transaction = M;
    the average number of times it is used, its velocity = V.

By a process often concealed in textbooks by something close to sleight of hand, T is replaced by the level of final output (Q) and P by the price level (usually still P), this holds constant, *inter alia*, the number of financial and intermediate transactions relative to financial ones and the structure of payments (that is how often people are paid and how goods are packaged and traded). V is assumed constant and M renamed money, so

    $M = KPQ$

In this case, a change in M is both necessary and sufficient for a change in PQ, nominal GDP. Alternatively one may assume Q constant or exogenously determined, in which case an increase in M leads to an increase in P.

    The arguments by anti-monetarists tend to concentrate within the framework on the stability of 'V'; in particular they argue that it is a function of the rate of interest. One may also question whether a unique medium of exchange exists and whether it determines or is determined by PQ.

B. The IS/LM Model[2]

Besides studying the velocity of circulation, there are other and probably more fruitful ways of examining the arguments between monetarists and non-monetarists. One is within the famous IS/LM framework, originally devised by Hicks.[3]

    This starts with the simple Keynesian model in which the equilibrium condition is that: planned savings (S) = investment (I).

    Usually one assumes savings rise with income (the Keynesian would also allow for some effect of credit policy and perhaps of interest rates) and investment is exogenous.

        $S = aY$

and $I = \bar{I}$

so $$Y = \frac{\bar{I}}{a}$$

One then incorporates fiscal policy in the form of government spending on goods and services 'G', which has the same effect on Y as changes in $\bar{I}$, so

$$Y = \frac{G + \bar{I}}{a}$$

Y can be either nominal or real income or the issue fudged by assuming constant prices.

Now, however, the model is expanded by assuming that investment depends on the rate of interest (r). One can expand the model to incorporate the Tobin/Fleming 'valuation ratio' by making the interest rate the inverse of the price of a representative composite asset:[4]

$$I = b - cr$$

Now

$$Y = \frac{G + b - cr}{a}$$

Thus there is an indeterminate relationship between Y and r, which is known as the IS curve when plotted on a graph with 'r' and 'Y' on the axes, as in Figure 1.1.

This is the goods market equilibrium condition. To complete the model and solve for 'r' and 'Y' the money market equilibrium is added.

A demand-for-money equation in which the demand for money (M^D) rises with the level of income (Y) and falls with the rate of interest (r)

$$M^D = k - lr + mY$$

One can derive the relationships between M and r in various ways; the most general argues that r represents the opportunity of holding money while the services derived from holding money rise with Y; these are services which include both the number of transactions performed and the ability to buy when one likes without first having to encash assets.[5]

The equilibrium condition is that money supply (M^s) is equal to money demand

$$M^s = M^D$$

Finally it is assumed that the money supply is controlled by the authorities, and variations in it represent changes in monetary policy.

$$M^s = \overline{M}$$

From these relationships one derives the LM curve:

$$Y = \frac{\overline{M} + 1r - k}{m}$$

One can then plot the two curves to determine Y and r, as in Figure 1.1. Expansionary fiscal policy moves the IS curve to the right (when $\overline{M}$ is increased), as in Figures 1.2(a) and 1.2(b), and as can be seen Y increases in both cases.

However, if the interest elasticity of the demand for money (e) = 0, then monetary policy is effective, whereas fiscal policy is not, as in 3(a) and 3(b), as

$$Y = \frac{\overline{M} - k}{m}$$

irrespective of the position of IS curve. Fiscal policy merely changes r.

However, if 1 = infinity (the 'liquidity trap') or the interest elasticity of investment (c) = 0, then monetary policy is ineffective. In the first case a horizontal LM curve cannot be shifted by monetary policy. In the second

$$Y = \frac{G + b}{a}$$

and monetary policy changes only the rate of interest. Table 1.4 summarises these results.

Thus the monetarist argues that the interest elasticity of the demand for money (1) equals 0, or can be treated as if it did. The extreme anti-monetarist argues that it equals infinity, or that the demand for money relationship is unstable.

Not surprisingly, empirical work produces a moderate answer — the interest elasticity of the demand for money (1) is equal to neither 0 nor ∞, but rather to a small value between 0.1 and 0.5.[5] Thus monetary policy is powerful but not exclusively so.

C. The Tobin Model[6]

The IS/LM curve model depended upon the substitutability of interest-bearing assets for money (i.e. its interest elasticity) and of the substitutability of new real capital for bonds (i.e. the interest elasticity of the demand for investment). This is generalised in the 'Tobin' model. Here there are n assets lying along a spectrum of liquidity: e.g. currency,

Table 1.4

Interest Elasticity of Demand for Money	Interest Elasticity of Demand for Investment	Monetary Policy	Fiscal Policy
0	0	Must be used in conjunction with each other	
0	Normal Value	Effective	Ineffective
0	∞	Effective	Ineffective
Normal Value	0	Ineffective	Effective
Normal Value	Normal Value	Effective	Effective
Normal Value	∞	Effective	Ineffective
∞	0	Ineffective	Effective
∞	Normal Value	Ineffective	Effective
∞	∞	Ineffective	Ineffective

Figure 1.1: The Determination of Y and r

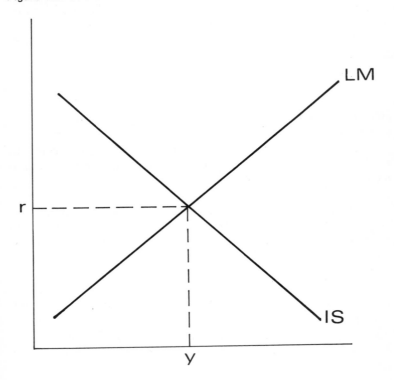

Figure 1.2 (a): Expansionary Fiscal Policy

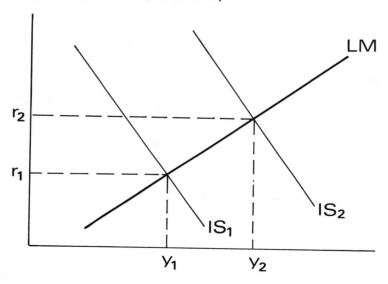

Figure 1.2 (b): Expansionary Monetary Policy

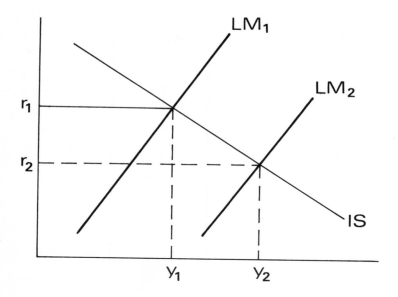

Figure 1.3: The Monetarist Case

(a) Fiscal Policy

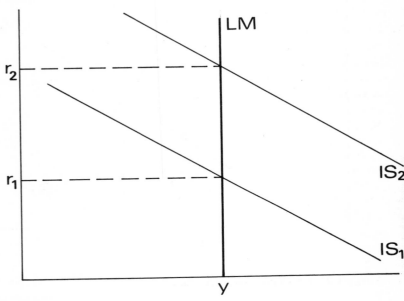

(b) Monetary Policy

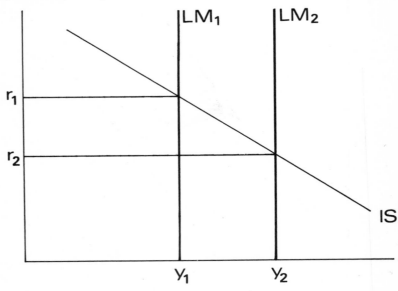

bank deposits, building society deposits, bonds, equities, factories, land, washing machines, each with a rate of return in terms of money or services derived from it.

The 'Tobinesque' approach to an increase in, say, the quantity of currency is that it leads to a switch to the next most liquid asset (its closest substitute) which drives down the rate of return on this asset, thus inducing a switch to the next etc., except that bond rates affect factories, so that the result will be to raise investment and/or the price of capital goods. Similarly, when land is reached land prices rise and finally the effect on washing machines is to raise their price or output. In this way monetary policy will affect prices and output, but only slowly and via an indirect route. In particular, observation of the bond rate and the dividend yield will be necessary and sufficient for monetary policy, rather than observation of a monetary aggregate.

The monetarists argue that there will be direct substitution between money and real assets. Money is an asset which is (more or less) equally substitutable for all other assets (and is defined as assets L_2 to $Ln - x$ where the elasticity of substitution is high up to and including $Ln - x$ but low between $Ln - x$ and $Ln - x + 1$). Thus a change in money will have a quick and direct effect on price and/or output.

Again the dispute is empirical and econometric work has produced a moderate, if not conclusive, answer. There is some direct substitution but more of the effects are Tobinesque.[7]

D. The Flow-of-Funds Approach

This approach to the monetarist-Keynesian controversy makes both positions seem rather untenable, theoretically extreme, propositions.[8]

As can be seen in Chapters 2 and 7, a change in the money supply involves a change in bank liabilities (deposits) and therefore necessarily a change in bank assets. Accordingly, after substitution one can write:

ΔM = Public Sector Borrowing Requirement + increase in bank lending to the private sector $\pm$ overseas adjustment $-$ increase in private-sector lending to the government.

The monetarist position argues that it does not matter which of the four 'right-hand side' supply side counterparts accompanies a change in the money supply $-$ a rather extreme proposition.

The Keynesian, on the other hand, argues that it does not matter how the PSBR is financed (he would argue that it does matter how it is composed, using Musgrave's 'fiscal leverage', for example).[9] A change in the PSBR can be financed by money creation, private saving or by a deterioration in the balance of payments, and it is ludicrous to argue that the effect of changing the PSBR is independent of its means of finance:

PSBR = change in bank lending to the government + change in private sector holdings of currency + change in private sector lending to the government + change in overseas lending to the government.

One may consider the following possible expansionary actions:

(a) increase in budget deficit (PSBR) of £100m financed by money creation, which can also be described as an increase in the money supply of £100m caused by a higher budget deficit;

(b) increase in budget deficit of £100m financed by private saving (normally accompanied by an increase in interest rates);

(c) an increase in the money supply of £100m caused by an increase in credit extended to the private sector by banks.

All parties would agree that all of (a), (b) and (c) would tend to raise prices and output. However, the extreme Keynesian would rank (a) and (b) as equal in their effects and (c) as a poor third. A more moderate Keynesian, accepting that raising interest rates tends to reduce private investment, would rank (a), (b), (c).

The monetarist would rank them (a) and (c) equal first with (b) a very poor third (or strictly without any effect at all). Thus one may regard the monetarist/Keynesian dispute in terms of the relative ranking of these expansionary actions. It is very hard not to conclude that (a) is the most expansionary of all. Thus the dispute at a practical level concerns the question of whether a bond-financed budget deficit or a money supply increase accompanied/caused by an increase in bank lending is the more expansionary.

E. Some Empirical Work: Two Further Models

Friedman endeavoured to prove that 'monetarism' was right by showing that 'money multipliers' were more stable than 'Keynesian' ones.[10] (Hahn has convincingly argued that both relationships are essential to any model.[11]) He estimated income as a distributed lag of past values of money and autonomous expenditure (the 'G + I' of the simple Keynesian model):

$$Y_t = f [M_{t-i}]$$
$$Y_t = f [A_{t-i}]$$

After a very long debate the main conclusion seems to be that neither model is very well specified, in particular the autonomous expenditure (A) concept of a Keynesian model is very woolly in reality, at least within a small model. For this reason most Keynesian models are very large — e.g. the 854 equations of the UK Treasury model.

The 'St. Louis' model is a similar but even simpler concept. Nominal GDP is estimated as a function of past values of the Budget deficit and money.[12] However, the statistical validity of this work has been successfully challenged.[13]

F. Causality and Endogenity: Further Empirical Work

Much of the monetarist/Keynesian debate has ranged over the direction of causality between money and income, or more technically whether it is endogenous to the system.[14] One solution to this is to try to find an exogenous variable which determines money, e.g. the money base or the three variables of Cagan's work (see Chapter 7).[15]

Another solution is to use statistical tests of causality to try to settle the question — for example, Box-Jenkins analysis or the 'Granger-Sims' test.[16] Unfortunately such work has so far yielded inconclusive results. The reason for this is almost certainly that both relationships are true — that is, income causes money *and* money causes income. Furthermore, some part of the relationship is simultaneous, which is not easy to incorporate into some of these techniques. One final problem is that such techniques are not yet as well refined as one would like. In particular, basically similar techniques produce contrary results.

G. Some Concluding Thoughts — the Defects of Monetarism

It will be clear by now that the author is neither a monetarist nor a Keynesian, and thinks 'money matters a great deal' in determining economic events, but is not everything. The defects of simplistic Keynesian systems of thought have been well rehearsed in the media in, at least, the Anglo-American world in recent years, so it seems reasonable to try to redress the balance by considering the defects of monetarism.

The first problem with monetarism is that it involves defining the money supply. This may seem a trivial problem but is in fact a very serious one. Money is used by monetarist authors such as Milton Friedman as a theoretical concept which may or may not exist in the real world. Certainly it does not correspond to any easily measurable definition. Like beauty, money lies in the eye of the beholder — that is, the definition must depend on how people regard an asset rather than upon the nature of the asset itself. Thus some individuals might regard a building society deposit as being 'money', while some other individuals might regard bank notes as not being 'money' in the technical economic sense. Thus it is not surprising that there are so many alternative definitions of the money supply available — for example M_1, M_3 and sterling M_3 as defined by the Bank of England, the US M_1 and M_2 as used by the IMF (see Appendix B). The answer of the monetarists to such criticism is to say that the definition of money should be determined by econometric work, or as Friedman puts it, 'money is whatever does the work of money'. This is fairly satisfactory for academic purposes even though it ignores the problem that the definition may change from year to year or even month by month. For policy making purposes, however, the problem of definition is a much more serious one. The problem naturally becomes even more important as the degree of sophistication of the financial system increases and there is an ever-increasing range of liquid assets available. Thus it is not surprising that monetarist results are much easier to establish for the USA than for the UK.

Monetarists lay great stress on statistical relationships, especially between various definitions of the money supply and movements in prices and incomes. Nevertheless such statistical results can only establish an association, not a causal relationship (see section F). Equally strong relationships can be established between, say, the number of storks in Lapland and the Swedish birth rate or, as a recent correspondent to *The Times* pointed out, 'between inflation and the incidence of dysentry in Scotland'. Even when there is obviously some relationship between two variables it is not clear which causes the other. If one event precedes another it does not mean that it has caused the subsequent event. For example, purchases of wedding rings precede marriages but it would be foolish to conclude that the act of purchasing a wedding ring causes a wedding. Yet this is the sort of deduction that has been made by monetarists.

The more sophisticated monetarists accept this criticism and seek to establish some behavioural explanation to justify their theory. This is the so-called 'portfolio balance' approach to monetary policy. The argument is that if one imagines two individuals, one of whom has a million pounds in cash and the other who has a million pounds invested in a family business, the assets of the first are far more liquid than those of the second. Thus the first individual is very likely to try to convert some of his surplus cash into other assets or to spend some of it. In doing this he will tend to increase the price of both goods and existing financial and real assets, thus setting off the inflationary pressures attributed to the increase in the money supply. Obviously there is a good deal of sense in this argument. Large cash holdings do tend to burn a hole in the pockets of either fund managers or private individuals. However, in the real world the gradations between different assets are minute and to attribute significantly different behaviour to, say, the holder of a Treasury Bill and a bank deposit may be mistaken, (hence the case for the Tobin model; see section C). This is particularly important if the authorities seek to control the money supply. In an economy without government intervention the size of the money supply might be a very good indicator of the degree of liquidity of the private sector. If the authorities try to control the money supply then it will be an inferior indicator. If they seek to control it by artificial means, such as ceilings, then it may turn out to be a very bad indicator.

Writing over two hundred years ago, the philosopher Hume defended the monetarist position by comparing the money supply to an underground spring. Whatever you do, it was bound to emerge to the surface somewhere or other. This is true but ignores the fact that it may matter crucially where and when it rises to the surface. Similarly, with monetarism, the transmission mechanism by which it affects income and prices may be crucially important. In particular, an increase in the money supply represents an increase in the liabilities of the banking sector. This increase may take the form of increased lending to private individuals, to property companies, or to industrial and commercial companies. Alternatively it may be increased lending to the public sector either in the form of Treasury Bills or gilt-edged securities (see section D). The list of possible bank assets is almost infinite, yet monetarism says that it does not matter which of them increases, the effect will be the same.

None of the above points means that money does not matter, merely that the precise rate of growth of the money supply should not be the 'be all and end all' of government economic policy. To assume that money is everything would be as big a mistake as to assume that the money supply does not matter at all.

Notes

1. See *Competition and Credit Control* (Bank of England, 1971). The system is discussed and/or described in *Monetary Policy in the U.K.* (OECD, 1976); M. Artis and M. Lewis, 'The Demand-for-Money: stable or unstable?' *Banker* (March 1974); E. W. Davis and K. A. Yeomans, 'Competition and Credit Control: the Rubicon and beyond', *Lloyds Bank Review* (March 1973); G. Pepper and G. E. Wood, 'Too much money?' *Hobart Paper*, 68, IEA, as well as the sources in Chapter 2.

2. E.g. J. F. Chant and K. Acheson, 'The Mythology of Central Banking', *Canadian Journal of Economics* (1972).

3. This phenomenon certainly creates the greatest 'mental block' in the minds of students when teaching monetary economics. The flow-of-funds approach which depends on this is described in the appendix to this chapter.

4. See that classic of invective debate: N. Kaldor, 'The New Monetarism', *Lloyds Bank Review* (July 1970); M. Friedman, 'The New Monetarism: Comment', and Kaldor's reply: 'The New Monetarism: Reply', which both appeared in the October 1970 issue.

5. See the Appendix; for a simple discussion of the difference see also C. A. E. Goodhart, 'The Importance of Money', *Bank of England Quarterly Bulletin*, Vol. 10, No. 2 (June 1970).

6. From 1952, control over 'hire purchase' (instalment credit) was achieved by a legal minimum down payment (deposit) and maximum repayment period. From 1956, hiring, chiefly of importance for TV rental, was controlled by a parallel measure specifying a minimum number of weeks rental to be paid in advance. The controls were completely lifted only between July 1954 and February 1955, October 1958 and April 1960 and from July 1971 to December 1973.

The range of goods covered varied but was normally restricted to consumer durables. The main exception was in 1956–8 when industrial machinery was also included. The minimum deposit and maximum repayment period varied from good to good, but normally the restrictions on cars were tightened.

The power to enforce these regulations depended solely on the Enabling Power (Renewal) Act which was passed annually. This power would disappear as a result of the Consumer Credit Act 1974, which implemented the recommendations of the Crowther Report 1971. The relevant sections would not take effect until the licensing provisions of the act came into force. This was originally scheduled for April 1977 but for various reasons has been delayed.

7. R. Mundell, *International Economics* (New York, Macmillan, 1968).

8. J. P. Hutton, 'A Model of Short-term Capital Movements, the Foreign Exchange Market and Official Intervention in the U.K. 1963–70', *Review of Economic Studies* (February 1977).

9. The best description of the bizarre events of 1955 can be found in S. Brittan, *The Treasury under the Tories 1951–64* (Secker and Warburg and Penguin, 1964), from which the quotation is taken.

10. *Committee on the Workings of the Monetary System – Report*, Cmnd. 827 (HMSO, 1959).

11. The report offers no guidance on how to measure 'liquidity'. This is the author's attempt to express the concept in a (conceptually, at least) quantifiable fashion.

12. E.g. paragraph 508.

13. There were two letters of interest, 23 November 1967 and 22 May 1969. Both appear in *Hansard* but are reprinted in, and more accessible in, J. E. Wadsworth (ed.), *Banks and the Monetary System in the UK, 1959–71* (Methuen, 1973). Most authors refer only to the second one but the first also contains

various articles analysing the impact of ceilings. Other studies are R. Alford, 'Indicators of Direct Controls on the U.K. Capital Market 1961–9', in M. H. Peston and B. Corry (eds.), *Essays in Honour of Lord Robbins* (Weidenfeld and Nicolson, 1972) and various articles in H. G. Johnson (ed.), *Readings in British Monetary Economics* (Oxford University Press, 1972); H. G. Johnson and W. Day (eds.), *Issues in Monetary Economics* (Oxford University Press, 1974).

14. *Competition and Credit Control*, ibid.; 'Key Issues in Monetary and Credit Policy: text of an address by the Governor to the International Banking Conference in Munich on 25th May 1971', hereafter 'Key Issues'.

15. R. Allard, 'The Impact of Hire Purchase Restrictions', Government Economic Service, Occasional Paper 7.

16. F. P. R. Brechling and R. J. Lipsey, 'Trade Credit and Monetary Policy' in H. G. Johnson, *Readings*.

17. E.g. the Deputy Governor in *Bank of England Quarterly Bulletin*, Vol. 13, No. 2 (June 1973), p. 193.

18. E.g. G. Schwarz, *Bread and Circuses 1945–58* (Sunday Times, 1959) (reprints of his weekly column).

Notes to Appendix

1. The quantity theory originates with Oresme in 1376, if not earlier, and has been restated many times in the six centuries since. The modern form is due to Fisher. The equation is set out in V. Chick, *The Theory of Monetary Policy* (Gray Mills, 1973), Chapter 3–1.

2. This is set out in: Chick, ibid., Chapter 3; D. Laidler, *The Demand for Money* (International Textbook Company), Part One; and C. A. E. Goodhart, *Money, Information and Uncertainty* (Macmillan, 1975), Chapter 9 A.

3. J. Hicks, 'M. Keynes and the Classics', *Econometrica* (1937), reprinted in M. J. C. Surrey (ed.), *Macroeconomic themes* (Oxford, 1976), 1.2.

4. See J. Tobin, 'A general equilibrium approach to monetary theory', *Journal of Money, Credit and Banking* (1969) Vol. 1, No. 1; J. Fleming *et al.*, 'The Cost of Capital, Finance and Investment', *Bank of England Quarterly Bulletin*, Vol. 16, No. 2 (June 1976), p. 193; J. Fleming *et al.*, 'Supplementary note: company profitability and the cost of capital', *Bank of England Quarterly Bulletin*, Vol. 17, No. 2 (June 1977), p. 156.

5. See Baumol's and Tobin's articles reprinted in Surrey, ibid., 4–1 and 4–2.

6. Tobin (1); Chick, ibid., Chapter 6.

7. Goodhart, ibid., Chapter 9 B.

8. On flow-of-funds analysis, J. R. Gaster, 'Financial Prospects for 1975–6', *Banker* (August 1975); P. Johnson, 'Pluses and Minuses of the Flow of Funds', *Banker* (August 1975); Bank of England, 'Introduction to Flow of Funds Accounts' (1972); B. Tew, *Monetary Theory* (Student Library of Economics, 1969); A. D. Bain, 'Flow of Funds: a Survey', *Economic Journal* (March 1973); M. J. Artis and A. R. Nobay, 'Balance Sheet Analysis of Money and the Concept of DCE' in H. G. Johnson (ed.), *Readings in British Monetary Economics* (London, Oxford University Press, 1972), Paper 31.

9. In, for example, Musgrave's paper in R. E. Caves (ed.), *Britain's Economic Prospects* (Brookings Institute 1968).

10. M. Friedman and D. Meiselman, 'The Relative Stability of Monetary Velocity and the Investment Multiplier' in *Commission on Many Credit Impacts of Monetary Policy* (Englewood Cliffs, New Jersey, Prentice-Hall, 1963).

11. F. H. Hahn, 'Friedman's views on Money', reprinted as 9–3 in Surrey, ibid.

12. L. C. Anderson and J. L. Jordan, 'Monetary and Fiscal Actions: a test of their relative importance in economic stabilisation', *Federal Reserve Bank of St. Louis Review* (November 1968).

13. Schmid Waud, 'Critique of Anderson and Jordan', *Journal of the American Statistical Association* (1973).

14. See C. A. E. Goodhart, 'Importance of Money' and the Kaldor/Friedman debate above; *Bank of England Quarterly Bulletin*, Vol. 10, No. 2 (June 1970).

15. P. Cagan, *Determinants and effects of changes in the stock of money 1875–1960* (NBER Studies in Business Cycles, No. 13, New York, 1965).

16. D. Williams, C. A. E. Goodhart and D. H. Gowland, 'Money, Income and Causality: The U.K. Experience', *American Economic Review* (June 1976).

2 THE 'NEW APPROACH'

(i) The 'New Approach': An Overview

The authorities had chosen to introduce a new method of control (see Chapter 1, section ii). In 1971, the authorities feared that they could no longer control the magnitude of credit flows, nor their allocation. More disturbingly they were, to some considerable degree, ignorant of the volume of those flows designed to evade the system of controls. Thus the authorities lacked both a means of controlling credit flows and a means of measuring them.

Not surprisingly, they responded in the textbook fashion, by resolving to control credit and money by market means, that is by price, which in financial markets meant by interest rates and by interest rates alone. As the Governor put it, 'Basically what we have in mind is a system under which *the allocation of credit is primarily determined by its cost* [and in which] we expect to achieve our objectives through market means'[1] (italics in original). However, their choice was more surprising in that they elected to control money indirectly via the supply side counterpart (i.e. bank assets) rather than directly; this decision partly reflected the mixed objectives of the scheme discussed below.

Hence, the supply side control mechanism will now be analysed (see appendix to Chapter 7 for a more detailed analysis). For a closed economy:

Money (M) = Deposits (D) + Currency (C)

but deposits are a bank's liabilities and

bank assets = bank liabilities (the accounting identity)[2]

So (ignoring non-deposit liabilities and the banking sector's real assets, branch buildings, etc.)

Deposits = bank lending to the government + bank lending to the
                 private sector

so

money = currency + bank lending to the government + bank lending
              to the private sector.

The public-sector borrowing requirement is obviously equal to the sum of the amounts the government borrows from all possible sources, so:

PSBR = Change in bank lending to the government + change in
             private lending to the government + change in private sector

holdings of currency.

(N.B. Currency is a form of interest-free loan to the government.)

Or

Change in bank lending to the government = PSBR — change in private lending to the government — change in private sector holdings of currency.

And so, by substitution,

the change in money supply = PSBR + change in bank lending to the private sector — change in private sector lending to the government. (This is the DCE equation as used by the IMF.)[3]

The 'supply side' method of control seeks to control money by controlling the variables on the right-hand side of this equation rather than directly. This latter method is used in the US, which is discussed in Chapter 7.

In an open economy and one with various different forms of private lending to the government, this equation becomes:

$\Delta M_3 =$ (1) PSBR[4]

        (2) + bank lending to the private sector

        (3) — sales of local authority debt ⎫

        (4) — sales of Treasury Bills etc.[5] ⎬ to the non-bank private sector

        (5) — sales of gilt-edged securities (government bonds) ⎭

(This is equal to DCE)

        (6) ± external adjustment (negative represents a balance of payments deficit — see appendix to this chapter)

        (7) — change in bank's non-deposit liabilities.

Of these, item 1 (the PSBR) was then outside the ambit of monetary policy, while to use item 6 required a deliberate decision to worsen the balance of payments to reduce monetary expansion. Even if this had been desirable, one cannot imagine any government, especially a UK one, doing it. Item 7, non-deposit liabilities (mainly retained profits) is both small and relatively immune to official control. However, raising interest rates tends to increase bank profits and so interest rate policies have an extra small favourable impact. Thus the authorities' weapons had to work via the effect on either the private sector's borrowing from banks (item 2) or its lending to the public sector (items 3, 4, 5); these would be influenced by interest rate changes: 'The resulting change in relative rates of return will then induce shifts in the asset portfolios of both the public and the banks.'[6]

Of the forms of private sector lending to the public sector, gilt sales (item 5) are both the most important in terms of size, the most volatile and the easiest to control. Hence competition and credit control depended on the effect of interest-rate changes on non-bank private sector purchases of gilt-edged securities and on bank lending.

(ii) The Control of Bank Lending

Private borrowing from banks was in general to be controlled by interest rates and interest rates alone (there was an escape clause reserving the power to issue guidelines, discussed below). The *modus operandi* was to push up the marginal cost of banks' funds (wholesale money rates) and assume that this would compel them (as profit maximisers) to raise the cost of overdrafts (so that marginal cost still equalled marginal revenue). Banks would go on bidding for funds so long as but only as long as it was profitable to do so.

In this case, then, it would seem essential that there be an elastic and stable demand for credit and so one might expect that the authorities would have firm econometric or other evidence to substantiate this. It is perhaps surprising that the authorities' faith in economic theory was such that they adopted this without any such evidence. Obviously, the imposition of ceilings and their effect in driving credit markets 'underground' had made such work difficult.[7] Nevertheless, the problem remained. No one knew what the effect of any given change in interest rates would be on bank lending. No one knew how much bank lending was restrained by ceilings, and so by how much demand exceeded supply. Furthermore, it was not clear how much of any increase represented new transactions and how much transactions previously carried out by other routes. It must be stressed that when previously frustrated demands were satisfied this represented genuine monetary expansion, official comments notwithstanding.

(iii) The Gilt-edged Market

The change in approach in the gilt-edged market under the 'new approach' was if anything even more dramatic than in the credit market. 'The Bank were no longer prepared to respond to requests to buy stock outright, except in the case of stocks with less than one year to run to maturity.'[8] The exception was to permit smoothing of the effect of the maturing of a large issue.

But any modifications to existing arrangements to be complete had to provide for the implementation of an easy monetary policy under which it might come to be appropriate for expansionary open market operations to be engaged in. For this reason, the Bank reserve the right to make outright purchases of stock at their discretion and initiative.[9]

Previously, the Bank had 'leant into the wind' to smooth out price fluctuations so that the change from day to day was small. This had various disadvantages — it 'gave rise to very large speculative trans-actions and made the speculative management of portfolios altogether too easy'.[10] Less discretely, the Bank guaranteed large profits to any-one who wanted them, since by smoothing the Bank ensured that once a price movement in a given direction had started, it would continue for a long period and that the movement in the opposite direction would be equally well signalled. Thus one had ample opportunity to buy at the bottom of a bull market and sell just after the peak: profitable management of portfolios was indeed 'altogether too easy', although whether there was anything speculative about it was questionable.

Even more seriously, 'leaning into the wind' was making the whole of the public sector debt a very liquid asset — a thirty-year bond is a highly liquid asset if the holder *knows* he can always sell it at close to the current market price. Hence to all but the most extreme of monetarists, supporting the bond market to permit bond sales was self-defeating. The policy of 'leaning into the wind' had been justified by the so-called cashiers' theory of gilt-edged demand, that is that the market was dominated by short-period-maximising holders with extrapolative expectations, so one could only sell on a rising market, that is to say, when interest rates were falling. More formally gilt-edged sales by the authorities were a *negative* function of the *change* in interest rates. This contrasted with the 'economists' theory' that lower prices induce greater sales, that is that sales were a *positive* function of the *level* of interest rates.[11]

One should perhaps note that the authorities retained the 'tap system' of gilt-edged sales. The authorities would fix a price at which they were prepared to sell (more or less) unlimited quantities of (usually) the 'short tap' stock (say about four years) and the 'long tap' (usually about twenty years). These stocks were issued in large quantities, most of which remained with the authorities and were gradually sold later. By varying the relationship between the 'tap' price and the market price, and by varying the length of 'tap stocks', the authorities sought both to control the volume of sales and to indicate their policy stance. Statistical research has proved unable to discover any such systematic relationships between sales and these indicators.[12] The alternative would be a 'tender' method (as used sometimes in the US, and for Treasury Bills in the UK) where the market determines the price for a quantity fixed by the authorities, discussed in Chapter 9.

It is clear that the authorities were right in believing that there were extrapolative expectations present in the market, although they may have been induced by the authorities' own behaviour. These expectations, it seems, would have yielded profits, at least on a daily basis,[13] but not perhaps on a monthly basis.[14]

However, such expectations were inconsistent with the gilts market being a rational, efficient market[15] in the economists' sense — not surprisingly, since this assumes all market operators seek to maximise profits subject to risk. Such an assumption is invalid, as the authorities, the largest operators, obviously do not maximise profits. In the absence of intervention, one would have expected the market to be rational and efficient. A rational market is one in which operators take any known opportunity to make profits. Thus if one knows with a 90 per cent probability that a price rise on one day will be followed by another price increase, then one will buy after any price increase to take advantage of the expected profit. However, such buying will destroy the relationship from which the buying opportunity arose — since the price will rise immediately. In general, it is impossible for all members of a market in securities to expect the price to rise, since if they do they will buy and the price will rise immediately. There cannot be an equilibrium unless the expected price change for the market as a whole is zero, that is, average of the expectations of individual dealers weighted for wealth and risk.

The efficient market hypothesis is similar — it argues that the price must reflect all known information, since market operators will use all information 'efficiently'. As information includes that about profitable opportunities (and past price movements) then one may treat the rational market hypothesis as a special case of an efficient market. However, it is possible to do the same in reverse — information is merely one of the items to be processed 'rationally' within the 'rational markets' model.

These hypotheses depend on various assumptions about the number of market operators, transaction costs, etc. In reality, there are certain limiting factors, e.g. transaction and dealing costs, tax considerations, which prevent market operators adjusting their portfolio to take full advantage of foreseen opportunities. However, these limiting factors should not prove much of a brake on the profit-seeking day-to-day operations of professional investment managers in financial markets, particularly in the gilts market. They should be largely offset by the economies of scale in financial transactions, together with these operators' specialised experience of assimilating, and of advantageous access to, information on market developments, which in combination should make their transaction and dealing costs relatively low. So we might expect the UK gilt market to approximate to a rational, efficient market, with prices and yields following a random walk on a day-to-day basis, in the same way as has been observed in several other asset markets.[16]

In this case, then, the authorities' beliefs on which the 'cashiers' theory' rests contradict the rational and efficient market theory. It may be that the authorities can, as discussed below in Chapters 8 and 9, continue to manipulate the market but it does raise problems of whether such behaviour is consistent with efficiency and rationality and if not, what the implications are. The authorities can try to maximise sales by arranging for large, fast price movements in a down-ward direction and long, slow rises; this is in fact part of the post-1974 strategy. In fact, it ought to be possible to sell ever-greater quantities at ever-higher prices if this theory is correct. It is, in fact, an extreme version of the 'other sucker's theory' which, it is alleged, explains behaviour in speculative markets from the Dutch tulip boom of the 1930s via Wall Street in 1929 to the UK property boom of 1972–3. However, if the authorities act as described above, extrapolative expectations will continually be falsified, so for how long can they continue? Nevertheless, the author's study cited above shows this in 1972. The leopard in Threadneedle Street may not have changed his spots then, but casual empiricism suggests similar behaviour under the 'new "new" approach' (see Chapter 8).

A further problem with extrapolative expectations is that it is not clear whether an upward movement in interest rates will increase or reduce sales. Thus on its own terms, competition and credit control was inconsistent. The implication, accepted by the authorities, was that the main brunt of monetary policy fell on the interest elasticity of the demand for bank credit.

(iv) Special Deposits and Reserve Ratios

So far in this chapter, no mention has been made of another change that was part of the 'new approach' — the introduction of a 12½ per cent uniform minimum reserve ratio for banks and of a 50 per cent public sector lending ratio for discount houses. This is because they were very much of secondary importance and were primarily designed to increase the authorities' control over interest rates and to speed up the asset movements caused by interest rate changes. Special Deposits had a similar role. Before discussing them, it must be emphasised that (despite a certain superficial resemblance to a variable reserve ratio on the US model) they were not, and the UK has never had, a textbook minimum reserve ratio/reserve base scheme.

This statement that the UK has never had such a textbook system is somewhat controversial, so it is perhaps necessary to set out the evidence, consequences and precise meaning of this statement.

Bagehot shows that this ratio was not part of nineteenth-century practice. In the inter-war period both McKenna and Lord Norman explicitly denied the relevance of arithmetic ratios to monetary control in their evidence to the Macmillan Committee, which endorsed their view in its report.[17] The Radcliffe Committee expressed a similar view. In 1971 the Governor of the Bank could scarcely have been more explicit:

> It is not to be expected that the mechanism of minimum reserve ratio and Special Deposits can be used to achieve some precise multiple contraction or expansion of bank assets. Rather the intention is to use our control over liquidity, which these instruments will reinforce, to influence the structure of interest rates. The resulting change in relative rates of returns will then induce shifts in the current portfolios of both the public and the banks.[18]

Thus the authorities consciously ignored the basic rules of a text-book system —

(a) define the reserve asset tightly;
(b) be the sole source of issue;
(c) police it carefully.

In fact, the reserve asset was defined as a rag-bag collection — see below (compare the US or West German system in Chapter 7). Many of the assets were liabilities of the private sector, not of the authorities, and enormous loopholes were left such that the banks could create an extra £10,000m of reserve assets in 1972 (i.e. enough to expand M_3 by 320 per cent if the textbook 8:1 ratio held). (These loopholes are discussed below.) No figures were available of potential reserve assets. Furthermore, very crucially, the ratios were set as near to average levels in the past as possible, they were not designed to be a 'portfolio constraint' as are the textbook ratios.

Thus, whereas in the US and West Germany, the precise arithmetic relationship of the textbook model is an accurate description of the money creation process, it is not in the UK (nor in France or Japan). However, ratios do matter in bank management and in monetary control. The UK clearing banks use about 25 to 30 such ratios as rules of thumb in their portfolio management. None is fixed, each varies with the level and structure of interest rates and the level of the other ratios. These are used as approximations to the utility maximising asset structure of a price discriminating oligopolist and oligopsonist. Banks have to trade off liquidity, risk and expected return on all assets and the similar differential costs of liabilities. To equate marginal cost and marginal 'benefit' of all sources and uses of funds demands a degree of knowledge which is often impractical and, more important, always too costly.[19] Thus rules of thumb both reduce costs and facilitate fast, decentralised decision-making (compare a 40 per cent mark-up for first-class rail travel).[20] Thus the textbook ratio is a simplification of bank behaviour which seeks or should seek only to capture one element of it. (In this way it resembles the perfect competition model.) The danger is to assume it is an accurate description of the whole system rather than a stylised description of one element of it.

The banks were asked to maintain a sum equal to 12½ per cent of their eligible liabilities in 'eligible reserve assets'. Eligible liabilities were deposits in sterling, net of inter-bank items, with initially less than two years to maturity. Reserve assets — described above as a 'rag-bag' — comprised

> balances with the Bank of England (other than Special Deposits), British government and Northern Ireland government Treasury Bills, company tax reserve certificates, money at call with the London money market, British government stocks with one year or less to final maturity, local authority bills eligible for rediscount at the Bank of England and (up to a maximum of 2 per cent of eligible liabilities) commercial bills eligible for rediscount at the Bank of England.
>
> Eligible money at call with the London money market will comprise funds placed with members of the London Discount Market Association, with certain other firms carrying on an

essentially similar type of business (the discount brokers and the money trading departments of certain banks traditionally undertaking such business) and with certain firms through whom the banks finance the gilt-edged market, namely the money brokers and jobbers. In order to constitute an eligible reserve asset, funds placed with these firms must be at call (or callable, if not explicitly at call) and must be secured (in the case of the jobbers, on gilt-edged securities).[21]

Later the definition was changed marginally.[22] It should be noted that cash was never a reserve asset.

The discount houses were asked to keep 50 per cent of their borrowed funds in 'specified categories of public sector debt' — there were some minor categories of public sector debt that did not qualify, notably local authority bonds with more than five years to maturity. The overall role of the discount market is discussed in section (v), but it must be noted that this differential treatment was responsible for some of the 'loopholes' in the reserve assets scheme. The discount houses had a 50 per cent public sector lending ratio in which call and callable money were included. So if a bank exchanged £100 of Treasury Bills and £100 of its liabilities (say a Certificate of Deposit) for £200 of call money, the discount houses' reserve ratio was satisfied while the bank's reserve ratio rose — its reserve assets and liabilities had risen by the same amount. As in Table 2.1, the reserve ratio of both parties could increase. The transaction was, of course, only possible so long as the discount house trusted the bank not to 'call' the call money.

Neither party satisfied the ratio. If the next day is a banking Wednesday, the minima must be observed, so the bank exchanges £5m Treasury Bills and £3m of its CDs for £8m call money. Now the position in Table 2.2 ensues.

The regulations are satisfied.

The Bank had recognised the danger of 'transactions designed to substitute "window-dressing" arrangements for genuine observance of [the] minimum reserve ratio',[23] but in the technical sense these transactions are not window-dressing since they represent a legitimate commercial transaction for both sides.

Later,[24] the discount houses' ratio was replaced by two gross assets: own capital and unidentified (i.e. private sector) assets: own capital. This was not a penal ratio at all. Now a CD/call money swap was all that was necessary to create reserve assets.

Other loopholes were even simpler. A bank could exchange 1–5 year

Table 2.1

Bank			
Assets		*Liabilities*	(£m)
Reserve assets (of which Treasury Bills 5)	10	Eligible liabilities	100
Non-reserve assets	95	Non-eligible liabilities	5
	105		105

Reserve Asset Ratio 10 per cent

Discount House			
Assets		*Liabilities*	
Public lending	24	Own capital	5
Private lending	26	Call money	45
	50		50

PSLR = 48 per cent

Table 2.2

Bank			(£m)
Reserve assets (+ 8 call money − 5 Treasury Bills)	13	Eligible liabilities	103
Non-reserve assets	95	Non-eligible liabilities	5
	108		108

Reserve Asset Ratio 12.62 per cent

Discount House			
Public lending (+ 5 TB)	29	Own capital	5
Private lending (+ 3 CDs)	29	Call money	53
	58		58

PSLR = 50 per cent

gilts for a discount house's gilts with less than one year to maturity, or exchange local authority bonds for bills with the relevant local authority, and see its reserve ratio rise with no effect on the other party, who would be rewarded.

At this stage, the reader may be tempted to ask, 'Why did the authorities bother with reserve ratios?' After all, he or she might legitimately argue the authorities have other tools to control short-term interest rates. The answer is that the functions of the ratios were minor but not insignificant. If the speed of response were speeded up, then this was, obviously, of major assistance to the operation of monetary policy. It is not clear how much Special Deposit calls did achieve this. Casual empiricism, like economic theory, suggests that it was not much, while whenever the ratios threatened to be effective the authorities, as in June 1972, had to intervene.

The ratios did, however, provide some support for the market in public sector debt — banks were less likely to dump gilt-edged stock to try to meet an unexpected call for funds. This actually slowed down the movement of interest rates. Nevertheless, by inducing banks to always respond to short-term or unexpected cash-flow problems by borrowing in the overnight inter-bank market — the main operating area of policy — then the authorities made overall control easier.

(v) Day-to-day Operations, the Discount Houses and the Treasury Bill Market

The final major change in the 'new approach' was in the discount market's relations with the Bank. Here it is perhaps important to stress that the rather quaint survival of the (currently) eleven members of the London Discount Markets Association has no economic and little other logic to commend it. (Equally, there is little reason to abolish the system, unless one regards its rather élitist nature as being a factor in the higher social status of traditional finance over corporate finance and of both over industry in the UK.) The authorities could conduct open-market operations equally effectively by the Chancellor of the Exchequer having a bank account and an overdraft with the banks. He would then vary both the gross and net size of his balance according to the needs of monetary policy. In the UK this is normally done via the discount market, but the taboo on Bank/bank financial transactions has been dropped in recent years. The authorities also act as net lenders in the overnight inter-bank market, as does the corporate sector, and use variations in the quantity of this lending as one of the major operational tools in both domestic monetary policy and exchange rate policy.

As the banks are heavy net borrowers in this market, their demand curve for funds is in the short run very inelastic. As the firms lending have no alternative home for their funds, so is the supply curve (the lenders may be oil companies accumulating balances over a few days to pay oil royalties). Thus, with very inelastic curves the market has something of the atmosphere of a high-stake poker game: dealers (acting on behalf of banks) are fond of relating how they bluffed the rate up when they had a surplus to lend by pretending to be short. There is also a very large variation in rates within a day − an average of 10 per cent frequently includes a range of between, say 2 per cent and 15 per cent − and between one day and another − 10 per cent and 100 per cent (on an annual basis) within a week is not uncommon. Furthermore, rates are often very high − 1,256 per cent is the 'record' (in November 1967 after devaluation) and 200 per cent is a rate that occurs fairly often. The market is also used in most foreign exchange speculation, since if one borrows overnight in sterling, converts the proceeds into dollars and invests them in the overnight inter-bank dollar market, this offers an opportunity of profit if sterling depreciates. This transaction involves the loss of the difference between the sterling interest rate and the dollar interest rate. Nevertheless, this cost is normally much lower than a comparable forward discount and this method is much more flexible than a forward contract, as one may renew the forward borrowing and lending daily. Thus, the speculator has a chance to close out his position on any day simply by not lending and borrowing for a further period rather than the clumsier method of having to sell his forward contract.

All of this makes the market an ideal forum for official intervention. Withdrawing funds has various effects:

(1) it puts up the cost to banks of being short and they tend to readjust their portfolios quickly − even on a daily basis credit at 200 per cent p.a. is expensive;

(2) it raises the cost of speculation against the pound and this tends to reduce its volume;

(3) it induces an inflow of funds from the Euro-sterling market. As banks taking these deposits normally hold dollars and forward sterling (rather than holding sterling) this automatically raises the demand for spot sterling relative to the supply.

Thus, the overnight inter-bank market is crucial to the conduct of domestic and international monetary policy, which has reduced the role of the discount market in this context, whose other traditional role is in the provision of government finance. The nature of this stems from the Bank's preference for having bank lending to the government held as much as possible in the form of Treasury Bills rather than balances with the Bank. To this end, the LDMA, acting as a cartel, had agreed to 'cover the tender' — to enter a syndicated bid for any volume of Treasury Bills the authorities chose to sell at each Friday's auction. 'Outside bidders' were allowed to participate and received their share of the allocation, if their bid exceeded the LDMA bid at the price they tendered; the Bank 'creamed off' the 'consumer surplus'.[25] Under the new arrangement, the LDMA continued to 'cover the tender' by bidding for the whole amount of bills on offer but not at a common price. Thus, the percentage of bills obtained by each house would vary with its bid — most would get either 100 per cent or 0 per cent, unless the Bank's unofficial intimation of the desired rate led all to tender at the cut-off level unless they enter several bids.[26]

The discount market was also of relevance to monetary control in that the Bank's official interest rate was Bank Rate — the rate at which it would rediscount first-class bills of exchange for the members of the LDMA. This was the 'traditional instrument to affect short term interest rates', but 'we envisage using it more flexibly than in the past'.[27] Bank Rate was not affected by the 'new approach' but was altered later (see Chapter 3).

(vi) The 'Escape Clauses'

There were two escape clauses written into the 'new approach'. One was that 'the authorities would continue to provide the banks with such qualitative guidance as may be appropriate'. Taken literally, this amounted to reserving the power to drop the entire system and was inconsistent with

> We have in fact been operating a system of bank lending ceilings with declared official priorities almost continuously since 1965. We have, however, been increasingly unhappy about the effects of operating monetary policy in this way over a prolonged period. In this audience I do not need to labour the ill effects. It is obvious that physical rationing of this kind can lead to serious misallocation of resources, both in the economy and in the financial system.[28]

The most obvious reason for this inconsistency is that the authorities were not unanimous and that this represented a sop to those, especially in the Treasury, who wished to see direct controls on personal lending retained. More likely, however, it was viewed as being a necessary transitional step, while hire purchase controls remained, to maintain equity between finance houses and banks. In addition, the Radcliffean view that direct controls should be used so long as markets were imperfect enough to make them effective implied in the context of the 1970s that direct controls could be used in an emergency because they would still have a short-term impact, even if quickly reversed.

The other escape clause (paragraph 15) was that the Bank reserved the right to impose limits on the interest rate paid on retail deposits to protect building societies 'because the impact of such competition on savings banks and building societies would need careful consideration'. This is usually known as Regulation Q, after its US equivalent. It is ironic that the Hunt Commission were recommending its abolition about this time[29] and that the abolition of the scheme in the US coincided with its first use in the UK.

One would not be excessively cynical in believing that this was essentially included for political reasons and stemmed from a need to keep mortgage rates down; the four million mortgagees are probably the most carefully cultivated political lobby in the UK. One economic justification is offered by the slow speed of adjustment of building societies' rates (like SLAs in the USA), partly necessary in view of adjustment costs, partly reflecting inefficiency.

It does, however, seem iniquitous by any standards to make the holders of small bank deposits pay for the government's desire to subsidise those buying homes while allowing larger holders to receive the market rate. Government-ordered price discrimination in favour of the wealthy must be unique in being contrary to every political philosophy. It is in fact even worse, in that it enables the authorities to keep down the whole spectrum of interest rates available to small savers, again morally reprehensible on all possible criteria.

To the Bank's credit, this piece of outrageous political expediency would, they hoped, never be used and was temporary — 'the need for such limits would be open to reconsideration in the light of changed circumstances' — which means to those who specialise in Bankology, 'We hope to drop it'.[30] Bankology, incidentally, is a much less widely known art than the basically similar Kremlinology but its devotees, largely in the City, seem to find it even more fascinating. However, at the risk of spoiling this game, the case for a more open approach, like that of the 'Fed', seems unanswerable.

(vii) 'Competition': the Structure of Banking

Thus far this chapter has considered only the changes which occurred as a consequence of the credit control aspect of the new approach. This is probably a fair reflection of the relative importance attached to the two in official (if not government) minds; some time later, a disillusioned very senior Treasury official was heard to remark that he would sacrifice all the competition in the world for 'an ounce of credit control'. However, the authorities undoubtedly hoped to improve the structural efficiency of the financial system by the 'new approach'.[31]

In particular, the authorities surrendered the right to determine the overall level of bank loan rates to facilitate more competition. Previously the banks' rates were fixed in relation to Bank Rate, determined by the authorities. The banks could and did vary the amounts charged to different borrowers, but Bank Rate remained the 'base rate' (unless Bank Rates were below 5 per cent, the floor to base rate after 1955). The new approach allowed the banks to fix their own base rates in a competitive fashion. (Not surprisingly, the market has behaved in oligopolistic fashion.) This partly reflected a response to criticism of the banking system by both official bodies, notably the Prices and Incomes Board and the Monopolies Commission[32] and academics.[33] Much more, however, it represented a reaction to the clearing banks' loss of market share under the ceilings régime. The banks had started to bid (usually through subsidiaries) for whole-sale deposits, but lending ceilings were restricting this by reducing outlets for funds. Thus the Bank was desirous of helping them recover their position both out of a sense of fairness and a sense of duty, as the traditional champion of the City, especially of the more established elements of it; no doubt the Bank were made aware of the clearers' sense of grievance. There were other minor aspects of the scheme which slightly increased competition, e.g. the end of LDMA joint covering of the Treasury Bill tender, but this was basically the 'competition' element. It reflected a touching faith in the effects of the ending of official intervention, perhaps influenced by Keynes's oft-quoted scribbler.[34] Equally it is clear that many in the Bank had found the administration of ceilings very distasteful and the fixing of rates almost as much so. This was a perfectly legitimate response, as few people enjoy restricting others and fewer still would enjoy administering such discriminatory rules.

(viii) What was the 'New Approach'?

The authorities never made it clear whether they wished to control M_3

for its own sake or because it entailed controlling other variables, whether it was a target or an indicator or what it indicated. Thus it was never clear whether the authorities thought they were running a credit or a monetary policy. This intellectual confusion was probably a major political bonus in rallying support for the 'new approach'. The scheme could be thought of as:

(a) a credit policy. At last, the authorities believed they had found the whole balloon. It is not without significance that M_3 (the money supply definition preferred) is known as the credit proxy in the US.

(b) a monetary policy. One must note that the authorities (carefully) called M_3 a monetary aggregate or stock — not a supply, with its implication of a supplier.

(c) a DCE policy. M_3 and DCE are closely linked, differing only by the overseas influence on the money supply.

(d) a Radcliffean liquidity policy. One could argue that M_3 was the best available measure of liquidity *so long as it was controlled by market means* and the overtones of 'portfolio policy' were present, e.g. in the use of Special Deposits to speed up the (inevitable) changes caused by interest rate policy.

(e) a *laissez-faire* policy. That is an opportunity to end the problems of Bank/bank relations and distortions and inefficiencies caused by the ceilings. M_3, besides being a target/instrument of a money or credit policy was also presented as being an overall indicator of:

(f) credit, fiscal and interest rate policy.

(Of the three items in the equation on page 25, the PSBR can be taken as an indicator of fiscal policy, bank lending of credit policy and debt sales of interest rate policy (as any change in private lending to the government must represent a change in the size and/or allocation of private sector portfolios and must therefore be accompanied by a change in asset prices). Thus M_3 may be viewed as overall indicator of economic policy.

It was also argued that the money supply could be viewed as an indicator not merely of economic policy, but of the economy as a whole.[35]

This argument starts with the idea of a demand for money function relating the money supply to real income (or output), prices and interest rates. Then any view of the desirable path of these implies a view of the desirable path of monetary expansion, assuming that the money supply and demand are always in equilibrium.

For example, if the demand for money function were:

$$M = 30 + 1.0 \text{ (price level)} + 1.2 \text{ level of real income}$$
$$- 0.25 (100 + \text{rate of interest})$$

If the desired level of the price level is 110, of real income 120 and of the interest rate 5 per cent then it follows that if these are achieved, the demand for money will be equal to 57.75.

The Bank's argument was that one could turn this round and say that if the money supply were, say, 300 then the desired levels of price, output and interest rates were not achieved.

This is true so far as it goes but is open to the following objections:

(1) the demand for money may not always be in equilibrium, as excess or deficient demand are likely: see Chapter 4, section IV;

(2) the error in, and stochastic variations of, the demand for money are likely to swamp variations in output etc.;

(3) an infinite number of constellations of output, interest rates, etc. are consistent with any given level of the money supply. For example, with the above function, output may be 10 points lower and prices 12 points higher than desired but the demand for money is unchanged;

(4) finally, in the UK, the index of industrial production and the Retail Price Index are both available before the monthly money supply series, so one can monitor output and inflation directly.[36]

However, it remained to be seen how the new approach would work and how it would be interpreted.

APPENDIX: Overseas Influences on the Money Supply

The confusion surrounding the precise impact of different overseas transactions on the money supply problem arises from an anomaly in the public sector accounts. If the government purchases, say, shares in the British Aircraft Corporation, this is treated as being an increase in the public sector borrowing requirement. On the other hand, if the government purchases dollars, thus similarly acquiring an asset, this does not appear as an increase in the PSBR. However, both transactions will obviously have an equivalent effect on the government's need to obtain sterling and so on the growth of the money supply. Equally, government borrowing in dollars can never finance any of the PSBR since this has to be financed in sterling. If the government borrows dollars and uses these to purchase sterling then this does reduce the size of the domestic borrowing requirement and thus of the money

Table 2.3

	M_3	Domestic* Borrowing Requirement	Reserves	Bank Assets
1. UK export (for the economy as a whole currency account surplus)	+	+	+	+
2. UK import (for the economy as a whole current account deficit) foreigner holds UK Bank A/c.	−	=	=	=
3. Alternatively the foreigner may repatriate the receipts from his sales to the UK	−	−	−	−
4. Foreigners buy gilts or the government borrows from IMF or the Eurodollar market	=	=	+	=
5. Foreigners buy property, equities, etc.	+	+	+	+
6. Foreigners hold sterling deposits with UK bank	=	+	+	+

* An increase means that the government (via the EEA) supplies more sterling.

This table assumes an exchange rate at level that would have prevailed without transaction.

supply, but it is the act of intervention which reduces the money supply, not the act of borrowing.

Intervention when the balance of payments is in surplus is obviously much more likely to be in order to hold down the rate of exchange rather than to support it. Thus the government's intervention will consist of buying foreign currency, particularly dollars, in exchange for sterling. There are four things that the foreign holder can do with his newly acquired sterling. He can use it to purchase public sector securities, e.g. gilt-edged, or he may purchase UK private sector assets (property, equities, etc.) or he may hold a sterling deposit with a UK bank. If the foreigner chooses to hold his increased sterling assets in gilt-edged securities then the reserves rise but otherwise there is no impact on the UK monetary system. If, however, he chooses to hold sterling deposits with a UK bank, then both the total of bank assets and the domestic borrowing requirement rise. However, there is no increase in M_3 as overseas deposits in sterling are not defined as being part of M_3. This is somewhat strange as virtually all other countries include similar deposits in their money supplies (see Appendix B). In particular, the IMF, the USA and the·OECD all believe that such deposits should be included. If the foreigner buys some UK non-bank private sector asset then the effect is to increase M_3 as well as the other aggregates. Table 2.3 shows how the various possible transactions between the UK and the overseas sector affect various domestic financial aggregates.

If he holds a sterling deposit with an external bank this increases the size of the Euro-sterling market but does not affect the UK authorities as Euro-banks normally sell sterling spot and purchase sterling forward. Thus the effect on the UK public sector accounts is cancelled out and the support for sterling is transferred to the forward market.

Notes

1. *Competition and Credit Control* (Bank of England, 1971); 'Key Issues in monetary and credit policy': text of an address of the Governor to the International Banking Conference on 25 May 1971 (hereafter 'Key Issues'), pp. 7 and 8.
2. Goethe regarded such identities as the greatest achievement of mankind. Most economists are very sceptical of accountancy. Both a discussion of these criticisms and a description of elementary accountancy can be found in P. Bird, 'The Interpretation of Published Accounts', CAS Occasional Paper No. 14 (HMSO, 1974).
3. The concept of DCE was first used by J. J. Polak in 'Monetary Analysis of Income Formation and Payment Problems', IMF Staff Papers, 1958. The above equations are an example of the use of flow-of-funds analysis described in the appendix to Chapter 1. See the references in footnote 8 to the appendix to Chapter 1.
4. The PSBR can be broken down either by sub-category of the public sector – local authority, central government and public corporation – or by nature of economic transaction. The PSBR is the sum of the public sector's gross lending and its financial deficit. The latter could be divided into the current deficit (surplus) and the capital deficit, etc.
5. The 'etc.' comprises National Savings, Tax Reserve Certificates, Tax Deposit Accounts. Certificates of tax deposit and 'other non marketable debt' (mainly the 'Fund for Banks of Saving' – an obligation to Trustee Savings banks). Public corporation borrowing from the non-bank private sector has not occurred in recent years.
6. 'Key Issues', p. 9.
7. See for example, W. E. Norton, 'Debt Management and Monetary Policy in

the U.K.' in H. G. Johnson (ed.), *Readings in British Monetary Economics* (Oxford University Press, 1972).

8. *Competition and Credit Control,* ibid,; 'Competition and Credit Control: extract from a lecture by the Chief Cashier of the Bank of England' (hereafter 'Sykes'), p. 17.

9. Sykes, p. 18.

10. Sykes, p. 18.

11. See H. G. Johnson (ed.), *Readings,* Section VI, Debt Management, especially the papers by Goodhart (24) and the Bank of England (23).

12. See C. A. E. Goodhart and D. H. Gowland, 'The relationship between long-dated gilt yields and other variables', *Bulletin of Economic Research* (1978).

13. See. D. H. Gowland, 'Is the U.K. Gilts Market Efficient? Evidence from Daily Data'(forthcoming).

14. See C. A. E. Goodhart and D. H. Gowland, 'The relationship between yields on short and long dated Gilt-Edged Stocks', *Bulletin of Economic Research* (November 1977).

15. See for a discussion of rational and efficient markets, J. F. Muth, 'Rational Expectations and the Theory of Price Movements', *Econometrica* (June 1971); E. Fama, 'Efficient Capital Markets', *Journal of Finance* (September 1970).

16. See P. H. Cootner, (ed.). *The Random Character of Stock Market Prices* (MIT Press, 1964); C. A. J. Granger and O. Morgenstern, *The Predictability of Stock Market Prices* (Heath Lexington Books, 1971); D. H. Gowland, 'The Money Supply and Stock Market Prices' in M. Parkin and A. R. Nobay (eds.), *Current Economic Problems* (Cambridge University Press, 1975).

17. Governor of the Bank of England and Chairman of the Midland Bank and ex-Chancellor of the Exchequer respectively.

18. Bagehot, 'Lombard Street: a study of the Money Market', reprinted in *Collected Works,* N. St. John Stevas (ed.) (*Economist,* 1965); *Report of Committee of Enquiry into Finance and Industry* (Macmillan Report), Cmnd. 3897 (HMSO 1931). McKenna was also a member of the Committee: see *Radcliffe Committee on the Working of the Monetary System,* Cmnd. 827 (HMSO 1959); 'Key Issues', p. 9.

19. A linear programming solution is possible and is in fact used by some American banks.

20. For a discussion of such issues, see J. J. McCall, 'Probabilistic Microeconomics', *Bell Journal of Economics and Management Science* (Fall, 1971).

21. *Competition and Credit Control,* ibid., 'Reserve Rates and Special Deposits' (p. 13).

22. 'Competition and Credit Control: further developments', *Bank of England Quarterly Bulletin,* Vol. 13, No. 1 (March 1973), p. 53.

23. *Competition and Credit Control,* ibid., 'Competition and Credit Control: The Discount Market' (p. 12).

24. 'Competition and Credit Control: Modified Arrangements for the Discount Market', *Bank of England Quarterly Bulletin,* Vol. 13, No. 3 (September 1973), p. 306.

25. The system is described in 'The Treasury Bill', *Bank of England Quarterly Bulletin,* Vol. 4, No. 3 (September 1964).

26. For an analysis of the Treasury Bill Market see M. Parkin, 'Discount House Portfolio and Debt Selection', *Review of Economic Studies* (Oct. 1970) and R. G. Alford, 'Bank Rate, Money Rates and the Treasury Bill Rate' in *Essays in Money and Banking in Honour of R. S. Sayers* (Oxford, 1968).

27. 'Key Issues', p. 8.

28. 'Key Issues', pp. 7–8.

29. The Hunt Commission's analysis differs in some minor respects from the standard academic study: J. Tobin, 'Deposit Interest Ceilings as a Monetary Control', *Journal of Money, Credit and Banking* (February 1970).

30. *Competition and Credit Control*, p. 3.

31. 'Key Issues', p. 10.

32. *Report on Bank Charges*, National Board for Prices and Incomes, Report No. 34, Cmnd. 3292 (HMSO 1967); Monopolies Commission, *Barclays Bank Ltd., Lloyds Bank Ltd. and Martins Bank. Report on the Proposed Merger* (HMSO 1968).

33. H. G. Johnson (ed.), *Readings*, section IV; B. Griffiths, *Competition in Banking*, Hobart Paper, No. 51 (IEA).

34. Ironically, no economist so much fills the role of 'scribbler' influencing events twenty years later as Keynes himself.

35. See 'Does the Money Supply Really Matter?', *Bank of England Quarterly Bulletin*, Vol. 13, No. 2 (June 1973), p. 193.

36. For a more extended critique of some aspects of the proposition see: M. Artis and M. Lewis, 'The Demand for Money Stable or Unstable?', *The Banker* (March 1974).

3   THE HISTORY OF 'COMPETITION AND CREDIT CONTROL'

One can divide the period of the operation of the new approach into four distinct phases (although precise dating is not possible). In the first phase, from May 1971, the accent was on easy credit to try to reduce unemployment. This lasted until the sterling crisis of June 1972. From June 1972 until October 1972 there was an interim phase while the authorities reviewed the position. From October 1972 onwards, they were 'willing to wound, yet afraid to strike' and tried to control credit and money without increasing interest rates. In July 1973, the authorities accepted the consequences of their own system and raised Minimum Lending Rate by 4 per cent in two weeks, to an unprecedented 11½ per cent. From July to December 1973, the competition and credit control régime was operated in something like its intended fashion but in December the new approach was replaced by a 'new "new approach" '. This new régime and its workings are discussed in Chapter 7. In this chapter, the four phases are examined in turn.

(i) The Era of Easy Credit, May 1971–June 1972

In May 1971, the authorities produced their first draft of the new scheme[1] and introduced one of its key elements by ceasing to support the market in gilt-edged securities, on 17 May, except for stocks with less than a year to maturity. 'Purchases of longer-dated stocks will in future be made only at the Bank's discretion and initiative'.[2] On 28 May, the Governor's address laid down the main features of and philosophy underlying the new system (as discussed in Chapter 2) so it seems reasonable to date the new régime from now rather than its later formal implementation, even though both general and specific guidelines on credit remained in force. However, as the permitted growth in restricted lending in the quarter ending in June was 2½ per cent, scarcely restrictive, they had little impact in this period.

The Chancellor of the Exchequer had explained in his Budget speech that his overriding policy aim was to reduce unemployment and consequently he would cut taxes further and make no effort to reduce 'the rate of increase in the stock of money . . . until inflation abated'[3] (or less discretely, the government would adopt a passive monetary policy in so far as this was necessary to accommodate inflation and an actively expansionary one to reduce unemployment). In the first half of the year, the money stock (M_3) rose by over 5 per cent, partly the effect of large capital inflow (or the authorities' failure to 'sterilise' this, by offsetting action) and partly of large borrowing by local authorities. However, the private sector increased its borrowing by over £100m, about 13 per cent.

On 19 July, the Chancellor introduced a new package designed to stimulate demand, including heavy cuts in indirect taxation and the end of credit controls. The indirect tax cuts and an associated nationalised industry price restraint policy were designed to be associated with the CBI's policy of restricting price increases by private industry to 5 per cent p.a. The aim was to reduce inflation directly — 'at a stroke' to be mischievous — and to persuade unions to moderate wage claims and so indirectly reduce the inflation rate. The consequences were to be disastrous for the size of the public sector borrowing requirement and for monetary policy.

In the third quarter, the money supply (M_3) rose by 2.4 per cent. Large borrowing by the private sector (£604m) and a growing public sector borrowing requirement (£355m) were partly offset by large sales of gilt-edged securities to the non-bank private sector, amounting to £513m.[4] In September, the Bank repaid £395m of Special Deposits and in exchange forced the London clearing banks to subscribe £750m of three new government stocks (5¼ per cent Treasury stock 1973, 5½ per cent 1974 and 6¼ per cent 1977) as envisaged in May.[5] This closely followed the parallel of 1952 when the authorities had repaid a precursor of Special Deposits, known as Treasury deposit receipts. It is difficult to know whether this was intended to be a purely technical operation to slow down the impact of the repayment of Special Deposits. However, this was all it was in practice, as the banks only held the stock until the second quarter of 1972, when large quantities were sold to permit extra lending to the private sector from an individual bank's point of view. The effect was, of course, to increase the banking sector's assets in total (since bank lending to the public sector is determined by the public and private sector's actions) except in so far as the banks' actions changed the private sectors' behaviour.

During this period interest rates fell steadily. The Treasury Bill allotment rate was 6.77 per cent at the beginning of the year, 5.68 per cent on 30 April and 5.54 per cent on 16 July. The rate then rose for technical reasons in August but fell to 4.92 per cent on 3 September, after Bank Rate had been reduced to 5 per cent on 2 September from

6 per cent (its level since 30 April). This was one of the last agreed tenders by the discount houses acting as a cartel. Under the new arrangement (see Chapter 2, section (v)) the rate fell to 4.72 per cent by the end of September and 4.28 per cent by the end of November, but then rose slightly and finished the year at 4.41 per cent.

In the fourth quarter, there was a sharp acceleration in the growth of the money supply (to 4.4 per cent). The original published figure showed an even larger acceleration — to 5¾ per cent. The statistical appendix (Table C.3) shows the initial published figure for the key aggregates as well as the latest revised figure, as the authorities' actions should be judged in the light of the then available information. Here the argument that the authorities should have acted is reinforced by this consideration. Similarly the original figures showed bank lending to the private sector rising to nearly £800m, but later revisions reduced this to £588m. Very large sales of gilts to the non-bank private sector (£410m) (and total purchases of public sector securities of £576m) still left a substantial proportion of the PSBR to be financed by the banks (£891m).

The authorities' reaction to this development would obviously be crucial. It is difficult not to believe that this was the period when the authorities lost control of the situation. The authorities were so worried about unemployment that they decided not to act, in fact to encourage the trend. This reflected partly the attitude (which might not unfairly be termed panic) about unemployment. However, it must be stressed that there was general support in the City and the media for the policy — one prominent gilt-brokers' circular argued that monetary conditions were too tight and further relaxations should be implemented (by large purchases of gilts from the non-bank private sector and cuts in interest rates). Furthermore, the Bank of England's demand for money equations apparently suggested that very high growth in money supply was necessary. The article which emphasised this appeared in March 1972[6] — 'an apparently rapid rate of monetary expansion might actually be restrictive in its effect when associated with a strong increase in output', as the Chancellor hoped and forecast in his Budget speech. Later research in the Bank changed significantly the coefficients in the equations on which this conclusion rested.[7]

'Barberism' reached its apogee with the 1972 Budget.[8] Despite (or because of?) the government's defeat in the miners' strike of early 1972, the Chancellor cut taxation by £1,200m and expected to increase the PSBR by 200 per cent to £3,360 million. This swing occurred despite his forecast of high growth (5 per cent p.a.) which meant that the constant employment budget deficit rose still more (not that the UK authorities used this concept). This reflected the aim of reducing unemployment (then 3.8 per cent) at almost any price. The authorities also believed that increasing real take-home pay by tax cuts would buy off union militancy — incomes policy was still, apparently, ruled out on ideological grounds and as contrary to election pledges.

The Budget also included a provision to allow interest on loans to be offset against tax (restoring the pre-1969 position) so long as the interest charge exceeded £35. This cut the cost of borrowing for persons by the amount of their marginal tax rate, about a third for standard rate-payers and up to 95 per cent (the precise amount depending on whether earned income allowances could be claimed, etc.). It is not clear whether the likely effect of this on the demand for credit was considered — certainly it is not mentioned in any official statement at the time. Yet it is an incredible omission in view of the emphasis in *Competition and Credit Control* on allocation of credit by cost.

In the first quarter of 1972, the money stock rose by 4¾ per cent, largely fuelled by an increase in bank lending to the private sector of £1,610m. Inflows from abroad ceased to increase the domestic borrowing requirement (following the Smithsonian Agreement in December 1971). Sales of gilt-edged stock to the non-bank private sector were only £109m, against £726m in the same quarter of 1971 and £420m in the previous quarter. Total purchases of public sector debt by this sector were £279m, a fall of £326m on the first quarter of 1971. Thus the other forms of public sector debt partly offset the £617m fall in sales of gilts. This improvement was because the local authorities had repaid (short-term) debt on a large scale in 1971–3. Thus the gilts figures reflected the underlying deterioration better than the total figures. Another potentially worrying feature was that most of the new borrowing was by property and financial companies.

In the second quarter, M_3 rose by 7¾ per cent and even this was after large capital outflows in June had reduced the growth by about 2½ per cent. DCE rose by £2,110m (after £1,223m in the first quarter). Thus the statement in the September *Bulletin* is a considerable understatement: 'the money supply has recently been rising very fast'.[9] 'Barberism' had also been associated with a massive deterioration in the balance of payments. Virtually any theory of the exchange rate would have predicted a 'crisis' given the monetary and balance of payments consequences of the authorities' policy. Hence it should not have surprised the authorities when there was an outflow of over £1,000m in the second half of June, triggered off by a threatened dock strike. Nor should it have surprised anyone that the UK was forced to let the pound float and leave the EEC 'snake' (wherein exchange rate movements were limited to 2¼ per cent between member countries within the Smithsonian 4½ per cent band). From 23 to 27 June foreign exchange markets were closed and when they reopened sterling fell from $2.59 to $2.41 but recovered in July to $2.44, representing a 6¾ per cent devaluation on a trade-weighted basis against its Smithsonian parity.

(ii) The Reappraisal, June – October 1972

'Floating' was part of the dash-for-growth strategy (to avoid the overseas constraint which it was felt had prevented the Maudling experiment from succeeding in 1963–4)[10]. So it would have been illogical – but not necessarily impossible – for this to have triggered off the reappraisal. The authorities certainly allowed money market rates to rise with the overseas pressure put on them. They had drifted upwards in May but were still below January's level. In the second half of June, the rate on inter-bank deposits rose from 5.69 per cent to 7.75 per cent. The Treasury Bill rate similarly rose (by over 1 per cent) and Bank Rate was increased to 6 per cent on 22 June.

The fact that the clearing banks needed massive support from the Bank may have worried the authorities. A sale and repurchase agreement (involving £356m of gilts) from 23 June to 14 July was necessary to enable the banks to meet their obligations. Alternatively they could have borrowed on the overnight inter-bank market but rates here were already 200 per cent (or sold gilts with equally dramatic effects on interest rates). By any standards, the sterling outflow had precipitated a major banking crisis.

The first sign of the reappraisal was when the Governor of the Bank sent a letter to the banking system asking the banks to make credit less readily available to the property sector.[11] Their borrowing had risen from £447m to £1,019m in the year to August 1972. They rose to £2,094m in the next fifteen months, to illustrate the non-impact of the letter. Loans to 'other financial companies', many of them engaged in lending to property companies, rose to £2,737m in November 1973 (from £643m in May 1971). Furthermore, in November 1973 the authorities reclassified £600m of advances into these categories, so the total growth of this lending was over £4,000m.

Despite the letter, interest rates, the policy weapon of the new system, were not used further. In fact inter-bank rates fell until mid-

September and then levelled out at about 7½ per cent. (It must be emphasised, though, that the crisis had pushed base rates up to 7 per cent.) The authorities, on the one hand, were anxious to see that credit continued to stimulate the economy and yet that excessive credit and money growth were restrained. Almost harking back to the 'real bills' doctrine refuted by Ricardo,[12] they obviously wished to distinguish between speculative froth and the needs of trade. Unfortunately this implied a wish for sectoral controls which were inconsistent with 'a system under which the allocation of credit is primarily determined by cost'.

In the third quarter, M_3 rose by 4¼ per cent, bank lending to the private sector contributing £1,108m to this, while the offset from sales of public sector debt to the non-bank private sector, £199m, was the lowest total since 1970. This may have reflected the problems of selling gilts on a falling market (see Chapter 2, section (iii) and Chapter 8) but must have worried the authorities. Certainly policy seems to have switched decisively to at least wishing to see a more restrictive stance in this period.

(iii) Willing the End but Fearing the Means? October 1972 – July 1973

On 9 October the Bank announced and on 13 October implemented a new method of fixing its basic penalty rate. Bank Rate was abolished and replaced by 'minimum lending rate'. At least this change in nomenclature was sensible. Only one bill had been rediscounted since the Second World War and then, it is said, because the chairman of a discount house was curious to see how the mechanism worked. The Bank lent against the security of bills at a level it determined (it could and did fix this higher than either Bank Rate or MLR). At a policy level it permitted an increase in the rate without the problems of announcing one too overtly at a time of tricky negotiations between government and unions.

The new rate was fixed at 7¼ per cent, a 1¼ per cent jump. This was determined by a formula, the Treasury Bill average rate of discount plus ½ per cent rounded up to the nearest ¼ per cent. This was treated in the press as a move towards a more market-oriented formula – probably with official encouragement, though the *Bulletin* was careful not to say this. This implicit disclaimer was necessary as the authorities had, and have, continued to determine the Treasury Bill rate by signals to the discount market and reserved the right to override the formula if its signals were ignored. The Treasury Bill formula then offered a fig leaf to cloak policy changes, and in any case as Treasury Bills were one of the discount market's major earning assets, it was a logical basic relationship. Policy could then be implemented by lending below, at, or above the rate as seemed appropriate and by varying it by either of the methods described above. Of these, signals were expected to be the normal method, but the override power has had to be used quite often.

The change, though of interest technically, was more important as a change in policy stance. MLR continued to rise (to 7½ per cent on 27 October, 7¾ per cent on 1 December, 8 per cent on 8 December and 9 per cent on 22 December). This eventually triggered off an increase in the banks' base rate, the key to the method of control, of ½ per cent on 15 December and further increases during January, finally reaching 8½ per cent. MLR then fell back to 8¾ per cent, but base rates rose in February to 9½ per cent. Thus since June they had risen by 5 per cent but the tax relief meant that borrowing was cheaper for persons than in March 1971. While inflationary expectations had accelerated, as the CBI and FT surveys showed, despite the standstill on pay and prices announced on 6 November. The rise then was probably too small, if one assumes that it was necessary to rein back significantly the growth of money and credit, and was certainly too slow. The response to the acceleration in borrowing was so slow that it had taken a year to produce a change in rates, scarcely the response implied by the new approach. There were calls for Special Deposits of 1 per cent announced on 9 November (which 'had no significant impact')[1][3] and 2 per cent on 21 December which contributed to tightness in the money market and so helped to push up the minimum lending rate by market forces as well as being interpreted as a signal of official wishes.

In the first quarter of 1973 M_3 grew by 5.8 per cent, bank lending to the private sector rose by £1,464m and the Bank acted as a net purchaser of public sector debt from the private sector. In fact the growth would have been even higher but for the large outflow from sterling which cut M_3 by £250m. Thus the authorities were not tightening policy judged by their own criteria of the magnitude of credit flows and asset movements. In the second quarter growth in M_3 accelerated to 7¾ per cent using the banking month series while on a calendar quarterly basis the increase was 5.3 per cent. By any standards this was excessive but the discrepancy is a comment on the poor quality of official statistics and (perhaps) on the volatility of arbitrage funds, the merry-go-round, discussed in Chapter 4. These problems are partly a comment on the authorities' incompetence and partly a comment on the problems they faced. In the short term policy-making was hampered by poor statistics. On the other hand, the solution lay in the Bank's hand. Financial statistics had been improved since Radcliffe and upgrading them had been continuous. Nevertheless the authorities could and should have pressed the banks to provide better figures sooner.

(iv) Competition and Credit Control in Action, July — December 1973

During the first half of 1973 the interest rates had been allowed to fall, MLR had been reduced six times to 7½ per cent and bank base rates fell from their peak of 9½ per cent to 8 per cent. The authorities' policy was strange, given the developments of monetary aggregates and the rationale of competition and credit control. Declining rates had enabled large sales of gilt-edged securities to be made in the second quarter but these had not offset an avalanche of private borrowing from banks. This was the immediate background to the situation facing the authorities in July 1973. On a longer-term basis, bank lending to other financial companies was 175 per cent up, to companies 85 per cent up and to persons 175 per cent up on the third quarter in 1971: added to this, there was another sterling crisis in July — the pound depreciated by a further 5 per cent between 1 and 4 July (it fell from 89 per cent to 85 per cent of its Smithsonian parity). By 6 July it was down to 82 per cent and after a recovery in the next part of July it fell to 80.5 per cent on 26 July.

Thus it is not surprising that the authorities sharply changed their policy in July and forced MLR up by 1½ per cent on 20 July and a further 2½ per cent on 27 July, partly by a call for Special Deposits, partly by making its views clear to the market. The changed tone of official policy was very marked and clearly the authorities had accepted the need to let nominal rates rise sufficiently to achieve their goals. Unfortunately, one cannot determine whether it was in response to the pressure on sterling or to domestic developments. It is clear that both were in the authorities' minds. The kindest and most likely explanation is that the response to the immediate problems was determined by the longer-term credit and monetary environment.[14] A cynic might say that the crisis provided an excuse. The cynic with a long memory would have commented that the UK authorities have always responded like Pavlovian dogs with higher interest rates when there was a foreign exchange crisis.

Within the monetary policy framework of competition and credit control, the crucial development was that the bank base rates rose by 3 per cent (to 11 per cent) between the beginning of July and the end of August. The immediate response of the monetary aggregates was unfavourable. Gilt-edged sales were sluggish, as might have been expected, and bank lending to the private sector continued to surge ahead, by £2,115m in the third quarter (the largest increase in the year so far). Thus M_3 rose by 7.8 per cent in the third quarter (or by 8.5 per cent if one takes the difference in the levels series, rather than the change. It is understandable that if one calculates the levels and changes of a series separately they will differ slightly. However, this discrepancy is amazing and alarming). This may have been reinforced by arbitrage operations, but not so far as to change one's assessment of the position.

The authorities reacted by a Governor's letter (of 11 September[15]) calling for restraint in lending to persons and property companies. Lending to persons (other than for house purchase) was £1,658m in August 1972 (after £767m a year earlier). In August 1973 it was £2,346m on a comparable basis (and £2,943m on a revised basis). The other 'escape clauses' in competition and credit control were also involved — 'Regulation Q' was used to prevent the banks from paying more than 9½ per cent interest on small deposits, i.e. below £10,000.[16] Thus a rapid rise in interest rates and use of the escape clauses suggested that competition and credit control was being used as intended.

However, M_3 and bank lending continued to rise — bank lending by £1,000m in October alone — and further measures were taken in November when another 2 per cent Special Deposits were called (13 November) and minimum lending rate raised to 13 per cent by the Bank using override power (16 November). Furthermore, the clearing bank chairmen were ordered to raise loan rates to 13 per cent and complied. Thus it seemed competition and credit control was (at last) being used as intended. However in the fourth quarter M_3 grew by a further 7.3 per cent and the authorities decided to drop the scheme. The new 'new approach' is analysed in Chapter 8, but it is clear that the authorities felt that competition and credit control had failed.

They felt that it was necessary to control money and credit for both economic and political reasons. They also were unwilling to increase interest rates, or to see their volatility increase. Thus the mechanism of competition and credit control could not be used.

Notes

1. *Competition and Credit Control* (Bank of England, 1971), 'Competition and Credit Control: text of a document issued on 14th May 1971', p. 3.
2. *Bank of England Quarterly Bulletin*, Vol. 11, No. 2 (June 1971), p. 151.
3. *Hansard*, 30 March 1971.
4. All figures are latest revised version. See Appendix A for initially published

figures and below (pp. 52–3) for the impact of revisions on policy.

5. *Competition and Credit Control*, p. 14.

6. *Bank of England Quarterly Bulletin*, Vol. 12, No. 1 (March 1972), p. 43.

7. *Bank of England Quarterly Bulletin*, Vol. 14, No. 3 (September 1974), p. 284.

8. *Hansard*, 21 March 1972.

9. *Bank of England Quarterly Bulletin*, Vol. 12, No. 3 (September 1972), p. 314.

10. Thus Brittan could conclude: 'A case could be made for taking a calculated risk and attempting a home-based expansion provided there was an ultimate willingness to devalue.' (S. Brittan, *Steering the Economy* (Pelican, 1971), p. 232). It is clear that such expansionist arguments greatly influenced the government in its willingness to expand irrespective of balance of payments. It was felt that floating would avoid the balance of payments problem.

11. Reprinted in *Bank of England Quarterly Bulletin*, Vol. 12, No. 3 (September 1972), p. 327.

12. In the US, the controversy lasted until the establishment of the federal reserve system in 1913. See M. Friedman and A. J. Schwartz, *A Monetary History of the United States 1867–1960*. NBER Studies in Business Cycles, No. 12 (Princeton University Press, 1963).

13. *Bank of England Quarterly Bulletin*, Vol. 13, No. 1 (March 1973), p. 12.

14. This was the official line: 'The sharp tightening of monetary policy was most immediately occasioned by the upward trend of interest rates in foreign countries but has to be seen in the broad context of the state of the economy.' *Bank of England Quarterly Bulletin*, Vol. 13, No. 3 (September 1973), p. 277.

15. *Bank of England Quarterly Bulletin*, Vol. 13, No. 4 (December 1973), p. 445.

16. Even so, the Building Societies Association raised mortgage rates to 11 per cent.

4 COMPETITION AND CREDIT CONTROL: AN ANALYSIS

(i) The Reasons for Failure

That the scheme had failed in the authorities' view may be deduced from the fact that they replaced it so hurriedly in December 1973. As the money supply had grown by 60 per cent in two years this view is not surprising. Whether this growth was excessive, and what its effects were, are examined below. There seem to be three basic reasons why competition and credit control failed.

(a) The CCC policy was based on the authorities' willingness to raise interest rates when necessary, and to see interest rates fluctuate to a considerable degree (at least initially). The authorities were unwilling to let (nominal) rates rise sufficiently and they never caught up with the rising inflationary expectations, partially generated by the monetary growth itself. Even the 4 per cent rise in interest rates in July 1973 was too little too late. Given the problem (both economic and political) of mortgages, sufficiently high nominal rates were not really a practical possibility. The authorities' commitment to stability in interest rates abated little. Varying Shakespeare, even if they were willing to wound, they were afraid to use the knife.

One example of the retreat from intention to reality involves official reaction to bank sales of gilts. The Governor's speech had said: 'thus we shall not normally be prepared to facilitate movements out of gilt-edged by the banks even if these sales should cause the market temporarily to weaken quite sharply'.[1] Yet in June 1972 this is precisely what the 'sale and repurchase agreement' had done. Of course the circumstances were abnormal, yet so was the rapid rate of growth of money earlier in the year. One can argue that the Bank should have intervened to avert a banking crisis, but equally that the form of intervention was inconsistent with the spirit and the letter of competition and credit control. The authorities chose not to inflict any penalty on the banks for the position of their 'books' (which had left them without the ability to meet the outflow) which had resulted from the pace of their expansion of credit. If market mechanisms were to be used, then the loan should have been at a penal rate, rather than (effectively) costless.[2] A loan at, say, 15 per cent or 20 per cent p.a. for a fortnight would have been dramatic, yet it was the logic of the system in the circumstances. This

Table 4.1

3 months	Wholesale Money Rate	Base Rates	Margin
1971			
September	5.25	5	0.25
October	5.09	4.75	0.34
November	4.56	4.5	0.06
December	4.69	4.5	0.19
1972			
January	5.06	4.5	0.56
February	5.12	4.5	0.62
March	4.87	4.5	0.37
April	4.53	4.5	0.03
May	5.06	4.5	0.56
June	7.75	6	1.75
July	8.4	6.88	1.52
August	7.63	6.88	0.75
September	7.56	7.0	0.56
October	8.19	7	1.19
November	8.5	7	1.5
December	8.94	7.5	1.44
1973			
January	10.13	8.5	1.63
February	10.63	9.5	1.13
March	9.94	9.5	0.44
April	9.44	9	0.44
May	9.25	8.5	0.75
June	8.13	8.0	0.13
July	11.63	8	3.63
August	14.50	11	3.50
September	13.25	11	2.25
October	12.75	11	1.75
November	15.63	13	2.63
December	15.81	13	2.81
	Last working day	Last working Friday	

would have made the banks much more cautious about their future lending policy. In a reserve base system (like the US), one can avoid the necessity of such action because the banks fall below their minimum ratio and this is sufficient to induce the desired change in behaviour.

(b) The assumption was that raising the cost of bank funds would suffice to force up overdraft rates:

Of course the extent of the pressure we shall be able to bring to bear
on interest rates by our open market policies, backed up if necessary
by calls for Special Deposits will be affected by many factors: ...
However no limitation is envisaged in the Authorities' ability to
neutralise excess liquidity or *to bring about sufficiently strong
upward pressure on bank lending rates.*[3]

This was not so. Not surprisingly, when bank profits were over
100 per cent up on a year earlier, the banks were prepared to take losses
on marginal business to preserve market shares, to avoid the administrative and psychological costs of rate alteration and, even, to avoid
political criticism. Like public utilities in the USA, and banks elsewhere
in the 'old Commonwealth', the clearing banks in particular have been
targets for political criticism on many occasions and there have been
frequent suggestions that they be nationalised.[4] Thus this sensitivity is
not surprising.

However it is clear that the authorities were seriously worried by
their inability to force up base rates when necessary. Thus in
November 1973 the authorities took special action to ensure that base
rates rose by specifically ordering the banks to raise them. One can see
the need for this by examining the behaviour of the margin between
wholesale money rates, the marginal cost of bank funds, and base rates
(see Table 4.1) and the general tendency for the margin to fall when
rates rise. The sort of model the Bank was implicitly using would
predict the opposite (so long as the own rate interest elasticity of
money exceeds the interest elasticity of credit which the Bank clearly
believed — the proof of this is given in the simplest case in footnote 5).
Ironically, this problem was reduced in December 1973 when the banks
related the cost of some borrowing to market rates on wholesale
deposits.[6]

(c) Finally, there were two technical problems which once more
obscured the statistics, and complicated both control and observations
of monetary developments. One was arbitrage to take advantage of
overdraft rates being lower than deposit rates, the so-called 'merry-go-
round'. It was estimated by City sources that perhaps £600m was
involved in such transactions. The other, the 'CD tax loophole' was
perhaps twice as large. A Certificate of Deposit was defined as debt, and
as a result of the 1965 Budget trading in debts was not taxable (nor
losses offsetable against tax) — this provision was enacted to close some
loopholes in the tax laws. This meant that one could buy a one-year
CD on 1 January, for, say, £100,000 at 10 per cent and sell it on 30

December for £109,990 without paying tax (one paid tax on the
interest only if the CD were held to maturity or one were an 'authorised
dealer' in securities). However one could use the CD as security for a
loan and offset the interest on this against tax. At the top UK rate of
98 per cent this meant one could borrow at, say, 12 per cent and pay
net only £240. Thus a top-rate taxpayer could make £9,750 on an
investment of nothing while his bank was still making a very healthy
2 per cent profit.

This complicated control of the money supply because it meant that
some part of the growth of the money stock was almost entirely without the economic effects one would normally predict. More seriously,
it meant that trends in monetary developments, already obscured by
poor statistics, were further complicated because the arbitrage 'money'
was a very short-term phenomenon and tended to be concentrated in
the one-week money market. Thus the month-to-month pattern of
monetary growth was obscured by whether or not the arbitrage was
taking place. When it occurred, £600m was created; when the transaction was reversed this £600m disappeared. However, the extent of the
problem seems to be greatly exaggerated by the authorities (in the
Deputy Governor's speech, for example).[7] This was a phenomenon that
could be monitored by observation of the relevant (relative) interest
rates and the money supply figures adjusted accordingly. This was
done, for example, by Gordon Pepper in his *Greenwell's Monetary
Bulletin.*

(ii) How Large was Monetary Growth?

The authorities argued that the genuine growth in the money supply
was much less than that in the published figures.[8] There are a number
of reasons advanced for this.

(a) Arbitrage and the 'CD Tax Loophole'

The 'merry-go-round' and the CD tax loophole, which were discussed in
section (i), were obviously not part of the money supply in the sense
that they were likely to increase inflationary pressures directly. Their
main effect was probably to allow companies to guarantee that their
overdraft facilities ('lines of credit') could not be affected by the
reintroduction of a ceiling, discussed further below as 'precautionary
demand' (section (v)). However, the size of these factors can be
exaggerated: M_3 grew by 60 per cent in 1972 and 1973, of which about
6 per cent can be attributed to the CD tax loophole, even making the
extreme (indeed impossible assumption) that no one was exploiting it

in 1971: (i.e. if the 1971 figure for M_3 was not boosted by this factor) total growth in CD holdings was only £1,000m. More likely, about half of this latter figure (2½ per cent) can be deducted from the growth in M_3. It is harder to decide how much of the 'merry-go-round' money was in M_3 at this time. One month CD rates were favourable for arbitrage but short-term rates were not. The banks were attempting to police the 'loophole' more closely. The *Bulletin*[9] concluded that 'little arbitrage seems to have taken place'. In this case, one may safely decide that the overall rate of growth of M_3 over the two years was not affected by the 'merry-go-round', even if the quarterly movements were.

Moreover, as the Bank believed, and still believes, that such short-run fluctuations are of little economic significance, it is difficult to use this as an alibi for the overall conduct of policy. The CD loophole is a reflection on the problems facing the Inland Revenue in their perpetual guerilla war with tax accountants, and is perhaps an argument for simplification of the tax laws. The 'merry-go-round' existed because of a serious problem of monetary policy — the inability to force base rates up as effectively as had been envisaged. However, it is difficult to see how policy would have been changed significantly if the 'merry-go-round' itself had not existed. Conceptually, it may be important that M_3 was not an unsullied indicator of credit, money, liquidity, etc. However, central bankers should operate in a world of shades of grey, not of black and white, and the effect of these two factors on M_3 as an indicator was not significant. The growth of M_3 is not affected even by the exclusion of all CDs — in 1972–3 M_3 — CDs grew by 61 per cent; M_3 by 62 per cent. In any case some of the CD growth reflected changing banking practices, not the CD tax loophole.

(b) 'End-Ceiling' Effects and Reintermediation

It was argued that much of the growth in M_3 reflected the effect of the end of ceilings as depositors and borrowers strove to remove the excess demand for money and credit which had built up in the 1960s. However one must carefully distinguish two different types of 'end-ceiling' effect. One is to bring back within the banking sector transactions which had occurred outside it during the era of ceilings — 'reintermediation' as the Bank called it. The other is the satisfaction of previously frustrated demand. *The inflationary effects of satisfying the demand for credit are the same whether the demand has existed for one week or ten years.* In fact, one of the chief arguments against rationing is precisely this — that when the control is abolished steps must be taken to remove any excess demand. 'Catching up' in money and credit markets after the removal of ceilings is identical in effect to an increase in the demand for credit (or money) caused by a change in inflationary expectations, or any other factor.

The volume of reintermediation is hard to measure. One must first of all stress that it is not without economic effect. To take the simplest form of disintermediation — if A had lent money to B rather than holding a bank deposit and B holding an overdraft with the same bank. If A regards a claim on B as less liquid than one on the bank because of lower marketability or higher default risk then this is an economic effect of considerable significance — it is part of either a Tobinesque or Friedmanite argument for caring about banks (the money supply) or financial intermediation in general. The intermediation of a transaction obviously yields benefits to the transactors, otherwise it would not occur. These benefits may be lower transaction costs, but they normally involve either changing the maturity structure of the claims or increasing their marketability (for example, most financial institutions lend longer than they borrow, thus increasing the 'liquidity' of both sides in the Radcliffean sense). The monetarist position stresses the importance of banks in this context, the Tobinesque one stresses that all financial institutions matter — as in Gurley and Shaw's work.[10] However there is little practical difference between the propositions here.

The extent of 'reintermediation' depends on showing either that some transitions were switched from one market to another, or at least that the banks' share of some markets rose.

It is very difficult to do this precisely. Certainly no one has, because of the poor quality of statistics. It is possible, however, to use the Bank's flow-of-funds figures to make some attempt to do this for the personal sector (see Table 4.2).

Clearly the share of banks had risen dramatically from 30 per cent to 80 per cent, comparing the financial years 1970/1 (the end of the old approach) and 1972/3 (the heyday of the 'new'). Nevertheless, concentration on new personal lending by banks does not distort the picture very much, if expressed as a percentage of the level of M_3 in the first quarter of 1972 (or of personal disposable income or any other relevant magnitude). To know that new credit extended to persons has risen from 2.7 per cent to 13 per cent is not different in its implications for policy from 0.8 per cent to 10.9 per cent. Moreover, it includes the effect of structural change, discussed in section (c), as well as end-ceiling effects. However, here one's view of economic theory does matter somewhat in that the difference is of more significance in so far as one

Table 4.2

	1970/1 (£m) [a]	1972/3 (£m) [a]
New loans to persons by companies [b]	138 (23.9%)	100 (3.6%)
New loans to persons by OFIs [c]	269 (46.5%)	357 (12.8%)
New loans to persons by banks	171 (29.6%)	2,327 (83.8%)
	578	2,784

a. Financial years.
b. Other items, which includes trade credit to public corporations.
c. HP lending + 'other lending'.

cares about 'liquidity' or 'money', much less if one cares only about credit. The 'reintermediation' argument is more significant if one is an extreme 'Keynesian' arguing that credit matters, rather than money or Tobinesque 'liquidity'.

(c) Structural Change in Bank Behaviour

An argument related to that in section (b) is that the new approach led to a structural change in bank attitudes whereby they bid more vigorously for deposits and so created a new type of demand for banks' liabilities. Again we must be careful to see whether this represents a change in the composition of liquid assets, or an increase in their level. Increased competition by banks can lead to:

(1) a diversion of the demand for assets from other private sector assets. This would have little effect on the economy *except in so far as the bank asset is more marketable or has a lower default risk,* unless one takes a strict monetarist position. Certainly this is true of bank assets compared to finance house deposits;

(2) a diversion as in (1) but from public sector assets. Here the effect is to increase credit but not 'liquidity'; money again rises. Liquidity would actually fall if public sector assets were less marketable than private ones. In the UK, a claim on the Midland Bank is probably as highly regarded as a claim on a local authority so this does not matter;

(3) an increase in total liquid or near-money assets.

One can try to see which of these occurred by examination of alternative definitions of the 'money supply'. If the structural change hypothesis is valid there would be substantially less growth in monetary aggregates which are not affected by the change. For example, if bank deposits had replaced Treasury Bills then a wider monetary aggregate, including Treasury Bills, would show slower growth.

Before examining these aggregates two points must be noted. One is that the growth of Certificates of Deposit increased the 'moneyness' of interest-bearing deposits. A three-month Certificate of Deposit is almost identical to a three-month wholesale deposit, except that the former is marketable in a vigorous secondary market whereas all one could do with the latter is use it as security for loan. This has two implications for analysis of statistics. M_1 includes a lot (in December 1976, £2,495m (13.1 per cent)) of interest-bearing sight deposits. Any theory of structural change would imply that some of the growth in CDs represented a switch from these deposits, since a marketable interest-bearing deposit is a very much closer substitute for a 'sight' deposit than any previously existing security.

More generally, the increased bidding for deposits must have attracted funds from current accounts, if only because some current accounts earned implicit (tax-free) interest in the form of remitted bank charges (see Chapter 6). As the closest of substitutes for each other at the margin, a structural growth in M_3 must represent a structural fall in M_1. (Cheques can traditionally be written against deposit accounts; much of M_1 pays explicit or implied interest.)

Thus the slower growth of M_1 (21.1 per cent) can be discounted as proof of monetary orthodoxy on these grounds. In any case one would expect M_1 to grow more slowly than M_3 as transactions balances should grow less fast than output because of economies of scale, even without this substitution effect.

Adding other 'liquid assets' to M_3 does not change the analysis significantly; this aggregate grows by 50.2 per cent, M_3 by 61.5 per cent. Further, the public sector component of these assets grew by only 36.4 per cent, so 'credit' grew even further than this broad aggregate.

The appropriate definition of money is a long-debated question.[11] Within an eclectic framework, or a Tobin-Radcliffe one, all aggregates matter but here the similarity (adjusting for structural change) is such that one can be reasonable sure that the appropriate aggregate grew by about 50 per cent in the two years of the hey-day of the new approach.

(iii) Was Monetary Growth Excessive?

The authorities periodically argued that the level of monetary growth could be justified by the nature of the economic situation facing them. To some extent there can be no *a priori* view of what is 'excessive' growth in any aggregate. The effects of any level of growth include

Table 4.3

	End 1971 [a,b]	End 1973	Per Cent Change
M_1	10,790[a]	13,100	21.1
$£M_3$	19,897[a]	31,540	58.5
M_3	20,411[a]	32,970	61.5
Treasury Bills[c]	54	22	−59.3
Trustee Savings Bank Ordinary Accounts	481	544	13.1
Trustee Savings Bank Investment Accounts	1,636	2,025	23.4
National Savings Banks Ordinary Accounts	507	537	9.9
National Savings Banks Investment Accounts	117	114	− 2.6
Local Authority debt 'short term'	1,802	3,026	69.9
Building Society Deposits[d]	491	596	21.4
Building Society Shares	11,695	16,022	37.0
Public Sector Liquid Assets	4,597	6,268	36.4
All Liquid Assets[e]	37,194	55,856	50.2

a. Adjusted for breaks.

b. As near to end year as statistics permit, all are between 30 September and 31 March, except for building societies.

c. March 1971 level plus subsequent changes as shown in *Bulletin* to give figures for December 1971 and 1973.

d. End of financial year for individual building society, probably centred around September.

e. This comprises all financial assets with an original maturity less than 3 months, except for corporate bills.

Sources: *Bank of England Quarterly Bulletin; Annual Abstract of Statistics.*

good and bad elements and these can be weighed against the objectives of the authorities to determine which is the optimal level. Thus it may seem strange to consider whether monetary growth was excessive before considering the effects of monetary growth on inflation, etc.

However, normal considerations do not apply here in that one can construct a theoretical case against any acceleration in monetary growth from about 8 per cent p.a. to 20–25 per cent p.a. (at least given the level of inflation in the UK). It seems reasonable to argue that inflationary expectations must have been about 6 per cent (inflation rates are shown in the appendix). If one wished to leave the level of capacity utilisation and employment unchanged, this implies about 9 per cent p.a. growth in money, whatever the theory of how monetary developments affect 'real' ones. Unless financial markets were affected by a strong 'bear' mood, when Tobin and Keynes would both have argued that monetary expansion should be used to try to offset this; however share prices had risen consistently since the Conservative victory in June 1970, by 25 per cent. In fact, if anything, the less monetarist one is, the *slower* should have been monetary growth in this period.

However the authorities wished to reduce unemployment. It is clear that in a modern economy as rigid as the UK's, it is virtually impossible for output to grow by more than 5 per cent p.a. This implies capacity utilisation rising by about 2 per cent p.a., employment by about 1 per cent in the first year, and unemployment falling by about ½ per cent p.a. in the first year and 1 per cent in the second and subsequent years. This may be an unpleasant fact about the UK economy, but it was accepted by Mr Barber — his policy claim was exactly this.

Thus, ignoring any perverse aims (like worsening the balance of payments) or any nonsensical ones (like increasing bank profits), the maximum desirable rate of monetary growth can be calculated so long as one can reach consensus on what rate of monetary expansion is necessary to increase output relative to the capacity ceiling. Unfortunately monetary theory is least well developed on this subject, and the answer would depend on speeds of adjustment, various income and interest elasticities and other factors, including the structure of the economy. However no economist who grants any importance to financial factors has ever argued that such growth would exceed twice the rate of output growth. In the context of 1972–3, this implies (prime facie) a maximum desirable rate of 12–13 per cent, about half that which occurred. It must be stressed that in the circumstances of the period one is lucky in that it is much easier to determine the highest desirable rate of growth of monetary growth. The neo-Keynesian, who would put emphasis on accommodating the expansionary effect of fiscal policy, and the Tobinesque variety of neo-Keynesian, who emphasises financial sentiment, would in fact support lower rates of monetary expansion than a 'monetarist'.

Hence the prima facie case that monetary expansion was excessive seems decisive. One should now, however, consider the counter-arguments before studying the detailed effects of the excessive growth, if excessive growth there was, in a later chapter. These arguments rested on either the need to reduce unemployment, i.e. the factors discussed above, or on the nature of the demand for money.

(iv) The Nature of the Demand for Money

As mentioned above (Chapter 3) the authorities argued that whereas
the theoretical arguments tend to assume a real income elasticity of
demand for money of approximately one, this view was incorrect for
the UK as this income elasticity was nearer to two.[12] As this view was
abandoned in a later *Bulletin* article[13] this issue can be ignored, though
its influence on policy was no doubt considerable. There are two more
important issues:

(a) did the authorities create an 'excess supply of money'?

(b) is it proof of a safe monetary policy if the supply of money does
not exceed the demand?

The first argument has been put very strongly by Artis and Lewis.[14]
Their proposition is that the 'supply side counterparts', especially bank
lending, created an excess supply of money and that this disequilibrium
was responsible for the adverse consequences of the new approach. In
the more academic of their two papers they develop the best model so
far in which to test the workings of the new approach. The supply of
money is determined by the interaction between the 'supply side
counterparts' (the PSBR and private demand for government bonds and
credit). This in turn, together with interest rates, influences GDP, which
in turn affects the demand for money. The supply and demand for
money are equilibrated over a period by movements in interest rates.
The proposition is that in 1972–3, the money supply consistently
exceeded demand with continuing inflationary effects.

This is a very powerful and useful model and illustrates the cleft
stick in which the authors of the new approach were caught when
defending its adoption. The scheme assumed a stable demand for
money, so if there were no such function the case for the new approach
disappears (using *modus tollendo tollens* for the rigorous-minded). On
the other hand, with a conventional stable demand for money function
the inflationary consequences of the policy's implementation are clear.

However, Artis and Lewis seem to imply there is some normative
significance in satisfying the demand for money, rather as the Bank
seemed to argue. That is, they argued that if there had been a structural
shift in the demand for money then this would be sufficient to justify
the implementation of the policy,[15] or at least to argue that the
inflationary or other consequences of such a policy would only be
those attributable to the level of interest rates (which might even be
exogenous, fixed by overseas influences).[16]

This argument seems misguided. In one sense, the quantity of money in existence must be demanded, *pace* Artis and Lewis: 'The view is regrettably heard too often that the stock of money in existence must be demanded. It is important to stress that this is fallacious.'[17]

The holders of money are willing to hold it, at least for an instant and under the constrained situation they face (ignoring cheques in the process of clearing and other 'transit items' such as bank notes in the post). There must always be a momentary equilibrium in that no one is forced to hold money in the way that a shopkeeper holds involuntary stocks since the nature of money is such that one can always get 'rid' of it. The holder in many cases may intend to dispose of some part of his money balances when conditions alter, e.g. someone living in a village may intend to buy goods or financial assets the next time he is in town (when the transaction cost falls within the neo-classical framework). Thus a perfect demand for money function would explain why the quantity of money in existence was held. Thus in this sense, money demand and supply would be in equilibrium (one might call it a temporary equilibrium, but for the different technical meaning of that term). However, either of these might be the case.

(a) The holder planned to dispose of his balance in such a way that only some 'inflationary development' (e.g. a rise in asset prices or nominal GDP) could restore equilibrium. This could be because of the constraints inducing the holder to be content to hold his balances, e.g. transactions costs, real or psychological. Alternatively, it might be that his intended reason for acquiring money was to perform some transaction which would put the money market back into a constrained equilibrium, which would involve some other transactor engaging in an inflationary transaction.

(b) The monetary equilibrium might only have been achieved by putting at least two other markets into disequilibrium (thus avoiding violation of Walras' law), and the resolution of these disequilibria would involve 'inflationary consequences'.

The effect of explaining the demand for money by different variables also depends on the nature of the transmission mechanism. For example, increased bidding in the CD market by banks would have a more powerful impact if transmission is by credit routes than by 'liquidity' ones.

Returning to the main argument, in the 'comparative static' world of the IS/LM curve it is true that if the demand for money function is

$$D^m = 30 + 1.1. \text{(output)} + 1.0 \text{ Prices}$$

and output is 110 and the price level 120, in period t, then if one fixes
the money supply for ever at 271 (the level demanded) this will not
have inflationary effects. However this result does not apply in a world
of continuous adjustment and many markets. The momentary equilibrium in the money market is a result of interaction between the demand
and supply curves of all other markets and the whole range of behaviour
of transactors involving *inter alia* adjustment patterns and expectation
patterns (the impact of these has been demonstrated by Mussa).[18]
There is no normative meaning to a demand-for-money function in this
context. Nor can one attribute any such meaning to a longer-term
equilibrium level of money demand. In this general equilibrium context
one cannot say that part of money demand which depends on the
existing price level is any different to that dependent on, say, the
building society being a 20p bus ride away.

(v) Why was Borrowing from Banks so Large?

One issue that must be considered in the analysis of competition and
credit control is why was the demand for credit so large? There are
various hypotheses that can be considered and the answer is important
both in itself and in determining the nature of the 'credit' effects of
competition and credit control as distinct from the monetary effects
(or if the alternative terminology is preferred in determining the extent
of the credit transmission mechanism). Furthermore, it has some
implications for the Artis-Lewis analysis of a large demand for credit
leading to excess money creation. Unfortunately it is impossible to
answer the question very precisely.

One explanation is that it represented pent-up demand frustrated by
ceilings. Another is that the very low, in fact significantly negative, real
rates of interest induced people and firms to borrow, especially as
inflationary expectations soared. Another concentrates on the high
rates of return available on property and some stock market invest-
ments. All of these imply similar effects on asset prices and consumer
spending. Another explanation argues that much borrowing was
precautionary, against the return of ceilings. Given prevailing interest
rates the cost of such borrowing, reinvested in short-term liquid assets,
was low. It certainly seems that such borrowing was very extensive.

One should, however, note that while the corporate sector as a
whole was borrowing from and lending to banks on a large scale, this
may not have involved individual firms engaging in both transactions.

Furthermore, precautionary borrowing of this type would not be without economic impact. 'Liquidity' is increased by borrowing and lending even on a short-term basis, as the bank loans were assumed to be of a much longer maturity than the assets. Radcliffean, monetarist and Keynesian could agree that it would be inflationary. However, its effect would be much more diffuse and longer-acting than if it were concentrated, fairly quickly, on financial and real asset prices. Paradoxically, precautionary borrowing is thus much closer in its implications to Friedman's version of the diffuse unpredictable nature of the effects of monetary policy, than is borrowing to permit speculation. Ironically the authorities argued that precautionary borrowing was large as an anti-monetarist argument!

With regard to Artis and Lewis, this form of borrowing creates its own demand for money, but without any implication that this legitimises the size of the money stock in any way.

(vi) Conclusions

In this chapter the reasons for the new approach being regarded as a failure have been considered. The proposition has been established that the period was one of excess monetary growth since neither structural change, statistical quirks nor appeals to the demand for money can change this. No conceivable objective of government policy could have been served by such monetary growth.

Notes

1. *Competition and Credit Control* (Bank of England, 1971); 'Key Issues', p.9.
2. The banks were allowed to keep the accruing interest on the gilt-edged, contrary to US practice.
3. 'Key Issues', p. 9.
4. The latest in *Banking and Finance* (Labour Party, 1976), which reviews some of the earlier suggestions.
5. Given a competitive banking system and the market cleared by price, the demand for deposits function may be written as

$$D^D = a + b \, r^D \quad \text{(where } r^D = \text{the deposit rate)}$$

and the demand for loans as

$$D^L = c - d \, r^A \quad \text{(where } r^A = \text{the advances rate)}$$

(r^A may be written as $r^D + r^m$, where r^m is the gross margin between deposit and loan rates).
So

$$D^L = c - d \, r^D - d \, r^m$$

From these equations

$$r^m = \frac{a + c}{e} - \frac{(d - b)}{e} r^D$$

dr^m/dr^D is negative so long as $d > b$, i.e. r^m falls when r^D rises so long as the interest elasticity of loans is less than that of the own rate elasticity of deposits.

6. *Bank of England Quarterly Bulletin*, Vol. 14, No. 1 (March 1974), p. 21.

7. *Bank of England Quarterly Bulletin*, Vol. 13, No. 2 (June 1973), p. 193.

8. *Bank of England Quarterly Bulletin*, Vol. 13, No. 2 (June 1973), p. 197.

9. *Bank of England Quarterly Bulletin*, Vol. 14, No. 1 (March 1974), p. 12.

10. J. Gurley and E. Shaw, *Money in a Theory of Finance* (Brookings Institute, 1960).

11. For a summary, see C. A. E. Goodhart, *Money, Information and Uncertainty* (Macmillan, 1975), pp. 13–19.

12. *Bank of England Quarterly Bulletin*, Vol. 12, No. 1 (March 1972), p. 43.

13. *Bank of England Quarterly Bulletin*, Vol. 14, No. 3 (September 1974), p. 284.

14. M. Artis and M. Lewis, 'The Demand-for-Money: stable or unstable?', *Banker* (March 1974); M. Artis and M. Lewis, 'The Demand for and Supply of Money' (unpublished): hereafter Artis and Lewis (2).

15. For a statement of the conventional, opposed view, see M. J. Hamburger, 'The Demand for Money in 1971: Was there a shift?', *Journal of Money, Credit and Banking* (May 1973).

16. E.g. *Bank of England Quarterly Bulletin*, Vol. 13, No. 2 (June 1973), p. 195.

17. Artis and Lewis (2).

18. M. Mussa, *A Study in Macroeconomics* (North Holland, 1977).

5 THE EFFECTS OF EXCESS MONETARY GROWTH

In Chapter 4 it was concluded that monetary growth was 'excessive' in 1972 and 1973. The effects of this will now be considered. Following the 'Tobinesque framework' (discussed in the appendix to Chapter 1), one would expect that there would be a large 'spillover' into building society assets, the next most liquid asset for most asset-holders. As 'credit' effects would also influence the property market via banks as well as the mortgage market, then, *a priori*, a major impact on property prices seems a reasonable expectation. There has been much written about the impact of the money supply on share prices — it is a favourite transmission mechanism of monetarists because it omits some of the steps in the Tobin mechanism while being close enough to it in spirit to appeal to Tobinesque economists. Hence this issue will be considered. The effect of the money supply on inflationary psychology and the gilts market will then be analysed, since the 'flight from money' attracted considerable attention in the media and the issue involves some interesting theoretical aspects. The impact of excess money growth on the exchange rate is then analysed. These provide some possible non-monetarist means by which the excess monetary growth might influence the price level, but the whole issue of the relationship between money and inflation is considered in the final section.

(i) The Residential Property Market

The 'new approach' seems to have had fundamental effects on both the owner-occupied residential property market and on the commercial property market. There was some overlap between the markets as developers bought large older homes for conversion into offices or flats, which were then resold to owner-occupiers. Large blocks of flats were also traded between developers and frequently the flats sold off to tenants or other buyers piecemeal ('flat-breaking'). However, at least outside London, the two markets were distinct.

The residential property market was and is dominated by building society loans, which finance most purchasers. In 1972 these loans amounted to 88.5 per cent of total loans for house purchase. Of the balance, local authorities accounted for 7.9 per cent (£325m), mainly for old properties and/or poorer households, where financing is

71

provided by public bodies in most countries, e.g. by Federal Housing Administration underwriting in the USA. Insurance companies provided 3.7 per cent, mainly in the highest price brackets, where the extra tax advantages of this form of finance sways borrowers. Some borrowers have been attracted by the availability of fixed-rate mortgages but they never amounted to more than a small fraction of the insurance companies' small share of the market.

The housing market was dominated by two phenomena:

(a) in 1972 and 1973 house prices rose at an annual rate of 34 per cent and by over 100 per cent in total during the period of the new approach. For comparison, the retail price index rose by 9 per cent p.a. and real personal disposable income by 5.5 per cent p.a. in 1972–3;

(b) the total of building society advances rose from £2,021m in 1970 to £3,649m in 1972 and £3,540m in 1973.

The issue is the causal relationships of these two and monetary developments. Economic theory would suggest the following:

(a) the increase in the money supply leads to a reshuffling of portfolios and as a result;

(b) there is an increase in building societies' funds and this leads to an increase in their lending. This probably takes the form of reducing 'equilibrium rationing' as they satisfy previously rationed-out demand by, *inter alia*, cutting the income : mortgage ratio and raising the loan : house price ratio;[1]

(c) because of (b) there are now more buyers in the market and each has greater purchasing power. This increase in 'effective demand' leads to some increase in new building, but most of the effect is seen in higher house prices.

Certainly developments in the housing market are largely consistent with this picture. In 1971 the number of houses started in the private sector rose by 25.4 per cent (from a very depressed level) but then the industry was near its capacity and 'starts' rose by only 9.5 per cent in 1972 and actually fell by 5.3 per cent in 1973. This is the response one would expect to such an increase in demand, either as a 'St Louis' monetarist predicting an initial increase in output and a delayed price effect, or as a more orthodox economist arguing in terms of capacity and relatively inelastic supply.

However, the building societies denied their responsibility for the increase, and tended to blame either costs or rising demand. The first is basically the proposition that there was an exogenous shift in the replacement value of houses which led to a rise in prices. This is unconvincing *a priori*, as it should have led to a fall in the number of houses built, and it is rather bizarre to expect such a sudden shift in building costs. The evidence is that it did not occur — construction costs rose by only 11.2 per cent in 1972 and 23.5 per cent in 1973. With the upsurge in demand it would be a normal response for wages (and overtime hours) to rise as builders tried to satisfy extra demand. One would expect the economists' 'less suitable resources' to be employed in building, e.g. as unskilled and inexperienced workers were employed.

More of the 'supply side' theorists have, however, concentrated on land prices rather than construction costs. This ignores the point, going back at least to Ricardo, that land prices do not affect the price of houses but are determined by the demand for houses. This would not be the case if, for example, alterations in planning regulations greatly reduced the amount of land available but this was not the case — and is again inconsistent with the increase in house-building. It was also argued that speculators were responsible for the 61 per cent increase in land prices and so for the rise in house prices. Again, they were given the opportunity to make (very easy) profits by the boom but could not have caused it except, perhaps, by a ring buying up all the available building land and reducing supply, or some other implausible scenario.

Thus it is reasonable to conclude that a shift in demand was responsible for the rise in prices but it was argued that this was much more a rise in underlying demand than in 'effective' demand, i.e. due to changes in other factors rather than building society practice.

One obvious such factor would be a rise in incomes but clearly no plausible income elasticity could explain the behaviour of the housing market, whereby a 5 per cent increase in real incomes is associated with a 25 per cent increase in relative prices. It has been argued that the Housing Finance Act of 1973 may have switched demand from the local authority housing sector to the private sector (by raising rents on public-sector housing). This is possible, but there is no evidence for it and the likely size of any switch is very small.[2]

It is very unlikely that any underlying demographic change could have such a marked effect in such a short period, especially as the only major trend (downwards in the birth rate) might have been expected to produce the opposite result. New household formation was very high in this period but this probably reflects a response to the low cost of mortgages and the availability of finance rather than any underlying demographic changes; it consisted largely of an increase in single-person households.

It should be noted that the low turnover of the housing stock (around 8 per cent p.a.) and loan-financed nature of the transactions makes it peculiarly vulnerable to variations in price. Thus the building societies have a responsibility to try to ensure some stability, which they have accepted by the formation in 1973 of a Joint Action Committee with the Department of the Environment and the Bank of England.

It is thus clear that building societies can be 'blamed' for the rise in house prices but one must note the very attractive nature of housing as an investment in this period, with mortgage rates of 8 per cent p.a., offsetable against tax. A very high rate of return was offered even at the historic inflation of house prices of 9—10 per cent p.a., let alone when expectations responded to the acceleration in house prices. The boom, like any speculative one, was of a self-fulfilling nature. Capital gains on one house encouraged people to buy bigger ones, and provided the deposit ('margin' in US market parlance). The rise in prices encouraged people to bring purchases forward and to buy bigger houses. Prices were justified on the 'other sucker' theory (that they could be resold at a high price) at least as much as on the underlying nature of the house.[3] The picture of a speculative market is reinforced by the enormous ratio between cash put up and the effect on the value of houses. The value of houses probably rose by £60,000m in 2½ years. The amount of new money is harder to calculate. Total loans for house purchase were about £13,000m. Applying a 40 per cent ratio of own to borrowed funds suggests that the total own funds were £8,000m and this depends on a very high ratio: for the new purchasers 15 per cent is a more typical figure. Some of this £8,000m was provided by the capital gain on a house already owned by those 'trading-up' (who tend to provide the largest share of own capital). Allowing for these factors, perhaps the total of 'new' money was £2,000m, and some of this may have been provided by bank borrowing or borrowing from relations to pay the deposit. Thus this provided the leverage for £60,000m of capital gains. Reported widespread 'gazumping' (breaking a contract to resell at a higher price) and dealings in rights to purchase unbuilt houses reinforce this picture of a speculative market.

The effects of this enormous rise are hard to judge. The personal sector's financial wealth was about £125,000m at the end of 1971. Net of mortgages, owner-occupied houses were worth about £35,000m and landed wealth was about £25,000m (net of mortgages). Thus the impact was considerable on both the net worth of the personal sector and its composition, and economic theory suggests that these will have some effect on spending and the allocation of savings. Even if one assumes only £60 extra spending on average by each owner-occupier (less than 1 per cent of the gain), this amounts to about £500m.

Owner-occupiers can realise their gains and move: the choice is rented property or a smaller/cheaper house. The former is and was probably unattractive on both psychological grounds and because of the future expected trend in rents. The demand for housing is probably price elastic[4] but there is a countervailing force: the desirability of a house as an asset offering protection against inflation. So while the higher price may reduce the demand for housing (a movement along the demand curve) a higher price will also generate expectation of higher prices and therefore increase demand (a shift of the demand curve). Almost certainly the latter effect could be large enough to ensure that the effects of rising house prices will exclude the sale of a house and moving.

The increase in wealth could still, however, probably have had significant effects. One would expect both more spending and some attempt to re-allocate wealth away from the non-interest-bearing illiquid form in which a greater proportion of it now is. Since houses are indivisible, one cannot sell part of them except by borrowing against the security of a house. One way in which this can be done is by means of a second mortgage; certainly increasing housing prices must be at least a permissive factor in second mortgage loans. There are no figures for other borrowing against houses, e.g. borrowing from a bank with a house as collateral. Even for second mortgages, there are no good data since 1968, despite general agreement, for what that is worth, that they have expanded rapidly. In 1968 the Crowther Report quoted both an estimate of £25m by the Association of Finance Agents, and an offical estimate of £14m, which omitted some significant lenders.[5] In addition, building societies usually lend about £30–35m p.a. in further advances.

Theoretically a change in the wealth of owner-occupiers is partly offset by a (notional) increase in expenditure on housing. It is possible that this is an accurate representation of how people view an increase in house prices in that they do not noticeably alter their behaviour at all. But it must be stressed that a wealth effect may only be subconscious – a person may feel better off because of his house being worth more, and so buy something he otherwise would not buy.

The effects of rising house prices on aggregate demand can be examined from the viewpoint of neo-classical price theory, which separates the income and substitution effects of higher prices. To take the latter effect first; if the rise in house prices reduced the demand for housing then, if other goods are a substitute, more of them will be bought, and if a complement, less. If, however, more housing is bought for expectational reasons, the demand for complements will rise and for substitutes fall. At least for this period the latter seems more likely. The income effect is complex for existing owners, but for new buyers and potential new buyers it is clearly negative. To expand this point, they will probably save more both to pay an increased deposit and because of greater uncertainty about the size of deposit to be paid. New buyers will also have higher mortgage burdens so gross saving may be higher in future years. Expectations of rising house prices may also, as discussed above, have meant that houses are bought earlier and/or larger houses purchased. If so, the burden of mortgage payments would have risen still further. Hence for new buyers, it seems that both income and substitution effects worked to cut their demand for other goods.

In the sense that he will finish up owning a more expensive house than when he started, everyone who 'filters up' is a new buyer. However it seems reasonable to assume the capital gain on the house sold will cover the higher deposit on the new one, so the effects will be small. As for people in the rented sector, it seems likely that they will suffer from a negative income effect and thus their spending will be lower.

Among other effects a rise in house prices will also affect two other groups directly — builders and landlords. While rent controls restrict the rise in rents (even under 'fair rents'[6]), there is probably some direct connection between house prices and rents. In addition the capital gains can be realised if and when the tenant leaves. During the period the implicit deflator of the price of housing services rose; the increase was less than half the rise in housing prices, but it is still a considerable increase in income for both property companies and private landlords. The capital gains would be even larger, although perhaps not immediately realisable.

The increase in house prices will also affect builders; the increase may permit them to increase the price of new houses whilst building them. Alternatively the profit will go to purchasers or speculators. Reports of a premium on options for new houses (above) suggests some of the latter were in operation; however, there are no data on this phenomenon. The general result will probably be to increase builders' profits in the short term, and is bound to be to increase them in the long run. The increase in demand and/or profit may also lead to an increase in building wages (as discussed above) and so to an increase in wages generally, therefore bringing about some spillover effects on other prices. This is either a cost-inflationary effect or the monetarist/Tobinesque transmission mechanism at work, depending on how these effects are interpreted. One might also expect some effect on the general level of prices by an influence on price expectations and by a tendency to increase cost pressures if the need to save for a higher deposit increased union wage claims. These factors can lead to either a higher natural rate of unemployment, more inflation or, most probably in the circumstances of 1972–3, both; which of these three depends on theoretical and empirical magnitudes. In 1972–3 all plausible theories would suggest similar effects. Thus the qualitative effects of monetary expansion are clear, if not their magnitude.

(ii) The Commercial Property Market

The residential property market may have exhibited all the signs of a classical boom but it fails to match the excesses of the commercial property boom in the same period, which must rival the Dutch tulip boom of the 1630s,[7] the South Sea Bubble[8] and Wall Street in 1929[9] amongst the great speculative dramas of all time. The UK property market has always had a fringe of somewhat dubious operators, largely because it (with the stock market) was the least regulated section of the economy and for this reason and for tax ones has offered the maximum opportunity to 'get rich quick'. (It is, to digress, one of the inevitable effects of a mixed economy – or the German 'social market' one – that the 'spivish' element tend to concentrate in a few markets.) Thus the UK property market has produced many colourful characters (and multi-millionaires) and has attracted much attention both from politicians and journalists.[10]

It is a paradox of markets that has been commented on before[11] that the riskiest of speculation can offer the safest of security for loans. Certainly banks have been willing to lend on the security of property as the most solid of all security. Under the 'old approach' they had lost a lot of business to insurance companies through the workings of the ceilings (see Chapter 1). Hence they were very eager to increase property lending and there were plenty of developers and dealers anxious to borrow, because of the effects of the controls on London office-building as well as the above factors.

Thus it is not surprising that the property market was the scene of a sustained boom in which properties were traded on a very low margin, as it was very easy to borrow on such security. Such loans generated price increases which generated further loans and so on, if not *ad infinitum*, at least until late in 1973.

At this point the bubble was burst and many institutions found that they had overlent to property companies. Many of their assets were unsaleable or insufficient to cover the loan or both. It is difficult to ascertain movements in commercial property prices but some indication is available from movements in the yields expected on prime property, which were (on an annual basis) 7.5 per cent in 1970, 4.75 per cent in 1973 and 8 per cent in 1974; in the UK property prices are normally calculated as a multiple of the current rental. This multiple obviously varies according to the nature of the review clause included in a contract, the quality of the tenant, etc. Even these figures understate the volatility of the market in lower-grade properties. Using these yields and the Department of the Environment survey for 'City' rent figures, one derives the price index in Table 5.1, which shows that prices tripled, then halved.

It is difficult to ascertain the impact of these operations on the economy. It is clear that by necessitating official action to rescue banks, 'the lifeboat' described in Chapter 6, it complicated the task of monetary policy. It almost certainly contributed to the 'inflationary psychosis' of the era. It may even have pushed rent levels upwards and thus increased the cost pressure on companies. The movement of rents is suspicious enough to lend credence to this hypothesis, especially the large rise in 1973. However, the impact on costs is lessened as neither shops nor factories shared in the boom. It should certainly have made it temporarily easier for companies to obtain funds by a 'sell and lease-back' arrangement — and much harder to do this in 1974. To that extent it must have increased the pressure on resources in 1973 and reduced it in 1974, thus intensifying the amplitude of the cycle.

(iii) Share Prices

Belief in a relationship between the money supply and share prices seems to be surprisingly widespread in academic and city circles. It is surprising that it survived the year commencing May 1973; in which M_3 rose by 23 per cent and the stock market fell by 39 per cent measured by the FT-Actuaries 500 Share Index. It is less surprising that it survived the author's attempt to disprove the relationship.[12] Thomas Whitebread, one of the victims of the 'Popish Plot' agitation, complained in 1680 that it was the hardest thing in the world to prove a

Table 5.1: Index of Commercial Property, 1970 = 100

	Price	Yield (per cent)	City Office Rents	Factory Rents
1970	100	7.50	100	100
1971	134	6.75	120	98
1972	195	5.00	130	105
1973	277	4.75	175	128
1974 (Nov.)	174	8.00	185	140
1975	144	6.50	125	153

negative: 'We are to prove a negative and I know 'tis much harder to prove a negative than to assert an affirmative.'[13] By the end of the study, it was very easy to sympathise with him. Nevertheless it seems very clear that there was no systematic relationship between money and share prices over any 'short period', i.e. less than six years. This seemed to me to dispose of any relationship of either plausibility or economic interest (but I discovered I was wrong — see the discussant's comments). Nevertheless, this conclusion still seems valid as far as monetary policy is concerned. The paper showed that neither spectral analysis nor a modified form of Box-Jenkins analysis could find any systematic relationship (over any measurable period) between share prices and various definitions of the money supply, either monthly or quarterly. Nor could any of the US results be replicated for the UK. Nor did previous work on the UK seem to satisfy either economic or statistical criteria, and furthermore their equations all forecast badly.

Despite this work there are some further points to be made. The first is that problems arise in reconciling systematic relationships and 'efficient' or 'rational markets'. The other is that there may be an unsystematic relationship between the two. Various reasons have been advanced why this relationship might exist:

A portfolio readjustment effect. If money holdings increase there will, *ceteris paribus*, be a tendency to buy other assets, including equities, to get back to a desired portfolio balance and thus the price of equities will rise. (This argument can be restated in terms of a demand-for-money function in which the return from holding equities appears and if increased money holdings are to be induced, this opportunity cost must be reduced — i.e. the price of equities must rise.)

A credit effect. Some equity holdings are financed by bank borrowing. The faster the money supply increases, the easier it will be to borrow money for such purposes, and the faster prices will rise (and vice versa).

An expectation effect. The best indicator of changes in activity (and profits) may be the money supply. Hence movements in the money supply will influence share prices even if they incorrectly reflect future movements in earnings.

A risk premium effect. Two versions of this have been suggested, one by Leroy and one by Hamburger and Kochin. The former's is relatively simple and, largely, a deduction from the 1966 'credit crunch'. This was accompanied by an increase in the differential yield between US Treasury securities and Aaa Corporate bonds. This suggested to Leroy that the risk premium on all corporate securities had increased and, thus, that this premium is related to the movement of the money supply.

Hamburger and Kochin's risk premium thesis is more complex. They argue (1) that wealth holders desire types of income whose variations will have a different cyclical pattern from the rest of their income and specifically, from that of earned income; (2) that earned income will be related to the money supply. From (1) and (2) they deduce that the most desirable investment income will not be related to the money supply.

Thus as in any case share prices and money supply are linked, 'as the variability of money rises so does the variability of the economy (and so) the risk premium rises and stock prices fall'.[14]

This argument might apply with different force at different times. For example, the 'credit effect' may have been powerful in 1971–2 but not at other times. The study found that interest rate movements did influence share prices. Thus, developments in official policy do affect the stock market – it is worth remarking that this relationship, established up to the end of 1972, obviously 'explains' the movement in share prices in 1973–4 much better than a money one. Thus one may accept a relationship between policy and the stock market boom of 1972–3 even while accepting that 'empirical work in both the time and frequency domain seems to prove that there is no relationship in the U.K. between money and share prices'.[15] However, the connection between money and share prices in this period is principally that both reflected the response to 'Barberism' and the mood of the times, rather than any direct relationship.

(iv) Inflationary Psychology

Many observers in the media, especially the American ones, argued that 1972–3 saw a significant shift in attitudes in the UK as an 'inflationary psychosis' took a grip and behaviour changed in response to this new attitude. The relevant theoretical reasoning in this context is Cagan's analysis of hyperinflation, wherein such a change in attitude is the major factor in inflation becoming hyperinflation. Certainly there were many signs of such a change in attitudes in, for example, the craze for purchasing the most bizarre of objects as hedges against inflation, satirised by *Punch* in a recommendation to buy articles recommending hedges against inflation. However, it is not clear how widespread this was at a popular level, probably much less so than in 1974–5.

There is no real evidence of a 'flight from money'. The savings ratio in fact rose in 1972 to 10.1 per cent (from 8.3 per cent) and rose again in 1973 to 11.4 per cent (and rose in 1974 to 14.2 per cent). Uncertainty (partly induced by inflation) and the wealth effects induced by inflation were more important than any 'flight from goods'.[16]

It would seem reasonable to conclude that while monetary growth contributed to the speculative fever which gripped markets, it had little to do with 'inflationary psychosis' in 1971–2, if only because of the little attention given to monetary development by the City and the media.

This changed during 1973 when 'monetarism' ceased to be only an academic theory and started to become part of the conventional wisdom, especially in the City; previously its only non-academic adherents had been two Conservative back-bench MPs, Bruce-Gardyne and Biffen. Under the influence of Peter Jay and Sam Brittan, economics editors of *The Times* and *Financial Times* respectively, the respectability of and publicity accorded to monetarism grew steadily to produce a fascinating circle of monetary effects.

High monetary growth led to a belief that interest rates must rise, both in response to a need to cure monetary growth and because of the inflationary effects of this growth. However, this depressed gilt sales and so led to a faster monetary growth. . . . Moreover, both Keynes[17] and Friedman[18] have made the impact of expected interest rates on actual ones a crucial element of their theories. This means that to curb monetary growth the authorities have to raise interest rates above the 'expected level' (Wicksell's natural rate in some analyses). Thus monetary growth meant that the level of interest rates necessary to curb it grew as the authorities' response was delayed; a fatal error in the period (fatal to the 'new approach' at least).

(v) The Exchange Rate

One of the most basic propositions in economics links quantity and price. Thus it is not surprising that the quantity of sterling and its international price, the exchange rate, have been linked. More formally, this is the monetary theory of the balance of payments, outlined in the appendix.

The effect of monetary expansion on the exchange rate must be considered. As stated in Chapter 3, any theory would predict that there would be pressure on the exchange rate as a result of 'Barberism'. Almost certainly, this theory has sufficient validity to be a major underlying cause of the floating of sterling in June 1972. However, it is also necessary to consider whether it was a proximate cause as well.

There are various methods by which monetary expansion could trigger off a foreign exchange crisis. One is by undermining foreign confidence. Another is that the ease of borrowing in London may facilitate speculation against the currency, as the cheapest method of speculation is normally to borrow sterling and lend dollars or marks. Closer to the theoretical model, accumulations of sterling in the hands of multinational companies may lead to an attempt to restore a normal ratio between currencies by selling sterling — certainly an increase in the amount of a weak currency held would be unacceptable given the pattern of interest rates in 1972.

It is impossible to test these hypotheses but they seem sufficiently convincing to make one believe that both the timing and the extent of the depreciation of sterling were determined by monetary developments. The consequences of this depreciation and its timing are harder to ascertain. The cost inflationary effects, though, were very large and in conjunction with the prevalent stance of monetary and fiscal policy made inflation inevitable.

Certainly the movement of the exchange rate casts considerable doubt on the government's argument that inflation in the UK was largely caused by world commodity prices. This in any case ignores the benefits of stable commodity prices in 1970–1, but more importantly, sterling commodity prices did rise by about 45 per cent in 1972 and 1973, prior to the OPEC increase in oil prices. However sterling depreciated by nearly 20 per cent in the period. So one can argue that nearly half of the 'worldwide rise in commodity prices' was caused by sterling's depreciation. This assumes that dollar prices of commodities were unaffected by the UK's depreciation (the 'small country'

assumption of economics). This does not seem to be wildly unrealistic. Certainly the effect on wheat, copper or soya prices would be very low. For a few commodities the impact would be larger (lamb, for example) but here one would expect that it would be less for a depreciation during a commodity boom than during a depression. Thus the timing of the depreciation was very unfortunate in that it probably maximised the cost inflationary impact. It was equally bad in its relationship to the incomes policy cycle in the UK. Accelerating inflation in 1973, when 'phase 3' was being introduced (and the depreciation 'worked through'), was very badly timed indeed. Price increases need to be as low as possible during the defreezing period of incomes policy to minimise 're-entry problems'. It is quite likely that indirect tax cuts and subsidies to buy down the Retail Price Index were counter-productive in their effort to reduce militancy. The indirect (and direct) inflationary impact of these increases in the PSBR (and thus M_3) were not only large but, perhaps worse, unfortunate in their retiming of inflation, that is they reduced it in 1972 but increased in in 1973–4, when its effects on the wage-price spiral were catastrophic.

(vi) The Money Supply and Inflation

The first part of this chapter has considered some of the indirect effects of the excess monetary growth on inflation, or some of the transmission mechanisms, but this still leaves the crucial question of how much the monetary growth was both directly and indirectly responsible for the increase in inflation.

As was described in the appendix to Chapter 1, the implications of both theoretical and empirical work on the problem are mixed. For example, the attempt to replicate Sims's study for the UK found that while some of the results 'suggest a possibility that there might be unidirectional causality from money to prices'[19] the general conclusion was indecisive.

No work done in the UK has, as yet, proved the case for monetarism, or even established a definite causal link from money to prices or nominal GDP. The nature of the arguments about the exogenity of money and the direction of causality is such that they may never be resolved. Virtually any results can be interpreted to fit most of the contending theories (see appendix to Chapter 1). *Post hoc ergo propter hoc* is certainly not sufficient to settle this dispute. The indicator/ target/instrument debate similarly bedevils the issue. Even if these issues were settled, the effect of the openness of the UK economy would still have to be considered.

It is nevertheless possible to lay down a series of propositions with which virtually all economists would agree:

(1) it is true that an increase in the money supply would be a sufficient cause of inflation;

(2) an increase in some monetary aggregate, or in the range of assets used as a means of payment, is necessary for inflation to continue;

(3) a reduction in the rate of monetary expansion is a necessary condition for reducing inflation.

These can be agreed without resolving all the fundamental issues. For this purpose it does not matter whether the money supply is a causally important variable or merely an indicator of the overall thrust of economic policy. Nor does it matter how money is defined, if all plausible definitions give similar results (the narrow definition — M_1 — grew more slowly than the other definitions, but given the obvious structural change effects and the interest elasticity in the UK between demand and time deposits, no theory would regard this as important).

These limited, generally acceptable propositions have important implications for the period 1972—3. In particular, they imply that the government's incomes policy had no chance of succeeding in 1973, given its monetary policy. Thus the drama of the miners' strike of 1973—4 (and the consequent fall of the government) were in one sense irrelevant to the success or failure of the incomes policy, though not to the events of 1974—6. One may consider various ways in which incomes policy is weakened by a lax monetary policy. Most obviously, the choice facing firms between resistance to wage claims and surrender to them is tipped in favour of surrender by easy credit to finance higher wage bills. Nevertheless this is in one sense irrelevant; the pressure on the policy would build up somehow or other and wreck the policy. How and where is crucial to the consequences of the breakdown — once more it may be that Hume is right about the inevitability of underground springs coming to the surface, but it does matter when and where. Following the analogy, an underground spring has disastrous consequences if one seeks to prevent flooding wherever and whenever it emerges. But it would still matter where, when and how it emerged.

More controversially, it is clear that monetary expansion had a significant role in the acceleration of inflation between 1971 and 1974. How much this was permissive and how much causal is less clear. To some extent it does not matter. Certainly the inappropriateness of the monetary policy pursued is clear. Whatever one's attribution of its role in conjunction with other policies in overall economic management, one must accept that the monetary policy pursued was a necessary component of the government's failure to achieve its objectives.

One cannot do more than speculate on what would have happened if the NUM executive had not voted by a majority of one to institute an overtime ban in 1973 so as to break the incomes policy.[20] Nor if the Arab–Israeli war had not broken out. Nor again if the incoming Labour government had not decided to postpone the adjustment to the oil price increase, and had not believed that the events of November–February 1974 made it impossible to resist wage claims. One can say with a reasonable degree of certainty, however, that inflation would have continued to accelerate in the UK, at least up to 15–20 per cent p.a., although the contingencies above may have pushed it up by another 10 points. Strict monetarists can justly claim that the whole of the inflation of 1974–5 and its timing were consistent with their theory. The peak of inflation followed the peak of monetary expansion (and likewise the slow-down) almost perfectly in line with Friedman's eighteen-month lag. However, one's judgement need not be significantly changed by taking a more eclectic position. All can agree, except the most extreme of cost-push inflationists or the most ardent defenders of the then Conservative government (which excludes the present leadership), that the monetary expansion was necessary for the acceleration of inflation in the UK and was a sufficient cause of, at least, the tripling of the inflation rate to nearly 20 per cent, even if other factors contributed to the explosion which reached nearly 30 per cent p.a. at its peak.

APPENDIX: The Monetary Theory of the Balance of Payments

This starts with the identity that:

the change in the Money Supply (ΔM) = Domestic Credit Expansion (D) + the overseas impact on the money supply (O)
O is also the 'total currency flow' (TCF) or 'overall balance of payments' with the sign reversed.

Most theories allow D or M to be the dependent variable in this relationship. In Friedman's analysis, for example, either a money target is set and D adjusted in response to variations in O by 'sterilising' open market operations or O increases the high-powered money base. However, this theory[1] argues that M and D interact to determine O (TCF) or the exchange rate.

D is taken to be exogenous, determined by the authorities: $D = \bar{D}$
M is determined by the demand for money relationship
$M^D = k + aY - br$ (where Y = nominal GDP and r the rate of
     |interest)
so $TCF = \bar{D} - k - a\Delta Y + b\Delta r$

Y and r can be determined within the system, as is done below, or assumed constant. However, the theory proceeds as follows. With a fixed rate régime the total currency flow must be supplied by the authorities to maintain an equilibrium between the supply and demand for the currency and so keep the exchange rate at the official level. If the authorities cease to be able or willing to do this, then devaluation or a switch to a floating régime must ensue.[2]

With a floating rate régime, then the final TCF must be zero, that is the exchange rate must adjust so that someone is prepared to hold an amount equal to the TCF implied by $\bar{D}$ and M^D. Thus one has another function to explain this demand for the currency (Dc):

$$D_c = p + qr - s\,(ER)$$

This relationship rises with the rate of interest paid and falls with the exchange rate (ER)

So $\Delta D_c = \bar{D} - a\Delta Y + b\Delta r$

So $\Delta ER = \dfrac{(q-b)\Delta r - \bar{D} + a\Delta Y}{S}$

Thus the exchange rate is determined by Y, r and $\bar{D}$. Obviously to complete the system Y and r have to be determined (see below), but this partial relationship holds, a rise in $\bar{D}$ lowers the exchange rate (whereas the effect of a change in Y is reversed).

Determination of Income and Interest Rates

Given that

$$\Delta M = D + O$$
$$D = \bar{D}$$

and rewriting the demand for money as a change

$$\Delta M_d = O\Delta Y - b\Delta r$$

The overseas influence on the money supply can be decomposed into the current account (BP) and capital flows (CF), a surplus and an inflow respectively increasing the money supply.

$$CF = Z_1 + c\Delta r$$

the capital inflow is partially exogenous and partially dependent on the rate of interest[3]

$$BP = Z_2 - dY$$

or alternatively

$$BP_t = Z_2 - d\Delta Y_t - dY_{t-1}$$

The balance of payments is partly exogenous (reflecting the exchange rate and other factors held constant) and partly determined by the level of income. The parameter 'd' captures not only the marginal propensity to import but also the effect of higher capacity utilisation on the desire to export and, perhaps, the effect of higher prices on competitiveness.[4]

Now we have

$$\Delta M_t = D_t + Z_1 + c\Delta r_t + Z_2 - d\Delta Y_t - dY_{t-1}$$

and

$$\Delta M_t = a\Delta Y_t - b\Delta r_t$$

from which

$$Y_t = \frac{\overline{D} + Z_1 + Z_2}{a + d} + \frac{(b + c)}{a + d} r_t - \frac{(b + c)}{a + d} r_{t-1} \frac{(+ a) Y_{t-1}}{a + d}$$

This LM curve has all the conventional features — notably an upward slope and that it shifts to the right when domestic monetary policy changes. However, it has two odd features: its position depends on the level of income and interest rates in the previous period, making the argument for a stable money supply (or a steadily growing money supply) much weaker as the LM curve is unstable.[5] Furthermore, its slope depends not only on the interest elasticity of the demand for money (b) but also on the interest elasticity of capital flow (c). The 'monetarist' case (a vertical LM curve) depends on both elasticities being zero, not just the interest elasticity of the demand for money. In both aspects, then, it is a rather 'Keynesian' LM curve.

Turning to the IS curve, it is assumed in the usual way that consumption (C) rises with income, that government spending on goods and services (G) is an exogenous policy weapon, and that investment (I) has an exogenous element and an element dependent on the rate of interest:

$$C = eY$$
$$I = Z_3 - fr$$
$$G = \overline{G}$$

The national income identity is

$$Y = C + I + G + BP$$

so

$$Y = \frac{Z_2 + Z_3 + \overline{G} - fr}{1 - e + d}$$

Not surprisingly, the effect is like that of 'opening the economy' in any other model; the main effect is that the size of the multiplier falls.

Thus the IS and LM curves provide the means of determining Y and r for a fixed rate régime economy.

For the floating régime there is the ER equation as above, and this provides a 3 equation, 3 unknown system (r, Y and ER) which has a unique solution.

Notes

1. See the figures in G. Hadjimatheou, *Housing and Mortgage Markets* (Saxon House, 1976) and *Housing Policy: A Review*, Cmnd. 6851 (HMSO, 1977).

2. The maximum likely switch seems to be 5,000–10,000.

3. This statement is based on causal empiricism but seems uncontrovertible.

4. See C. M. E. Whitehead, 'A Model of the U.K. Housing Market', Buvis (November 1971); Hadjimateou, *Housing and Mortgage Markets.*

5. Consumer Credit: *Report of the Committee*, Cmnd. 4596 (HMSO, 1971).

6. The history of rent control in the UK is long, since 1914, and the legislation confirming — Mckinnon LJ once termed it a 'mass of chaotic verbiage'. Under some circumstances, arbitrators (rent tribunals) fix the rents and this is called a 'fair rent'. Most landlords are forbidden to charge as much as the 'fair rent'.

7. The classic description of this boom can be found in C. Mackay, *Extraordinary Popular Delusions and the Madness of Crowds* (Bentley, 1941 and NEL, 1952). The only modern (abridged) edition is published by Unwin Books, 1973.

8. J. P. Casswell, *The South Sea Bubble* (Cresset, London, 1960).

9. J. K. Galbraith, *The Great Crash 1929* (English edition) (Hamish Hamilton, 1954 and Pelican, 1961).

10. O. Marriott, *The Property Boom* (Hamish Hamilton, 1967, revised edition 1969).

11. E.g. in Galbraith, *The Great Crash*.

12. 'Money Supply and Share Prices' in M. Parkin and A. R. Nobay (eds.), *Current Economic Problems* (Cambridge University Press, 1975).

13. The case is discussed in J. Kenyon, *The Popish Plot* (Oxford, 1974).

14. Extract from Parkin and Nobay, *Current Economic Problems*.

15. Quoted from Parkin and Nobay, *Current Economic Problems*.

16. See J. Townend, 'The Personal Savings Rates', *Bank of England Quarterly Bulletin*, Vol. 16, No. 1 (March 1976), p. 53 for a discussion of the effect of inflation on saving.

17. J. M. Keynes, *General Theory of Employment, Interest and Money*, Vol. VII of his *Collected Works* (Macmillan, 1971).

18. M. Friedman, *'A Theoretical Framework for Monetary Analysis'* (NBER, 1971). This originally appeared in the *Journal of Political Economy* (1970 and 1971) and is reprinted in M. J. Surrey (ed.), *Macroeconomic Themes* (Oxford, 1976) and G. Clayton *et al.* (eds.), *Monetary Theory and Monetary Policy in the 1970s* (Oxford University Press, 1974).

19. D. Williams, C. A. E. Goodhart and D. H. Gowland, 'Money, Income and Causality: The U.K. Experience', *American Economic Review* (June 1976).

20. See David Butler and M. Kavanagh, *The British General Election of February 1974* (Macmillan, 1974).

Notes to Appendix

1. The theory is set out and/or analysed in H. G. Johnson and J. Frenkel (eds.), *The Monetary Theory of the Balance of Payments* (Allen and Unwin, 1975), and is reviewed by J. Williamson in *Economic Journal* (August 1976); R. Dornusch, 'Devaluation, Money and Non-traded Goods', *American Economic Review* (September 1973); F. H. Hahn, 'The Monetary Approach to the Balance of Payments', *Journal of International Economics* (August 1977); D. A. Currie, 'Some criticisms of the monetary approach to the balance of payments', *Economic Journal* (September 1976).

2. See J. P. Hutton, 'A Model of Short Term Capital Movements, the Foreign Exchange Market and Official Intervention', *Review of Economic Studies* (February 1977) for a model of how the choice is made.

3. This is a stock adjustment model, following W. H. Branson and R. D. Hill, *Capital Movements in OECD Area* (OECD, 1971) and Hutton, 'A Model of Short Term Capital Movements'.

4. See J. P. Hutton and P. Minford, 'A Model of U.K. Manufactured Exports and Export Prices', Government Economic Service, Occasional Paper 11.

5. The dependence on past values of r stems from the stock adjustment model of capital flows. However, the dependence on past values of Y is implicit in the model.

6 COMPETITION AND SUPERVISION: THE AFTERMATH OF THE NEW APPROACH

There are various possible approaches to the question of how the authorities should try to increase the structural efficiency of the monetary system and ensure the protection of depositors and others compelled to use the money transmission mechanism.[1] The nature of banking is such that no one suggests that 'normal' market mechanisms should be allowed free rein. The consequences of bank failure are catastrophic for individuals and companies and so for the economy, as the 'knock on' effects are so much greater than for any other industry. They were the basis of the plots of so many Victorian novels[2] and even caused many novels to be written.[3] The macroeconomic effects are as serious. Friedman and Schwartz have convincingly demonstrated the role of bank failures in the great depression in the USA.[4] The consequences of the liquidation of a bank's loan portfolio can be almost equally devastating, even without failure. Thus there is need for some form of guarantee against bank failure, but it is necessary to do this without producing too rigid a banking structure. One solution to the problem has evolved in the USA. This is based on the compulsory insurance of all bank deposits with the Federal Deposit Insurance Corporation, established by the Glass-Steagall Act of 1933. The FDIC guarantees the first $40,000 of any depositors' deposit. In fact it usually tries to preserve all deposits, as is shown in its intervention in the affairs of the Franklin National Bank and the National Bank of San Diego. In the latter case the FDIC arranged a take-over by the Crocker Bank, which safeguarded both depositors and borrowers, at the price of an injection of FDIC money. However, the consequence was to reduce competition in banking in Southern California. This was no doubt inevitable but revealed that even deposit insurance does not guarantee the compatibility of competition and safety. The US system also relies on the Comptroller of Currency to both enforce a number of laws designed to ensure prudent banking (as well as some similar Federal Reserve Regulations) and issue informal guidelines. The former restrict, for example, the ratio of loans to one company to total loans and loans to major shareholders and officers (as Mr Lance now knows![5]). The latter have also been controversial, e.g. when the banks were advised to restrict lending to Italy during 1974.

The US system is obviously in accordance with the dictates of conventional economic reasoning and is a 'welfare economics' solution to the problem. The Continental system (most clearly to be seen in Germany, Belgium and Italy) is very different and combines officially supported cartels with very close supervision over who is allowed to set up a bank. Once a licence is obtained there is very little supervision exercised, even in Germany. The efficiency of the German system is debatable — the English fashion for lauding all things German has brought it praise from Goschen in 1904[6] to the Labour Party NEC in 1976.[7] However, there is little evidence that it significantly reduces the cost of the money transmission mechanism or otherwise offers better or cheaper service. The greater success of UK banks in facing competition from public sector banks (the Post Office Savings Bank, now the National Savings Bank, the Trustee Savings Banks and the Giro) than the German 'D' banks in facing competition from Länderbänke and the Giro is suggestive. The history of Continental bank failures, especially the Hesse State Savings Bank in 1974, suggests that supervision is not as well exercised as in the US, though the problems with Real Estate Investment Trusts (REITs) and other property loans show that the US system is not perfect.[8]

(i) The UK in 1971

The UK system has been based on informal but very close supervision (of the City) by the Bank of England. The lack of statutory backing to the system was a matter of pride.[9] So was the inability to define a bank which provided a light-hearted introduction to legal textbooks.[10] It was assumed that a gentle warning could deter any dubious practices, while in this very gentlemanly world competition was not encouraged. The bank cartel was very welcome to the authorities as a seemly way to conduct business and because it gave leverage to monetary policy (see Chapter 2, section (vii)). The Bank's traditional attitude is well illustrated by its high regard for 'sponsoring associations' of the various types of dealer, bank, etc. through which it operated its system of informal regulation.[11] The system worked very well until the mid-1960s. For example, just as a tight legal system prevented IOS from operating in the US, so did informal supervision in the UK, while those who 'sincerely wanted to be rich' lost vast sums in virtually every other country.[12] However, the number of banks increased in the later 1960s with the advent of foreign banks and those seeking to evade ceilings. There were too many of these for the Bank's traditional close monitoring to be possible and in any case too many of them, it later transpired, were not prepared to abide by gentlemanly codes — some of their officers had very dubious records.[13] This was the system based on 'friendly personal relationships' with 'each bank being judged individually', and aimed to create a relationship akin to that with a confessor or marriage guidance counsellor.[14] Whether it was desirable is debatable; that it was no longer practicable is clear. The task had been one of the (less important) tasks of the Principal of the Discount Office and his staff (about 12 in all).[15] In 1967 three new Principals were added and by 1971 the total staff was 20, still inadequate to cope with the expansion in bank numbers and new banking practices, or as the Governor of the Bank (belatedly) realised, 'self-regulation and self-discipline can achieve a great deal. . . . But self-regulation can be put to too great a test if competition from the less regulated and less disciplined is too easily permitted'.[16]

The market for banking services can be subdivided into 'retail' and 'wholesale' transactions, that is by size, since small personal accounts and large (usually business) ones form clearly distinct markets, even if the distinction is blurred at the edges. The distinction is formally between business conducted at branch level and at head office, at least in the UK. Retail deposits were legally defined for M_2 statistics in the US — below $50,000 — and informally defined by 'Regulation Q' in the UK — £10,000. It can also be divided into loans, interest-bearing deposits and money transmission services (which, of course normally involve holding demand deposits (current accounts)). Thus there are in all six markets. The evidence for the degree of competition prevalent in them in 1971 is limited, and is mainly derived from official reports[17] and such ephemera as stockbrokers' circulars.

Nevertheless, it is clear that there was little competition in the 'retail' markets. Retail loans were nearly all in 'restricted' categories, being either to persons or to service industries. Thus the absence of competition is not surprising. The interest rates on retail deposits were fixed by Bank Rate, so there was no competition in this area. Retail 'transmission services' were a more competitive area but of a very imperfect kind. The banks (other than the Royal Bank of Scotland) kept the formulae by which bank charges were calculated secret, and customers bargained on an individual basis over the charges, and the remission for notional interest on current account balances. (This interest, in kind, was of course tax-free and therefore very attractive to high-rate taxpayers.) Impressionistic evidence suggests that quite a few customers switched to gain better terms, while more forced improved offers from their banks by such threats. Nevertheless competition was very limited and was reduced by a tendency for the banks to specialise in different types of business. The Midland Bank, for example, was more interested in personal accounts while the National Provincial (National Westminster after the 1969 mergers) was known to be especially solicitous to the needs of small businesses.

Wholesale competition was greater. The 'money transmission services' saw similar imperfect competition and price discrimination to the retail market, but as the customers were better informed, it was, *a priori*, more desirable.[18] 'Wholesale loans' were not as competitive. In some cases all the 'Big Four' acted as bankers; in others traditional ties restricted competition. In the late 1960s the wholesale deposit market became very competitive. Local authorities and finance houses had always bid vigorously for funds and provided effective competition for the banks. But the advent of foreign banks, secondary and fringe banks, money brokers and the like (not to mention the growth of the Euro-currency market) made this a highly competitive field, which the 'Big Four' usually entered through such subsidiaries as the County bank. The additional factor of the growth of the inter-bank market (and the banks' net debit position in it) provided much more scope for corporate financial management as one- and two-day deposits paid significant interest rates (see Chapter 2, section (v)).

(ii) The Impact of the 'New Approach': Competition

The 'new approach' led to 'base rate' replacing 'Bank Rate' as the base for the calculation of loan rates, as described in Chapter 2, section (vii). Its overall impact on competition is harder to assess, but certainly competition increased.

The retail 'money transmission' service market became much more competitive. During 1973 simplified charges were brought in and eventually standard tariffs were introduced — Barclays appear to have been the first to do so, in May 1973. However, banks remained unwilling to publish their scale of tariffs, so it is difficult to know precisely when they started to do this. Although both *Money Which?* and *The Economist* complained of the banks' unwillingness to display scales of charges, both were able to obtain 'representative' scales from the head offices for their surveys on charges. By December 1973 *Money Which?* was able to report that printed tariffs were available over the counter from Midland, National Westminster and Williams and Glyn's, but that these were not generally displayed in their branches. Further-more, the price of the services dropped successively as the banks increased the implicit interest rate by reducing the balance necessary for free charges.

In January 1974 National Westminster were the first of the clearers to introduce 'free' current account banking, provided a minimum balance of £50 was maintained. Ultimately free services were offered to any account always in credit by Williams and Glyn's on 1 March 1974 and the Midland Bank on 4 July 1974. Economists have argued in a wide variety of contexts for separate charging for all services to permit greater choice and facilitate greater resource allocation.[19] This, usually, involves the separation of advisory services from the primary transaction, as in this case. Whether such 'disbundling' is as desirable as economists have argued is not clear — the size of transactions costs makes it dubious, even if 'second best' problems can be ignored. However, a later (1976) development is much better in that the National Westminster Bank now remits 5 per cent of the average cleared balance from charges (rather than the formulae whereby a minimum or average balance secured total exemption). This is desirable to achieve the 'optimal quantity of money' — as Goodhart has argued, this rather arcane literature has a very practical aspect to it in this area.[20] Furthermore it avoids the problems caused by the clearers' *de facto* (and almost *de jure*[22]) monopoly on money transmissions and the consequent 'endowment profits' earned by the non-payment of interest on current accounts. The next step would be an explicit interest payment, thus replacing an oligopolistic with a competitive market or at least transferring the monopoly profit to the consumer.

Nevertheless, some caveats must be entered about the apparent growth of competition in this area. One can plausibly argue that the remission of charges and publication of tariffs were in response to the banks' exposed political position in view of their profits' acceleration. Equally, the later increase in charges might, one can argue, be a response to lower profits, not to a reduced need for funds. In March 1975 the clearers made an application to the Price Commission for an increase in certain charges. The decision by the Commission to block the application led to a dispute between the two parties which remained unresolved until the beginning of 1976. After tripartite discussions between the Bank, the Clearers and the Commission, Barclays successfully applied for approval to revise charges to personal and corporate customers, effective from 1 July 1976. This triggered similar applications from the other big clearers.

The increase in competition in the retail loans market is more genuine. The introduction of credit cards to the UK[22] and the advertising by banks of the availability of loans clearly demonstrates this. They also briefly entered the housing finance market during 1972–3. Their lending rose from £40m in 1970 (almost entirely to their staff) to £345m in 1972 and £310m in 1973, but then they withdrew from active competition with the building societies and their lending was only £90m in 1974. Competition for retail deposits did not increase much; the rate was tied to base rate, as it had been before at 2 per cent below Bank Rate. This again probably reflected political expediency – i.e. not competing with building societies. Later, 'regulation Q' made such competition impossible and the banks thereafter increased the margin between their loan and retail deposit rates, partly as a response to the IBELs ceiling.

The 'corset' also reduced competition for 'wholesale' deposits, as any ceiling must do and thus wholesale competition *declined* between 1970 and 1975. There was little difference in behaviour by banks towards the other segments of the wholesale market – increased competition for loans in 1972–3 disappearing later.(US banks also provided increased competition in this period but, it seems, this was of very little importance – certainly much less than was suggested in the press at the time[23].)

(iii) The Aftermath of the 'New Approach': Prudence and Control

The property boom discussed in Chapter 3 and Chapter 5, section (ii), collapsed in December 1973 and revealed just how imprudent many banks had been in their eagerness to lend on the security of over-valued and now unsaleable properties. The Bank had to decide how to react to the imminent collapse of a number of institutions. It took the view that it should ensure the safety of all deposits of all banks, even the 'Section 123' banks. As one of the threatened banks was Edward Bates, which had received its certificate only weeks before, the unwisdom of some decisions and the framework of the decision-making process, was clear. Nevertheless, at a very considerable cost in terms of public expenditure, the Bank was successful in redeeming its reputation and saving as much as possible of the City's. The Treasury bore the cost in terms of its foregone share of the profits of the Bank rather than an increase in the size of public spending as defined in official statistics.[24] Nevertheless the cost was probably close to £200m; the Slater Walker rescue alone probably exceeded £100m, and the temporary addition to the public sector's financing needs was considerably greater (as the Bank borrowed to relend to the 'lifeboat' discussed below). Whether it was worth it can never be answered but it was a continuation of a tradition going back at least to the 'Baring Crisis' of 1891, when the Bank's reaction was similar. In earlier crises (e.g. 1867[25]) the Bank had prevented 'knock on' collapses, but not the original bank failure.

The Bank's reaction has received general approbation and its detailed handling of the crises brought almost universal praise. Nevertheless it made one major blunder in using First National Finance Corporation as a vehicle for some of its intervention; this institution collapsed ignominiously later in 1974.

The Bank's basic vehicle was the 'lifeboat' wherein Bank and clearing bank funds were deposited with the threatened institutions — at its peak something over £2,000m was involved. United Dominion Trust alone received over £500m. The bodies concerned had suffered because 'many large depositors responded to the first exposure of weakness by withdrawing funds from a wide range of secondary banking companies, to the detriment of some whose reputation and prudence in management should ordinarily have sufficed to allay apprehension'.[26] Market rates were charged on the deposits so in theory the Bank and the clearers were not losing money. However, much of the interest was deferred and in many cases it was not merely a liquidity crisis but a lack of management skill:

> To be rather more specific, in the case of most of those we have assisted, experienced teams from the clearing banks or from firms of professional advisers have been reinforcing the management. Under guidance from the supporting consortium, these teams are imposing improved standards and disciplines. In some cases, more reliable and stable sources of finance are being developed. In others, the quality of assets is being upgraded.[27]

In some cases there was a huge deficiency which could never be covered even if the market in property recovered, thus creating a huge contingent liability on the Bank. Besides this, in 1977, there are still £650m of 'lifeboat' funds outstanding, despite the liquidation of some and the recovery of other of the banks.

The affair also reveals some strange features of the authorities' attitude in the UK. First of all, the involvement of the 'clearing banks' in the scheme is a good reflection of their position, half-way between public utilities and competing firms. Deposit insurance is a logical policy but making some, but not all, banks responsible for the defalcations of some of their competitors is odd.

Even odder is the apparent failure of the authorities to grasp the nature of a market:

> I think this episode raises a question about the role of the large depositors in the wholesale money markets. Often deposits seem to have been placed in response simply to the offer of a high rate of interest and without any closer relationship than the passing of a name, without commitment, by a broker. When unease developed, deposits were often withdrawn with the same apparent lack of discrimination, with which they were put there in the first place. More initial discrimination and a more thorough assessment of a company with whom money is placed, which would provide the basis for a more steadfast relationship, would seem to be required if a market of this kind is to work satisfactorily.[28]

This is ignoring the very nature of a competitive market which involves the impersonal nature of dealings. The Bank does seem to want to have its cake and eat it. Nevertheless, the authorities were forced to rethink their attitude to supervision by the events described here. Furthermore the EEC's Directive[29] was a further spur to action, perhaps more than it need have been, together with the backwash of the Crowther Report.[30] All of this culminated in a White Paper setting out the outline of a new system. The rest of this chapter examines the theoretical background to the Bank's choice (section (iv)), analyses the White Paper and its likely effects (section (v)).

(iv) Bank Supervision: Some Theoretical Issues and Policy Options

The authorities may choose to try to ensure prudent banking by a number of different methods:

(a) Licensing

The authorities may restrict the business of banking to those fulfilling certain criteria. These may be imposed on the institution, its officers or both. This may be compared with restrictions on who may drive cars in an attempt to reduce road accidents. Thus in the UK drivers have to meet minimum standards of health, age and eyesight and those suffering from certain disabilities (e.g. epilepsy) are banned altogether. In addition, would-be drivers have to pass a test of driving competence. Unfortunately, similar standards are much harder to lay down in banking. One can eliminate bankrupts and those with criminal records, but it is difficult to go much further towards achieving the necessary standards of probity and prudence.

Nevertheless fear of losing the licence may act as an incentive towards better standards. The positive aspect of licensing, demanding competence, is even harder. Despite examinations set by such bodies as the Institute of Bankers, there are no generally agreed components of banking skills. One could insist on a certain number of trained specialists, in accountancy for example. This is part of the tradition of the Franco-German approach to banking supervision. Minimum asset cover could be demanded for new banks, but such precautions are rarely easy to define satisfactorily, nor have they succeeded elsewhere. The UK system's step-by-step approach was logical. This meant that a would-be bank acquired the full status gradually – e.g. it had to be a 'Section 123' bank for a time before progressing to any more exalted status. The problems arose because the probationary period was not sufficiently restrictive and the overall level of supervision was inadequate. Certainly the close regulations on which 'banks' were allowed to advertise for deposits was both sensible from an administrative viewpoint and highly desirable on theoretical grounds. If the objection to full competition is lack of information for consumers, then allowing only the better-informed consumers to purchase the product is the textbook answer of the classical liberal. The problem is that it is likely that even informed customers will regard an official licence as an imprimatur guaranteeing respectability. Licensing is probably desirable in that its limited benefits outweigh its costs, administrative and otherwise.

(b) Asset Ratios

Another classic method of attempting to regulate banks is by prudential ratios. These can take the form of liquidity ratios or prudential ratios *pur et dur*. The former seek to ensure that a bank can meet any demand on it by its depositors – to avoid the classic 'run' on a bank. The latter seek to ensure the underlying safety of the deposits by concentrating on the quality rather than the maturity of the asset structure. Obviously the two are not independent, high-quality assets ought to be marketable (or at least provide good collateral), so ensuring safety ought to ensure liquidity. Nevertheless, if a bank, for example, invested all of its funds in ten-year government bonds and interest rates rose, thus reducing the market value of its assets, the bank would be unable to meet requests for repayment of deposits without becoming insolvent. Nevertheless (unless it sold any bonds) its depositors' funds would be safe. On the other hand, if a bank invested in high-risk assets of very short maturity, the reverse would be true (e.g. one-day IOUs of a would-be roulette player).

To the extent that the two are independent, separate ratios may be necessary. Certainly a bank matching its asset and liability structure is not either a sufficient or a necessary condition for safety, *pace* Professor Maynard.[31] The problem of liquidity ratios has been increased by the growth of 'roll-over' deposits. If this money is placed for five years, say with either a 'break clause' at three months' notice, or renegotiation every three months, banks often enter these in their balance sheets (and in the Bank of England Eurocurrency statistics) as five-year deposits. Clearly they are not: a deposit at three months' notice or subject to renegotiation every three months is a three-month deposit. Yet the banks have a point. The commitment of funds 'for five years' is at the overnight rate of interest prevailing over the period (usually called the LIBOR — London Inter-bank Overnight Rate). This does change its nature compared to a conventional three-month deposit. In particular, by eliminating the risk of capital loss for the company (and increasing the secondary marketability of the asset) it does reduce the risk of withdrawal, so inequity would arise, however the ratio was calculated. In fact this sort of inequity is the chief argument against ratios of any sort. No two banks have identical businesses, and therefore the necessary asset ratio is different for every bank and so a regulation would have to penalise most banks to be effective, since the riskier liability/asset structures would determine the ratios. This is analogous to the problem that arises with speed limits and blood/alcohol levels, to return to the motoring analogy. Some motorists can drive more safely at higher speeds or after drinking more than others but the law is enacted because it is believed that it will be effective in reducing accidents. Similarly, a regulation that no more than 15 per cent of a bank's assets can be invested in, say, loans to property companies will discriminate against a bank that has greater knowledge of the property market, but may still be desirable and perhaps essential. It is, of course, the case that regulations or at least their spirit can be evaded. The classic self-regulation argument is that (using the analogy once more) people will always drive 1 m.p.h. below the speed limit. However, in banking, it may be that informal supervision can only work within the framework of rigid ratios. Certainly the US Comptroller of Currency and the 'Fed' use ratios in part as a device to screen out which banks need informal supervision of the traditional UK kind.

It is clear then that ratios have a role to play. There are two general points about them. One is that maxima should be calculated on the basis of the maximum loss rather than the sum invested where the former is greater, e.g. in the foreign exchange market, where, *inter alia*, Lloyds of Lugano lost large sums. By accident, the UK's exchange control regulations, by restricting the size of open positions, have averted such problems. The other is that ratios should be calculated as a percentage of deposits rather than assets. What a bank does with its shareholders' funds does not require special legislation, except in so far as they are necessary for the protection of depositors. Here one could insist that deposits do not exceed a multiple of own capital, as with the UK discount house ratios. One can insist that certain transactions are financed solely out of shareholders' funds (or loans other than deposits) but this is a maximum of 0 per cent on the deposit base. Finally, it might be desirable for banks to offer 'earmarked' deposits paying a higher rate of interest and accepting some risk in exchange for this. This might have made sense with the REITs in the US or with some property loans in the UK. Effectively the bank would be using its services as a financial intermediary without risking its depositors' funds. As it is desirable to utilise a bank's enormous skills (comparative advantage) in this area without this rise it offers something of the best of both worlds. It is a version of syndication, but smaller funds would probably be aggregates.

Asset ratios of both a liquidity and a safety nature are clearly desirable. So are multiples of deposits to own funds. Rigidity may be a consequence, but once the system was well established, then some of the benefits of informal regulation could be incorporated even in a 'mechanistic' system since, with experience, over-fulfilment of one ratio could be allowed to permit the maintenance of a less prudent ratio elsewhere. The authorities could then produce a horrendously complex (but flexible) system where each ratio depended on the rest; closer to the way banks operate normally as discussed in Chapter 2, section (v). Thus (simplifying and using an imaginary formula) the maximum percentage share of property loans to deposits might be $10 + 0.7$ (the deposits : own capital ratio) $- 2$ (the percentage of loans to the Third World). Such flexibility could only come slowly as the authorities and banks acquired the experience to lay down such formulae. Nevertheless they would overcome many of the objections to ratios. Returning to the motoring analogy, they are like speed limits which vary with the type of road, vehicle and load.

(c) Compulsory Insurance

Following the motoring analogy, compulsory insurance seeks to mitigate the consequences of disaster rather than to avoid them. However, financial compensation is obviously adequate recompense for financial loss in a way that it can never be for loss of life, or serious injury.[32] One can safely conclude that while *ex post* compensation may not be adequate in other spheres, it is in the banking case. Thus one need not consider the effect on depositors. However, there is the 'moral hazard' case against insurance,[33] i.e. that it may induce dishonestly reckless behaviour by economic agents. Imprudent banking may become an attractive business as it will be easier to attract funds, and a 50–50 bet on bankruptcy or becoming a millionaire may be appealing. Thus the need for asset ratios, licensing, etc. in addition to insurance. However, the combination of all three does not eliminate the risks involved in any one of them.

Another argument against insurance is the equity one, that it is unfair that careful (or lucky) banks should pay insurance premiums to cover up the mistakes, or worse, of the imprudent and dishonest. This is a trifle disingenuous as an argument. All banks have a vested interest in the overall reputation of banking, so the avoidance of any failure is in their interest. Friedman and Schwartz have shown the adverse long-term effects of the 1929–33 bank failures in the US.[34] Until 1929 the deposit-currency ratio was on a rising trend but this was reversed as a result of the failures. In 1960, the ratio was still below the 1929 level, whereas the upward trend has continued in the UK. It is impossible to compute the business lost by banks as a result of the 1929–33 crash (it involves, *inter alia*, knowledge of the 'Fed's' reaction function) but it is obviously substantial. Such insurance is probably desired by operators in financial markets but is impossible to arrange because of classic 'public good' problems. Where these can be overcome, e.g. on the Stock Exchange, then such insurance arises from market self-interest in the UK as well as from official (SEC) prodding, in the USA. Banks, as in the US in 1907, do try to avert failure by other banks even without official prodding.

In any case, the banks are normally compelled to rescue their weak sisters, as with the lifeboat. So the FDIC merely converts an unpredictable levy, e.g. the 'lifeboat' contributions, into regular premiums. As the former will come at times when the banks are having problems with their own 'books', then regular insurance payments should be preferred.

Thus in conclusion, insurance, asset ratios and licensing all have a role to play in banking but none is sufficient in itself.

(v) Official Reaction: The Consumer Credit Act of 1974 and the White Paper of 1976

There have been three major developments in supervision legislation in the UK in recent years. The first was the Consumer Credit Act of 1974, which introduced a system of licensing of all institutions granting credit to consumers, including shops. This was to be administered by the Office of Fair Trading for purely prudential reasons — any purposes of credit control were disavowed during the Parliamentary debates on the Bill. This rationalised a chaotic system of regulations, and lack of them.[35] Some of the system was a successor to medieval usury laws, some a remnant of wartime regulation, the rest had, like Topsy, 'just growed'. The problems that have arisen in administering it may be teething troubles but probably reflect an official underestimate of the importance of, and work involved in, such supervision. One can also have legitimate doubts about the adequacy of the proposed checks on credit-granting bodies contained in the legislation and on the penalties for non-compliance. Nevertheless the framework of this Act seems unexceptionable. Indeed it was very welcome as the first step towards a comprehensive supervisory control system of the US type.

The EEC Draft Directive[36] laid down a massive battery of ratios, licensing regulations and the like, but the UK authorities had, it seems successfully, drawn its teeth in negotiations.[37] The ratios had become optional. Power to exempt institutions had been written into the directive. Other clauses had been watered down, so the licensing clause became meaningless, for example. Thus this mountain which had been referred to so often in official documents[38] (and presumably in their thinking) had brought forth a mouse, or rather a potential mouse.

The White Paper of August 1976[39] has not been enacted into law, nor does it seem likely that it will be in the near future. Nevertheless it is still of vital importance in that in the atmosphere of the UK banking world an intention to legislate has almost the force of law. Furthermore, it involves such a radical transformation of the Bank's attitude to control. For example, paragraph 9 of the White Paper contains the following sentence:

Exacting criteria for such recognition, covering such matters as minimum capital and reserves, the type or range of banking services required to be provided, and the reputation or status needed, will be determined by the Bank with the agreement of the Treasury and will be published.

This reflects a very different attitude to the confessor/marriage guidance counsellor referred to above.

The White Paper suggests a two-tier system. Licensed deposit-takers will be subject to detailed scrutiny before and after the granting of a licence.

> No company will be granted a licence unless its capital and reserves exceed a minimum figure. The Government will have to strike a balance, in fixing the figure, between the need for it to be high enough to provide sufficient assurance of financial substance and the need for it not to be so high that it constitutes an undue deterrent to otherwise suitably qualified persons who wish to enter the deposit-taking field. Institutions will also have to satisfy the Bank of England that their management is honest, trustworthy and suitably qualified to undertake the kind of business which they intend to conduct. In deciding whether to grant a licence to an existing institution, the Bank of England will also look at its past performance and will assess whether it is likely to be able to meet the standards of liquidity and solvency appropriate to a deposit-taking institution.
>
> Institutions which receive a licence will thereafter have to satisfy the Bank of England that they continue to meet those criteria and conform to the required standards in conducting their business. In assessing a deposit-taking institution's business, the Bank will examine appropriate balance sheet relationships and ratios relating to the capital adequacy and liquidity of the institution, the degree of risk attaching to various assets, the matching of liabilities and assets in both sterling and other currencies, the reliance placed on deposits from connected companies and the institution's lending to connected organisations, the distribution of its lending among economic sectors and the provisions and profits that have been made. This information will be interpreted flexibly taking account of the particular circumstances of each institution. The Bank will be able to attach further conditions to the granting and renewal of licences covering such matters as the appointment of directors or management, and the injection of extra capital. They will be able to revoke or suspend a licence if they consider that the company no longer meets the standards required of a deposit-taking institution. There will be a right of appeal to the Treasury against the refusal or revocation of a licence.[40]

'Banks' will be exempt from these restrictions and can use 'bank' in advertising (para. 10). Exemption will be granted to banks subject to criteria laid down in para. 9, quoted above.

A 'Deposit Protection Fund' will be set up to guarantee the first £10,000 of deposits with both licensed deposit-takers and banks. This introduces deposit insurance to the UK (para. 11).

There are some exclusions from this system:

Building Societies, Giro, Trustee Savings Banks and Friendly Societies.

13. The supervisory arrangements described above will not cover the building societies, trustee savings banks, the National Savings Bank, the National Giro and friendly societies which are already satisfactorily regulated and supervised under statute. But the trustee savings banks have recently begun a transformation process which will, over the next few years, enable them to expand progressively their range of banking services. The Government envisage that they will be brought within the arrangements proposed in this White Paper at the appropriate stage in their development. The arrangements will also not apply to stockbrokers who are regulated by the Council of the Stock Exchange.

'Deposits' with Estate Agents and Traders.

14. 'Deposits' will be defined in the legislation in a way which will exclude part payments for future acquisitions or services. The legislation will, therefore, not apply to deposits taken by solicitors, estate agents and a wide range of other traders who take deposits as such part payments.

These seem reasonable, although estate agents' deposits need separate legislation as the protection for house-buyers at present is inadequate.

A final feature of the Act is that the criteria for exemption must be approved by the Treasury, and there is a right of appeal to the Treasury in individual cases, where there will be a tribunal of enquiry (para. 19). This both clips the Bank's wings somewhat and introduces a welcome element of due process to the system.

There is one serious criticism that can be made and that is that the 'exempt' banks are subject only to the existing system of supervision: 'The arrangements for their supervision will remain unchanged, although in the considerably strengthened manner that has recently been introduced in response to the experience of the early 1970's.' It is very doubtful whether the 'considerable strengthening' has amounted to very much or will provide adequate safeguards. The case for formal ratios for 'banks' as well as for 'licensed deposit takers' seems conclusive. In general the emphasis on flexibility seems excessive.

The White Paper, in essence, accepts a (relatively weak by Continental standards) system of licensing and deposit insurance. It has rejected rigid ratios — i.e. the US system — in favour of sole reliance on informal methods. Only the future can and will reveal whether this will be adequate. However, in the light of recent history, there seems to be a strong case for a very rigid system that is relaxed as evidence becomes available to suggest the appropriateness of such relaxation.

Notes

1. For a survey, see C. A. E. Goodhart, *Money, Information and Uncertainty* (Macmillan, 1975), Chapter 13.
2. E.g. Mrs Gaskell's *Cranford.*
3. Notably Scott after the failure of James Ballantyne and Co., consequent on the collapse of Constable and Co.
4. M. Friedman and A. J. Schwartz, *A Monetary History of the U.S.A. 1877–1960*, N.B.E.R. Studies in Business Cycles, No. 12 (Princeton University Press, 1963). Chapter 7: reprinted as *The Great Contraction* (Princeton University Press, 1965).
5. Mr Lance was forced to resign as Director of the Office of Budget and Management in October 1977 after revelations, *inter alia*, of his breach of this regulation as an officer of the Calhoun National Bank and National Bank of Georgia.
6. Goschen's remarks were in a pamphlet, *Essays on Economic Questions* (London, 1905).
7. *Banking and Finance* (Labour Party, 1976).
8. See, e.g., *Fortune* (July 1977).
9. See 'The Supervision of the Banking System', *Bank of England Quarterly Bulletin*, Vol. 15, No. 2 (June 1975), p. 188 (hereafter Blunden).
10. E.g. Minty, *Law Relating to Banking and Foreign Exchange* (New Era Publishing Company, no date), Chapter 1, Section 1.
11. E.g. the foreign banks in London were encouraged to form associations, both a comprehensive one and on a country basis, and when the Bank decided to supervise commodity markets more closely in 1973–4, a rash of associations resulted. The various types of bank are defined in Blunden.
12. C. Raw, A. Hodgson and B. Page, *Do you sincerely want to be rich?* (Andre Deutsch, 1971), Chapter 9 (USA), Chapter 13 (UK).
13. For a not always accurate account of the racy backgrounds of fringe bankers, see the magazine *Private Eye*.
14. The analogy and quote are both from Blunden.
15. *Bank of England Quarterly Bulletin*, Vol. 14, No. 1 (March 1974), p. 54 (hereafter Governor).
17. See the sources listed in Chapter 2, footnotes 32 and 33.
18. A good summary of economic theory relating to competition can be found in D. Swann *et al.*, *Competition in British Industry* (Allen and Unwin, 1974), Chapter 3.

19. E.g. the IEA in the Hobart papers, and economists of various regulatory agencies and committees. The theoretical justification can be found in I. D. M. Little, *Critique of Welfare Economics* (Oxford, 1961).

20. Goodhart, *Money, Information and Uncertainty*, Chapter 13 B.

21. Entry to the Clearing House is restricted by the banks themselves, but as the Bank of England is a member the restriction has official backing.

22. 15 April 1971.

23. The source is private conversations with various employees of American banks.

24. I.e. it appears as a reduction in revenue.

25. The Gurney crisis: see R. S. Sayers, *History of the Bank of England* (Cambridge University Press, 1976).

26. Governor, p. 54.

27. Governor, p. 54.

28. Governor, p. 55.

29. The latest version of this is 'Co-ordination of loans, Regulations and Administrative Provisions relating to the taking-up and pursuit of the business of Credit Institutions' (F946/77/EF13, EEC Convention, Brussels).

30. *Consumer Credit: Report of the Committee,* Cmnd. 4596 (HMSO, March 1971).

31. In a paper presented to the Money Study Group in 1975, he argued that it was a sufficient condition.

32. Some economists have argued that financial compensation will be sufficient for any loss (see, e.g. M. Jones-Lee, *The Value of Life: An Economic Analysis* (Martin Robertson, 1976), but there is no need here to get involved in this fascinating literature.

33. K. J. Arrow, *Essays in the Theory of Rich Bearing* (North Holland, 1970).

34. See footnote 4.

35. Consumer Credit Act.

36. See footnote 30.

37. Source: rumours circulating in the City.

38. See Blunden; Governor; *Competition and Credit Control*, ibid.

39. *The Licensing and Supervision of Deposit-Taking Institutions*, Cmnd. 6584 (HMSO, 1976): for the sake of completeness the working party with the clearing banks should be mentioned, despite its anodyne conclusion: see 'The Capital and liquidity adequacy of banks', *Bank of England Quarterly Bulletin*, Vol. 15, No. 3 (September 1975), p. 240.

40. Paragraphs 7 and 8.

7 TECHNIQUES OF MONETARY CONTROL: A SURVEY

In December 1973, the authorities had to find a new system of monetary control. They had already used:

(a) quantity controls on bank assets (1952–71);
(b) price controls on bank assets (1971–3).

They were to choose:

(c) quantity controls on bank liabilities.

The three systems used in the UK are analysed elsewhere in this book, but it is necessary to examine the alternative systems (this is done more formally in the appendix). These are relevant for several reasons. One is to provide some background against which to evaluate the decisions made by the UK authorities. Another is to provide alternatives, which it is argued below[1] the UK will have to consider.

However, it is perhaps advisable to start this consideration of the alternatives facing the UK authorities by considering the objectives of monetary policy. This is most appropriately and generally defined as changing financial flows and asset prices so as to affect prices, output, exchange rates, capital flows and other ultimate targets of government policy. This definition has two implications. The first is that there can be no conclusive, *a priori* arguments in favour of one means of control rather than another. One must judge, within the relevant institutional framework, which techniques will be most effective and at what cost. The other is that monetary policy can only work if it changes someone's behaviour. Thus it can work only if it causes inconvenience, and, probably, pain. The belief that monetary policy can work without hurting anyone is persistent, despite having been attacked by economists ranging from Galbraith[2] to Friedman.[3] Perhaps the responsibility for this belief lies with the cynical motives attributed to central bankers by some.[4] More reasonably, however, it can be attributed to the universal but dangerous search for some simple, costless and effective economic policy which has so confused popular economic debate.

(i) The German and US Systems: Portfolio Constraints on Banks

There are differences in both the technical details of the German and US systems and the policy objectives pursued within them,[5] but both are basically identical in having a tightly policed, carefully defined reserve base whose issue is controlled by the monetary authorities (see Chapter 2, section (iv) for a comparison with the UK).

Thus starting as before:

Money (M) = Deposits (D) + Currency (C)

The authorities lay down a legal minimum ratio between reserves held by a bank (R) and its deposits:

$$\frac{R}{D} \geqslant \frac{x}{100}$$

(for simplicity it is assumed profit-maximising banks hold no excess reserves). A behavioural relationship is added:

$$C = eM$$

(it is assumed the private sector holds a constant fraction of its money holdings as currency).

$$\text{So as } D = \frac{R\,100}{x}$$

$$M = D + C$$

$$= eM + \frac{R\,100}{x}$$

$$= \frac{100\,R}{(1-e)x}$$

By altering R or x the authorities can vary M.[6] It is not clear what the consequent variation in rates will be. Assuming perfect competition, perfect certainty, perfect information (and thus all markets clearing by price) then the change will be the same as in the competition and credit control system. Otherwise it will be less. Such schemes assume that monetary control (not credit control) will be the prime goal of the authorities.

To examine the US system in more detail, authority is exercised by the Federal Reserve System (the Fed.), although the Comptroller of Currency has some powers to regulate banks, and the various federal credit agencies (especially the Federal Housing Administration) are of some importance. The Federal Reserve System consists of the Board of Governors in Washington and the twelve regional Federal Reserve Banks; the city in which each is located is known as a reserve city. Policy is determined by the Federal Open Market Committee (FOMC) which consists of seven of the Board of Governors (including the Chairman, Dr Arthur Burns) and five of the Governors of the regional banks. (Conventionally the other seven, and various aides, attend the meetings but do not vote.) The way in which the Fed. determines policy is worthy of note. By far the most intellectual and rational of the central banks, it relies much less on 'market feel' and much more on objective targets and quantitatively reasoned arguments. This is perhaps one reason for its openness, which is quite exceptional by European standards. For example, the minutes of the FOMC are regularly published and include details of disagreements over policy and how each member voted.

This intellectuality and frankness is perhaps related to its concentration on one target — the growth of the money supply (M_1), though supplementary targets are set for M_2. This is pursued by the classical monetary policy instruments of the discount rate and open market operations to control the reserve base.

The discount rate's importance stems from the seeming paradox that if the government both borrows from and lends to the banks it acts as an expansionary force, as Table 7.1 shows (a 10 per cent reserve ratio is assumed).

In practice banks usually owe money to the government (and irrespective of the institutional arrangements in force, this is the equivalent of a government deposit) and respond to open market operations by increasing this borrowing ('lender of last resort'). Open market operations cut net indebtedness to the banks, but gross bank holdings of the reserve base determine money. Hence, the rediscount rate ('penal rate') is set at a level to make the open market operations 'effective' — i.e. to discourage banks from borrowing. To summarise, the basis of the system is that banks are compelled to hold a sum equal to a certain percentage of their deposits in the form of certain specified assets (reserve assets). The quantity of these assets is controlled and in consequence so is the maximum size of deposits. The quantity of the reserve assets is controlled directly by buying and selling them (open market operations). However, as the lender of last resort, a central bank must supply reserve assets to a bank on request. Nevertheless, it can control the price at which it supplies them (the discount rate).

The definition of the reserve base in the USA is relatively simple: a bank's holdings of currency plus its deposits with the Federal Reserve System. This differs from the UK's in two ways, in addition to the crucial distinctions discussed above. First, 'till money' is permitted as a reserve asset. Second, no reserve asset yields a return to the bank holding it. Regulation D, which determines the reserve requirements, is occasionally revised to alter the definition of a deposit — for example,

Table 7.1

A.		Bank's Balance Sheet	
Reserve base	10	Private deposits	100
Lending to private sector	90		
Liabilities	100		

B. The government borrows 10 from the banks, increasing their reserve base, and re-deposits it.

Reserve base	20	Private deposits	100
Private lending	90	Government deposits	10
	110		110

C. Now, however, the banks can lend more (as their reserve ratio is 18 per cent) and (by the operation of the credit multiplier): Money creation continues until the ratio is once more 10 per cent.

Reserve base	20	Private deposits	190
Private lending	180	Government deposits	10
	200		200

in recent years both federal fund market borrowing from non-banks (February 1970) and liabilities under repurchase agreements (July 1969) have been reclassified as deposits (these agreements are explained below).

The former was a purely technical change so that all liquid liabilities to the private sector were defined as deposits. The latter was more important in that liabilities to the Fed. were classed as deposits, whereas they clearly are not money. However, the object was to increase the effective penal rate for any given discount rate. (If 10 per cent of 'lender of last resort' borrowing has to be redeposited interest-free, this means that $10 has to be borrowed if $9 is needed, thus pushing the effective cost up by 11 per cent.)

The most important change of recent years, though, has been to bring US banks' borrowings from the Eurodollar market within the orbit of the regulations (July 1969).[7] The Fed.'s powers in this area were further extended by the Act of Congress in December 1969. The current reserve requirements for Eurodollar borrowing is 4 per cent.

Currently the other reserve requirements are 6 per cent against time and savings deposits, and against demand deposits, 16¼ per cent for 'reserve City' banks.[8]

The way the reserve ratio is calculated is also interesting. For every week, the average daily holding of a bank's reserve assets is calculated. This must exceed the required percentage of its deposit liabilities of two weeks earlier (a change instituted in September 1968). The banks can 'carry forward' an excess or inadequate holding of reserves of up to 2 per cent. Thus the reserve ratio is a very complex moving average rather than the one-day-only UK system or the German system whereby the statutory minimum must be maintained every day.

It is usual to divide reserves into 'borrowed and non-borrowed' reserves. (The former consist of reserves borrowed from the Fed.) Reserves are also divided into 'excess reserves' and 'required reserves' — i.e. the total in excess of the statutory minimum, and the minimum itself. Finally, excess reserves less borrowed reserves are termed free reserves. Non-borrowed reserves plus currency is the Fed.'s principal operational target, though since 1972 increasing attention has been paid to the Friedmanesque concept of 'high-powered' money.

As mentioned above, banks are often forced to borrow from the Fed. to fulfil their reserve requirements. This borrowing takes place at the Federal Discount Rate and is controlled by Regulation A. Each of the twelve banks has the power to fix its own rate, but in practice the FOMC determines a rate for the entire system (the last time major divergence occurred was 1920–1).

Banks can obtain funds from the Fed. by either advances or purchases, depending on whether the Fed. grants a loan against the security of an asset or buys it. Advances are more important, but purchases are quite common. This is in marked contrast to the UK where classic rediscounting, i.e. purchasing, has occurred on only one occasion in the last thirty years. Of particular importance are repurchase agreements where the asset is sold but either the Fed. or the bank can reverse the transaction within fourteen days.

The Federal Funds Market (properly called the inter-bank market for Federal Reserve funds) cannot be ignored in any analysis of US monetary policy. As its name implies, its participants borrow Federal Reserve Deposits from each other, thus permitting a bank with less than the required reserve to use the excess reserves of another bank rather than visit the Federal discount window. It is similar to the UK inter-bank market but differs significantly in various ways. One of these is that legally the dealers buy and sell assets rather than borrow and lend (thus a participant exchanges one cheque on a Federal Reserve bank for another of a later date). Another difference is that the normal minimum transaction is much smaller — $10,000 is not uncommon. A third is that all deals are on an overnight basis, another that one broker

(Gavin Bante) arranges half the transactions — at one time this share was 80 per cent.

A much more important difference, perhaps, is the great stability of the rate compared to the day-to-day fluctuations of the UK rate. Finally, because of the nature of the asset, the bulk of the trading is done by banks.

The market is of great importance to monetary policy. It acts as a transmission mechanism of the effects of open market operations — the FOMC operates in New York. New York banks (traditional net borrowers in the market) are squeezed, thus they increase their borrowings. This in turn affects the position of banks in other parts of the country. Its other role is to increase the efficiency of the use of reserves (i.e. to reduce the banking system's net excess reserves) and thus increase the effectiveness of changes in the reserve base.

The *modus operandi* described above applies only to those banks which are members of the Fed. Currently, any bank may belong to the system, but banks with less than $400 million deposits and whose head office is not in 'a reserve city' need not belong to it. Non-members are subject only to state laws which are much less onerous, especially on reserve ratios. Thus many banks do not belong to the Fed. and some have recently left it (the peak of the exodus was in the first half of 1974, when 26 banks with total deposits of $1.2 billion left the system).

This led to the fear that the control exercised by the Federal Reserve system over monetary growth is 'as poor as that of a fisherman trying to reel in a tuna on a line that was alternatively as unyielding as an anchor chain and as elastic as a rubber band', as Thomas O. Wagge (Senior Vice-President of the Federal Reserve Bank of New York) put it.

Over the last few years, the faster growth of the non-member banks has added 1½–2 per cent to the rate of growth of M_1. Since 1947 the proportion of total deposits held by Federal Reserve members has fallen from 86 per cent to 77 per cent (1976). The Fed., which shares these worries, has several times in recent years asked Congress for powers to impose uniform reserve requirements on all banks, whether members or not.

Thus the Federal Reserve system has now additionally asked Congress to permit the payment of interest on demand deposits (NOW accounts) by member banks, as this additional freedom of non-member banks has also encouraged their growth.

The US's monetary policy, it is clear, has been successful in achieving its objectives since the appointment of Burns as Chairman of the Fed.

Earlier the administration of policy was trenchantly criticised by Friedman.[9] On the whole his criticisms of inconsistency seem well merited. However, they are not really criticisms of the system of control but rather of how it had been used. The objectives may or may not have been well conceived but targets for M_1 growth have been set and achieved.

West German monetary control has three distinct characteristics: the relative success of its policies; its dedication, of almost textbook purity, to controlling money rather than credit, though interest rates are also regarded as important; and its constant battle to maintain an autonomous monetary policy in the face of vast capital inflows. Underlying this position is the semi-independent nature of the Bundesbank, which for institutional and political reasons holds a unique position *vis-à-vis* the government, under Article 12 of the Federal Republic's Basic Law.

The Bundesbank pursues the classic monetary policy, based on tight control of the reserve base (interest-bearing deposits of financial institutions with itself), a rigidly policed minimum level of reserves against deposits (which must never be infringed) and a concentration on monetary aggregates as a target. The use of open market operations has been limited, although since the introduction of 'liquidity paper' and 'mobilisation paper' in 1967 they have been of increasing importance. (Previously a shortage of assets to deal in restricted the Bundesbank's ability to pursue open market operations. These new securities supply suitable assets which are the equivalent of US Treasury Bills despite their Teutonic nomenclature.)

The Bundesbank has considerable powers to vary the minimum reserve requirements. The limits are the maxima imposed by law: 30 per cent for demand deposits, 20 per cent for time deposits and 10 per cent for savings deposits. The Bundesbank is unique amongst major central banks in imposing a penalty charge for breach of its regulations.

Bundesbank rediscount policy assigns a rediscount quota to each institution (which cannot exceed its quota) and defines quite strictly what is, and is not, eligible for rediscounting. It then follows closely US practice with Lombard credit, that is additional rediscounting at the discretion of the central bank and corresponding to 'borrowed reserves'. The dichotomy is revealed in the Bundesbank's policy target of 'free liquid reserves'. This includes all potential reserves (unused discount quotas are classed as reserves). Thus, as the Bundesbank cannot use rediscount quotas as a short-term policy weapon, the volume of Lombard credit is of key importance as an indicator. Finally, a policy unique to the Bundesbank, and illustrative of its monetarist purity, is its encouragement of the growth of short-term assets with maturities of over three months (including bank deposits). It views this 'monetary capital' as a useful offset to the growth of the money supply rather than as a complement to it.

The Bundesbank's successful monetary policy stems from four main factors: first, the very wide range of credit institutions treated as banks, and the key role of the big three 'D' banks in investment banking; second, the small size of the German money market; third, and of greater importance, is the fact that for institutional reasons corporations are almost wholly reliant on banks for credit during a squeeze and so the Bundesbank's influence through the banking system is felt directly. Finally, the German political climate has made a tight money policy far easier than elsewhere in Europe.

The major problem with German monetary policy has, ironically, been caused by its success: the very strength of the mark has induced capital inflows which have threatened to unleash inflation in Germany (by expanding the banks' reserves).

While other countries have been reluctant to deflate, the German authorities understandably have refused to suffer inflation so as to ease the problems of others. The other answer of revaluation (or 'floating' the mark), sufficient to choke off the inflow, has proved unsatisfactory. The limited nature of the German securities markets, and the size of the inflows, ruled out sterilisation operations. Thus direct controls were the only solution. Market mechanisms were used to the maximum extent, however, especially very heavy forward intervention, the so-called 'swap' policy. The 'coupon tax' introduced in 1964 was one device; non-resident purchasers of German bonds had to pay a 25 per cent withholding tax on the interest. Direct prohibition of interest on non-resident deposits is another available weapon. Most crucial has been the imposition of reserve requirements of up to 100 per cent against non-resident deposits, and the Bardepot.

This has enabled the authorities to insist that borrowing from abroad by German companies or banks be matched by a deposit of a percentage (up to 100 per cent) of the loan with the Bundesbank at up to −10 per cent interest. Negative interest rates are necessary because the possibility of revaluation of the D mark has meant that it was profitable to lend at, say, −5 per cent p.a. for three months to acquire a claim in marks, as a 10 per cent revaluation of the mark would make this equivalent to 37½ per cent p.a. interest on a dollar loan.

The German authorities have been as successful as the Americans in achieving their goals. However, they have used interest rates as the indicator of policy. Thus they have been monetarist about how financial factors affect the economy and how money should be controlled, but not about how the appropriate level of the money supply should be determined. This is almost the mirror image of the UK's competition and credit control rationale of using the money supply as an indicator of a Tobinesque policy, discussed above.

(ii) The French System[10]

The UK authorities might also be well advised to study the workings of the French system of monetary and credit control, which is also generally recognised to be a success. This is a full-blooded *dirigiste* system of control, aiming at the control of credit flows both by sector and in aggregate — in almost complete contrast to the US scheme.[11] It is based on banks being forced to deposit a considerable percentage of their deposits with the Banque de France, which then lends them back to the banks (at a profit!). By varying the terms of these loans, the Banque de France influences bank behaviour.[12] Normally a bank can borrow various tranches at ever-increasing rates of interest — the higher ones used to be known as 'super hell'. The size of the privileged quota (cheaper loans) depends on how closely a bank follows central bank guidelines. In particular, a bank is expected not merely to observe the regulations but to ensure that its customers do.

Even if a bank provides only 5 per cent of, say, a shop's funds it is expected to use this to ensure that all of the shop's activities are within the official guidelines — thus avoiding the problem that a loan notionally made available to finance X will in fact finance Y (X would otherwise be financed from a different source which is now used to finance Y). The social cohesion of French society, especially the pervasive role of the Inspectors of Finance,[13] and the relative lack of sophisticated financial institutions no doubt help this system of direction and rationing to work. Nevertheless, work it does — at a cost in terms of efficiency and economic freedom.

(iii) A Tax on Banking

Besides the schemes considered above and those tried in the UK, there are various other ways in which it is possible, at least in theory, to control the money supply through affecting the banking system.

One is a tax on banking, designed to increase the margin between bank deposit and loan rates so as to reduce the volume of lending and deposits. This is sometimes called a 'wedge' because of its effect on the gross margin between loan and deposit rates.

(iv) Conclusions

Perhaps the major conclusion which can be drawn from a comparison of different methods of monetary control is that any system of control can work, either the *dirigiste* (France) or the market-oriented (the US), either the monetarist or a policy based on sectoral allocation within a Keynesian framework. However, all have required vigorous use of the different policy instruments and so, by comparison with the UK, one might conclude that faint-heartedness is the only important error in monetary policy.

APPENDIX: Control of the Money Supply

Alternative Methods

In a closed economy:

$$M = D + C \qquad \text{(i)}$$

Bank assets = Bank liabilities so $\qquad$ (*)

$$D \text{ (bank liabilities)} = bLp + bLg \qquad \text{(ii)}$$

$$P = \Delta bLg + \Delta pLg + \Delta C \qquad \text{(iii)} \qquad (**)$$

so

$$\Delta bLg = P - \Delta pLg - \Delta C \qquad \text{(iv)}$$

as

$$\Delta M = \Delta C + \Delta bLp + \Delta bLg \text{ (substituting (ii) into (i))} \qquad \text{(v)}$$

therefore

$$\Delta M = P + \Delta bLp - \Delta pLg \text{ (substitution of (iv) into (v))}$$

It should be noted that this is the IMF DCE equation and that a change in the money supply must be associated with a change in at least one of (and must be caused by one of):

   (a) the budget deficit (i.e. fiscal policy);

   (b) bank lending to the private sector (i.e. credit policy);

   (c) private sector holdings of government debt, which represents a change in the allocation and/or size of private sector portfolios and must therefore be accompanied by a change in asset prices, i.e. interest rates. This association leads to two conclusions:

   (i) monetary variables may be thought of as an overall indicator of all other economic policy;

   (ii) one cannot talk of monetary policy apart from its credit/ fiscal effects, nor credit and fiscal policy apart from their monetary effects.

Further, this equation is sometimes known as the supply side counterpart to the monetary stock.

Thus as

$$\Delta M = \Delta D + \Delta C$$
$$= P + \Delta bLp - \Delta pLg$$

This leads to various alternative ways of controlling the money stock:

(a) by quantity controls on D (i.e. bank liabilities, as in the UK 1974–   );

(b) by price effects on D.

If it is assumed that deposits are non-interest-bearing, then the demand for them will fall if interest rates on alternative assets rise. If, as in reality, some are interest-bearing, then relative interest rates matter as well as the absolute level.

(c) by altering the size of P;

(d) by quantity controls on bLp (as in France or the UK 1952–71);

(e) by price effects on bLp.

It is assumed that the interest elasticity of the demand for credit is negative.

(f) by quantity controls on pLg.

The authorities can order private individuals to hold public sector debt, e.g. by trustee legislation, as in various Continental countries.

(g) by price effects on pLg.

The authorities can induce private individuals to lend to them, probably by higher interest rates.

It can be seen that the impact of interest rates on the money stock can occur in any of (b), (e) and (g).

Furthermore:

(h) the authorities can impose portfolio constraints on banks, as in the US and Germany.

For example, a minimum ratio of public sector debt to deposits

$$\frac{bLg}{D} \geqslant x\%$$

If profit-maximising banks minimise holdings of bLg, that is if the ratio is set higher than the desired level in the absence of the requirement

$$D = \frac{bLg}{x}$$

then

$$M = C + \frac{bLg}{x}$$

bLg can be changed by any of (c), (f) and (g). However, raising x gives the authorities an extra control mechanism. Further, if the reserve base is a subset of bLg, then by affecting the distribution of bLg between non-reserve and reserve assets the authorities can also affect M. Normally (as above) the demand for currency is assumed to be

$$C = eM \qquad \text{so}$$

$$M = \frac{bLg}{x(1-e)}$$

If deposits pay interest then the demand for currency will depend on this e.g. $C = pM - qr^D$

then if the banking system is competitive

$$M = \frac{bLg}{x(1-p)} - qr^D$$

but r^D is also determined endogenously to equate the demand for deposits with the constrained supply and will depend on the nature of the demand for deposits function, in which both own and competitive rates will appear. If any of the competitive rates are under official control, e.g. government bond rates, then this adds a further weapon to the official armoury.

(j) taxation of banks.

In a competitive banking system, if the supply of deposits to banks is

$$D = a + br^D - cr^g$$

and the demand for loans:

$$bLp = d - fr^A$$
$$= d - fr^D - fr^M$$

so

$$r^D = \frac{d}{f} - r^M - \frac{bLp}{e}$$

by substitution:

$$D = a + \frac{bd}{f} - br^M - \frac{b}{f}bLp - cr^g$$

by raising r^g the government can reduce deposits (b) above.

However, by increasing r^M they can also reduce D. This can be done by a tax on banking. Similarly one can show that it will reduce bLp.

(k) restrictions on interest rates.

This – 'regulation Q' – is a hybrid of (a) and (b). The restriction of interest paid on bank deposits induces the private sector to hold less, but as the bank is constrained it is like a quantity control. It is rarely used for reasons of monetary policy in any case.

KEY

Money = M

Deposits = D

Currency = C

Bank lending to the private sector = bLp

p   = private sector

g   = government sector

b   = banking sector

P   = government borrowing requirement

r^D = rate paid on bank deposits

r^A = rate changed on bank advances

$r^M = r^A - r^D$ (gross margin)

r^g = rate paid on government bonds.

(*)   owners' capital and the bank's assets in buildings etc. are assumed equal to simplify the equations. In practice, changes in these items are small enough to be ignored. However, in so far as bank profits rise with higher interest rates, then there is a favourable impact on the money supply, since higher retained profits count as part of bank liabilities and thus reduce the size of deposits for any given size of lending.

(**)   In this economy the government can borrow from the private sector in either an interest-bearing form, i.e. pLg, or a non-interest-bearing form, i.e. currency. The remainder of the borrowing requirement is provided by the banking sector. This may be a behavioural relationship in that the banks provide residual finance as in the UK, or it may be purely an identity in that the amount the government borrows in total must be equal to the sum of the amounts it borrows from all possible sources.

Notes

1. See the author's 'Techniques of Monetary Control: The U.K.'s choice', Economic Policy Analysis Group, Discussion Paper Number 1.

2. Amongst other places in *The Great Crash* (Hamish Hamilton, 1955) and *The Liberal Hour* (Houghton Mifflin, 1960).

3. Especially in his Presidential address to the AEA: 'Role of Monetary Policy', *American Economic Review*, Vol. 58 (March 1968).

4. E.g. J. F. Chant and K. Acheson, 'The Mythology of Central Banking', *Canadian Journal of Economics* (1972).

5. For a description of the US and German systems see: *Monetary Policy in Germany* (OECD, 1973); *Monetary Policy in the U.S.A.* (OECD, 1974); D. Hodgman, *National Monetary Policies and International Monetary Co-operation* (Little Brown, Boston, 1974); J. M. Boughton, *Monetary Policy and the Federal Funds Market* (Duke University Press, Durham, N. Carolina, 1973); K. Holbick (ed.), *Monetary Policy in 12 Industrial Countries* (Federal Reserve Bank of Boston, 1973).

6. The relationship is used extensively in: M. Friedman and A. Schwartz, *A Monetary History of the U.S.A. 1867–1960*, NBER Studies in Business Cycles, No. 12 (Princeton University Press, 1963); P. Cagan, *Determinants and effects of changes in the stock of money 1875–1960*, NBER Studies in Business Cycles, No. 13 (New York, 1965).

7. Regulation M.

8. The precise size of required reserve depends on the size of deposit (calculated on a progressive scale);

Type of deposit, and deposit interval in millions of dollars	Requirements in effect 31 May 1977 Per Cent
Net demand	
0–2	7
2–10	9½
10–100	11¾
100–400	12¾
Over 400	16¼

Type of deposit, and deposit interval in millions of dollars	Requirements in effect 31 May 1977 Per Cent
Time:	
Savings	3
Other time:	
0—5, maturing in —	
30—179 days	3
180 days to 4 years	2½
4 years or more	1
Over 5, maturing in —	
30—179 days	6
180 days to 4 years	2½
4 years or more	1

	Legal limits, 31 May 1977	
	Minimum	Maximum
Net demand		
Reserve city banks	10	22
Other banks	7	14
Time	3	10

9. See Friedman's articles in *Newsweek* over the period 1964—69. Some of these are reprinted in *Dollars and Deficits* (Prentice-Hall, 1968).

10. See the references in footnote 5 and *Monetary Policy in France* (OECD, 1974), and *Demand Management and Monetary Policy in France* (OECD, 1975).

11. A minor point is that it seems that whether a bank is nationalised or not is almost completely irrelevant for monetary control purposes.

12. There have been minor variations following the two Wormser reports (1967 and 1971) but the basis of the scheme has remained intact throughout.

13. The classic study of 'L'Enarchie' is still P. Lalamière, *L'Inspection des finances* (Paris, 1959).

8 THE NEW 'NEW APPROACH'

(i) The Scheme

In this chapter, the 'new "new approach"' is analysed. This examination analyses its rationale and thereby considers various issues running through the period. Next the history of the period is examined in some detail, and finally some conclusions concerning the period are deduced in the light of the earlier analysis.

In December 1973 the authorities dropped competition and credit control and replaced it by a ceiling on bank liabilities, rather than (as before 1971) on bank assets. The new scheme more strictly controlled one category of bank liabilities — interest-bearing eligible liabilities (IBELs). The ceiling is policed by 'supplementary Special Deposits'. If a bank exceeds the prescribed level by x per cent, it has to lodge a variable percentage of the excess as a (non-interest-bearing) supplementary Special Deposit with the Bank of England.[1] More specifically, if the excess were 0–1 per cent this was 5 per cent, between 1–3 per cent 25 per cent, above this 50 per cent (on 1 April, the bands became 0–3 per cent, 3–5 per cent and 5 per cent upwards). The deposits being interest-free, in contrast to orthodox Special Deposits,[2] the scheme has some aspects of a 'tax' about it — a 50 per cent interest-free deposit is equivalent to a 50 per cent tax on banking — but while at the 5 per cent level it might act as a tax on banking, at 50 per cent or higher it is prohibitive and acts as a ceiling.[3] Thus it is open to evasion by techniques similar to those employed in the 1960s. So far these have not been so prevalent as to interfere with the workings of the scheme for two reasons:

(1) the 'secondary banking' failures have reduced the appeal of evasion as the necessary agents are less trusted;

(2) the depression has cut the demand for funds so the ceilings have not 'bit' very much anyway.

'Terms control' on hire purchase was also reintroduced.[4]

The authorities have also relied on a much more aggressive policy in the gilt-edged market. The new sales technique is based on an amalgam of the two previous theories and argues that sales depend on:

(1) the level of interest rates — the higher the level the larger are sales, as in 'the economists' theory';

(2) the change in rates — a fall in rates induces sales, as in 'the cashiers' theory';

(3) the differential between long and short rates; the higher the margin the greater are sales.

To take advantage of this the authorities raise both long and short rates dramatically. They then (gradually) reduce short rates. This increases the demand for gilts and so generates sales and a rising market (falling rates). However, absolute rates are high so all three factors work in the authorities' favour. This has worked very well and over all but the short term, the authorities' control of money has been exemplary (whether by good luck or good management is discussed below). Some general problems facing the authorities over the next few years are given in the final chapter.

(ii) Some Issues

The period of the 'new "new approach" ' has also seen the adoption of explicit money supply targets by the UK, with a target of 12 per cent growth in M_3 for the financial year 1976/7 and a 9–13 per cent range for sterling M_3 for the financial year 1977/8 (the various monetary aggregates are defined in Appendix B). This represents a major change in official attitudes in the UK. There are various reasons why they might have adopted the targets:

(a) together with 'cash limits', it is a method of curbing public spending.[5] This is using the 'supply side counterpart' equation yet again (see Chapter 2 and the appendix to Chapter 7). By setting a limit on a monetary aggregate then (depending on forecasts for the private sector's desire to lend to the public sector and to borrow from the banks) one can deduce a desirable level for the PSBR. However, the PSBR can be cut by sales of assets (e.g. BP shares as in 1977) and by financial transactions whereas those seeking to curb the PSBR are usually more interested in cutting public-spending *per se*;

(b) the authorities, especially the Treasury, had come to believe that the financial community is monetarist even though they still believe the world actually works in a Keynesian way. Therefore, money supply targets are necessary to inspire confidence, but have no economic significance;

(c) finally, one may believe, that the Chancellor, Mr Healey, believed that control of the money supply is a necessary if not a sufficient condition for control of the rate of inflation. The Budget speech of 6 April 1976 gives some credence to this.

> Second, it remains my aim that the growth of the money supply should not be allowed to fuel inflation as it did under my predecessor. To this end, I aim to see that the growth of the money supply is consistent with my plans for the growth of demand expressed in current prices.[6]

The argument that international pressure forced money supply targets on the authorities can easily be rejected — in particular the advent of the IMF, led to an de-emphasis on money. 'But our target will now be in terms of DCE not M_3.'[7] Equally, the argument that the government was monetarist seems fallacious, given its emphasis on incomes policy. While all of (a), (b) and (c) are probably of importance, it would seem that (b) has probably swayed the Treasury civil servants and the Bank and (c) the Chancellor.

The growth of the monetary aggregates — see the statistical appendix — has been both within the targets laid down by the authorities and in accordance with the prescriptions of 'gradualist monetarism', that is of slowly reducing the rate of growth of the money stock and keeping it below the level of inflationary expectations. Given the consensus that excessive monetary expansion would accelerate inflation, then the growth of money at around 10 per cent p.a., relative to inflation coming down from 25 per cent to 15 per cent p.a. between 1974 and 1977 seems a sensible policy. However, one can argue that in the context of the depression the authorities have been lucky, or indeed that they may have caused considerable damage by their policy. All these propositions involve different views about the nature and effects of the high level of the public sector borrowing requirement (PSBR) over the period, and the various announced cuts in the level of public spending. One should perhaps start by emphasising that Mr Healey entered office intent on cutting the PSBR from the high level left by Mr Barber, and in fact in his first Budget planned to reduce it by £1,500m, to £2,750m. However in the course of the year, electoral necessity and growing fears about corporate liquidity and unemployment led him to reverse this plan.

The line that a hagiographically-minded supporter of the government would take is that the government has had the problem of both maintaining adequate growth of money and avoiding excessive growth.

Thus the authorities had had to manipulate public spending and taxation (and so the PSBR) and the market in government bonds to achieve this. Thus the initial increase in the level of public sector borrowing from banks was necessary to offset the very depressed level of private borrowing and so maintain (relative) stability in money. There have been so many rounds of public expenditure cutting because there were costs (in terms of unemployment, inefficiency and the loss of desirable expenditure) in over-large cuts as well as in not cutting enough. Therefore a gradualist approach was necessary.

The alternative argument is that the authorities have been very 'lucky'. They have lost control of public expenditure and have been spared hyperinflation as a result of this only because the depression has reduced private borrowing so much. The frequent changes of policy reflect confusion, cowardice and incompetence and (possibly) an ill-founded belief in fine tuning, not gradualism. The monetary aggregates do not in any case reflect the full damage done to the economy as much of the money creation has 'leaked' abroad (see Chapter 9), thus leading to a lower exchange rate. Domestic credit expansion over the period 1974—6 has been £20,000m, whereas M_3 grew by only £11,500m.

Both of these groups accept the same sort of flow-of-funds approach to the analysis of money creation that the authorities use, differing in whether the high level of bank borrowing by the public sector and low level of bank borrowing by the private sector were associated by a lucky accident or by design. Another group would argue that they were associated not by either, but as cause and effect. This is the 'crowding-out' hypothesis much discussed in the media and in financial circles.[8]

The whole debate reflects the extent to which monetary policy has been much more central to economic management in the period now under review. Hence, the whole issue of public spending control and crowding out is discussed at some length in the concluding sections of this chapter and this chapter includes more analysis of overall economic management than did Chapter 3, the corresponding analysis of the new approach.

(iii) A New Scheme and a New Government, January — October 1974

In December 1974 the government announced not only the 'new "new approach"' (and a £1,200m package of public expenditure cuts) but also the 'lifeboat' discussed above. The government was also facing an overtime ban by the National Union of Mineworkers, in opposition to phase three of the government's incomes policy. Following a pithead ballot (the result was announced on 4 February) the NUM called an all-out strike commencing on 11 February.

This led, *inter alia,* to a three-day working week (on 13 December) and a general election on 28 February which in turn was followed by a change of government, Mr Wilson heading a minority Labour government with Mr Healey as Chancellor.[9] The new Chancellor introduced his first Budget on 20 March and announced a complex package of tax increases and expenditure increases and reductions. The effect was to, he believed, leave the PSBR at £2,700m for 1974/5 against £4,200m out-turn for 1973/4.

The new government was obviously most concerned with 'getting the country back to work' but the first signs of the working of the new measures were encouraging. The reimposition of terms control had a significant impact. In 1973, the personal sector borrowed £183m 'on hire purchase'; in 1974 it repaid £76m. The swing is £259m (implying that consumers' expenditure was £160m lower in 1974 than it otherwise would have been). (The monthly figures for credit outstanding are shown in the appendix.) The September directive reinforced by the impact of the new method of control had also 'worked' (see the statistical appendix for details). Loans to the personal sector (other than for house purchase) fell by £253m in the year to November 1974. Loans to property companies continued to rise rapidly into 1974 (as the developers' need for funds rose with the three-day week and other restrictions on building) but in the year from February 1974 rose by £173m. In this period loans to the 'other-financial' sector fell by £189m. So total loans for property, direct and indirect, were probably constant. As liquidation of loans on a very large scale was impossible in the prevailing conditions, this was as much compliance with the directive as could have been achieved.

In the first quarter of 1974 the money supply (M_3) rose by £1,214m (and DCE by £1,593m). This (3.6 per cent) was marked by a deceleration in the rate of growth. The deceleration seemed greater on the initial figures which showed growth of 3.1 per cent; the subsequent revisions were downward (to 2.8 per cent) before the latest figures showed an upward revision. The underlying growth was clearer, as the Bank bought large quantities of commercial bills in both the fourth quarter (£204m) and first quarter (£118m) to smooth the impact of the measures. The change was even more marked on a monthly basis. In the month to 12 December, M_3 grew by 2.6 per cent, in the month to 16 January ('banking December') by 2.2 per cent, in banking January by 1.3 per cent and in the next two months by 0.3 per cent and 0.4

per cent. In the first (calendar) quarter bank lending to the private sector was £1,267m. As might have been expected, sales of gilts were fairly low (£214m), but other categories of public sector debt were purchased on a large scale, so even after the open market operations the total 'offset' was £586m. Three-month inter-bank sterling deposit rates had risen from 12.25 per cent on 9 November to 16.25 per cent on 21 December, but fell back thereafter as the ceiling on 'IBELs' bit.

Obviously the new scheme deterred banks from bidding for deposits, since growth in interest-bearing deposits was penalised, so it was to be expected that the rate paid on deposits would fall. Consequently as a by-product of the scheme short-dated public sector securities became more attractive and reduced the rate of growth of M_3, but not the private sector's liquidity, an interesting example of how the desirability (of the effect) of a policy depends on one's theoretical perspective. The Bank's minimum lending rate was reduced by a ¼ per cent on 4 January and 1 February and so ended the quarter at 12½ per cent. Base rates were unchanged at 13 per cent. Longer-dated bond yields continued to rise, the Bank's 20-year rate (calculated by yield curve[10]) had been 12.37 per cent at the start of the quarter, and 14.69 per cent at the end of it (and 10 per cent in March 1973).

Thus conditions were ideal for using the Bank's new method of selling gilts. Long rates were high relative to short rates and, it seemed, absolutely. So, if they were pushed slowly downwards, a large volume of sales would be generated. They were. During the second quarter of 1974, sales of public-sector debt to the non-bank private sector exceeded £1,000m, and included in this was a very substantial un-winding of the open market operations of the previous quarter; gilt sales were £679m. In consequence the (seasonally adjusted) growth in M_3 was £685m (2.0 per cent). DCE growth was much higher, at £1,459m, which was not surprising in view of the UK's balance of payments deficit (£4,000m p.a. at an annual rate). Nevertheless DCE growth was the lowest since the first quarter of 1972, and M_3 growth lower than any quarter since the third quarter of 1971, in effect since the introduction of the 'new approach'.

Interest rates fell during the second quarter; the 20-year rate dropped to 13.6 per cent at the end of May. They then rose again to 15.2 per cent at the end of June — the first of several 'selling seasons' in which stocks were sold on expectations of a continuing fall in rates and the expectations falsified. Base rates fell by ½ per cent in April and by ½ per cent in May to finish at 12 per cent, MLR was cut on 5 and 11 April (by the override power) and 24 May by ¼ per cent on each occasion, to end at 11¾ per cent. During the quarter the government lent £100m to the building societies, and promised a further £400m, to avoid an increase in the mortgage rate. This compared with Mr Barber's subsidy of £15m in May 1973 to achieve the same end.[11]

The Chancellor introduced another Budget in July. He was perhaps encouraged by the slow-down in monetary growth, and by the banks being some 2 per cent below the IBELs ceiling. The worsening state of the corporate sector's financial position may have worried him, their financial deficit being £689m in the first quarter and £957m in the second. But electoral considerations must have influenced him in his package of measures, which added £340m to the forecast of the PSBR. In fact the commitments in the two budgets to keeping prices down had created an open-ended drain on the public purse. The 'threshold' system left by the previous government created problems (wage increases were triggered by rises in the RPI[12]) but to continue the policy of buying down the Retail Price Index was to prove as disastrous for the size of the PSBR as it had when Mr Barber tried it.[13]

In the third quarter M_3 rose by £1,215m (3.5 per cent) and DCE by £2,014m. Compared to the second quarter, gilt sales were somewhat lower (£341m) and there was no longer any significant offset from the unwinding of (commercial bill) open market operations. MLR fell to 11½ per cent on 20 September, but otherwise base rates and MLR were unchanged. Bond rates fluctuated quite sharply but fell nearly ½ per cent over the quarter, to 14.89 per cent. The variations may have helped gilt sales without contradicting the authorities' theory if sales were concentrated in the periods of rising bond prices. Otherwise it seems to suggest that fluctuating bond prices and gilt sales are not inconsistent with each other, i.e. to refute the validity of the cashiers' theory.

(iv) Company Liquidity and the Social Contract, October 1974 – June 1975

On 10 October there was another general election and shortly there-after (12 November) Mr Healey introduced a third Budget which inaugurated a new phase of economic management. The Budget included massive tax relief for companies as well as an easing of the price code. This raised the PSBR forecast to £6,300m, compared to £5,500m without the measures. The two packages were responsible for less than half the difference between the Budget estimate and the revision. The rest was due to inflation, in particular the additional cost of the subsidies. In fact the final figure would be £7,602m. This incredible error is discussed below but it must be true that excessive levels of public spending and the overseas deficit (excessive relative to planned levels) offset each other as far as M_3 was concerned.

In the fourth quarter, M_3 rose by 3.1 per cent (£1,107m). (The banking figures show a very large increase in the month ending 17 January but there was no sign of acceleration towards the end of the year as in the original figures, or deceleration as in the revised ones). The Bank *bought* in considerable quantities of debt net, bank lending to the private sector was only £416m, nearly £1,000m down on each of the earlier quarters of 1974, and the lowest level since the second quarter of 1971. This was the beginning of a long period of low private demand for credit, and the economy was clearly depressed, a very different situation to that prevailing earlier. However, the overseas impact on M_3 was negative by over £1,400m; DCE grew by £2,527m. One way and another it was a rather unpleasant period for the economy, the balance of payments was in massive deficit and inflation accelerating — see the statistical appendix.[14] Longer interest rates rose markedly — the twenty-year bond rate rising to 17.39 per cent by the end of the year.

Thus as long rates had risen, indeed been pushed up, absolutely (by 2½ per cent) and relatively to (unchanged) short rates there was a good chance of selling gilt-edged securities by lowering rates and having all three factors working in the authorities' favour. It worked — spectacularly — and in the first quarter of 1975 purchases of central government debt by the non-bank private sector were £1,659m. As bank lending to the private sector was only £95m, DCE was 'only' £835m — the lowest since 1971 (despite the Issue Department's purchases of Commercial Bills — £268m, and a CGBR of nearly £1,500m). M_3 growth was £290m, the lowest in money terms since 1970 and (at 1.1 per cent) in percentage terms since 1969. Interest rates on bonds fell to 13.34 per cent at the end of March — but then rose rapidly in April, to 14.85 per cent at the end of April, again extrapolative expectations had been falsified. Base rates fell to 10½ per cent during the quarter, and to 9½ per cent in April. MLR was reduced six times to 10 per cent (on 17 and 24 January, 7 and 14 February, 7 and 21 March).

In the second quarter MLR fell by ¼ per cent on 18 April. This largely technical fall was reversed on 2 May. Base Rate was unchanged after the fall noted above, and the bond rate drifted down in May and June. In the quarter, M_3 rose by 1.4 per cent (£631m) — bank lending to the private sector was higher at £240m, virtually all of it in foreign currency. Gilt sales were lower (central government debt sales were £556m) but the Bank reversed the Issue Department's bill sales and the overseas impact negative by £1,800m, and DCE rose by £2,778m.

Against this background, the Budget (on 15 April) raised personal indirect taxation sharply and public spending cuts for 1976/7 were announced. The PSBR was forecast to be £9.1 bn against £7.6 bn in 1974/5, and over £10 bn, without the Budget changes. This, with a no-growth prediction and a forecast rise in unemployment to one million also included in the Budget, reflected the marked change in emphasis since the election. However, not until after the Common Market referendum on 5 June did the government introduce an incomes policy on 1 July, following the foreign exchange crisis of June 1975.[15]

During the first half of 1975 sterling fell from 79.6 per cent of its Smithsonian parity to 71.1 per cent, following remarkable stability in 1974 when it fell by only four points, despite a balance of payments deficit of over £3,300m. This ushered in a new phase of government policy — the era of the most orthodox and conservative management since the Second World War despite, or because of, a Labour govern-ment with a vocal left-wing element.

(v) Labour Conservatism, July 1975 — December 1976

The third quarter saw longer-term interest rates drift downwards, while inter-bank three-month rates rose (by about 1 per cent) to 10.62 per cent. Base rates rose by ½ per cent to 10 per cent in early August, following a 1 per cent rise in MLR on 25 July to 11 per cent. Sales of central government debt were very high (at £1,234m) but this was to a large extent (some) £500m in Treasury Bills. This was a by-product of low bank demand for funds, partly the effect of the IBELs ceiling, partly of low demand for credit. The margin between base rates and retail deposit rates rose from 2½ per cent to 4 per cent, reflecting similar factors. But an enormous CGBR (at £2,717m) meant that DCE was £1,193m even after repayment of £141m of bank borrowing by the private sector, while M_3 rose by 4.6 per cent (£1,743m) as the external influences ceased to reduce M_3 much below DCE growth.

Sterling also continued to be weak, and a rise of nearly 3 points following the pay freeze was reversed in August and September and sterling continued to fall, reaching 69.9 per cent by the end of the year. Thus it is not surprising that the authorities once more manipulated interest rates — the twenty-year bond rate was increased to 14.91 per cent on 5 November (1 per cent up on the level of one month earlier). MLR was forced up to 12 per cent on 3 October and reduced on 14 and 28 November, 24 December, 2, 16 and 23 January, 6 and 27 February and 5 March: by now it was down to 9 per cent. Base Rate went to 11 per cent in mid-October and fell in mid-January

(10½ per cent) and February (in two steps to 9½ per cent). Thus for the third time the authorities manipulated the gilts market. In the fourth quarter of 1975 they sold £1,897m of central government debt to the non-bank private sector (virtually all of it medium- and long-dated gilts) and a rurther £1,435m in the first quarter of 1976; gilt sales were £1,643m and £1,092m.

In the fourth quarter of 1975 the private sector repaid a further £56m to the banks and so (despite a low overseas adjustment and PSBR of £2,589m) M_3 grew by 0.6 per cent.

In the first quarter of 1976 growth in M_3 was faster: 1.0 per cent (£741m), a larger (negative) overseas adjustment partly offset £130m increase in bank lending.

These figures may have encouraged the authorities a little but the overshooting of the PSBR forecast (by £1,700m) at £10,800m must have depressed them.

The growing importance of cash limits began to control the money level as well as the volume of public spending. They are discussed below but their introduction in February 1976 was for this reason an important step towards the abandonment of 'post-war' demand management and towards the acceptance of financial, if not monetarist, policy.

The April Budget included the first semi-official money supply target in UK history (Jenkins in 1969 had spelt out the money supply implications of a DCE target):

> To this end, I aim to see that the growth of the money supply is consistent with my plans for the growth of demand expressed in current prices. If it became clear that this aim were not being achieved, I would be ready to use the appropriate mix of policies – not necessarily monetary policy alone – to redress the situation. After two years in which M_3 has grown a good deal more slowly than money GDP, I would expect their respective growth rates to come more into line in the coming financial year.

In July this was firmed up: 'For the financial year as a whole money supply growth should amount to about 12 per cent'.[16]

The other feature of the Budget was a conditional package of tax cuts – conditional on the successful negotiation of a phase two incomes policy with the TUC, After this was done, the total effect of the Budget was to increase the forecast PSBR for 1976/7 to £11,962m (instead of £11,287m) compared to £10,773m in 1975/6.

In the first quarter the current account deficit was only £60m but sterling lurched downwards from 70.0 on 2 January (and 69.8 on 27 February) to 65.9 at the end of March. The downward movement continued in April, down to 62.5 on 23 April and May (reaching 58.8 on 4 June). The authorities continually intervened heavily but only to hold the rate for a while and then let it slide again. This was a very strange policy, as it almost certainly maximised the cost to the reserves for a given downward movement as the brief periods of stability provided an opportunity for holders of sterling to get out without providing an incentive to them to stay in.

This policy necessitated continuous heavy borrowing. In these circumstances it is not surprising that overseas factors led to a 1½ per cent increase in MLR (to 10½ per cent) on 23 April and a further 1 per cent increase on 21 May — which with heavy intervention and a new loan enabled sterling to remain in the 59–60 range throughout June, July and August. In the second quarter government bond yields rose by about 0.2 per cent, the twenty-year bond rate ending the quarter at 14.03 per cent. In the quarter, M_3 rose by 4.0 per cent (£1,633m), a very large (£2,257m) expansion of DCE being partly offset by a large 'external adjustment'. Bank lending to the private sector was very much higher (at £805m), the PSBR higher (at £2,862m) while sales of public sector debt fell slightly (£1,262m instead of £1,600m) but this stability cloaked larger borrowing by local authorities and smaller sales of gilts. On 22 July, a further *credit control notice*[17] was issued emphasising the need to keep lending to the restricted sector under control (i.e. personal sector borrowing, property company loans and loans to finance 'purely financial transactions'). Further public spending cuts were announced on 22 July.

The third quarter saw another dramatic downward movement in the exchange rate — it fell from 60.4 on 3 September to 55.3 on 1 October. There was no change in MLR during the quarter but the 'override power' was used to force the rate up to 15 per cent on 7 October. The banks' base rate rose to 12 per cent in mid-September (and to 14 per cent by 22 October). Bond rates rose consistently; the twenty-year rate finished the quarter at 15.14 per cent.

The authorities had to cope not merely with these worrying overseas developments but also with a continuation of the acceleration in monetary growth — M_3 rose by 5.4 per cent (£2,276m) in the third quarter (DCE rose by £3,113m) as a further increase in bank lending (to £1,193m) and lower debt sales offset a lower PSBR. Thus the increases in rates described above are not in the least surprising. Nor was the Bank's reimposition of the IBELs ceiling on 18 November 1976: this time the growth rate permitted was about 6 per cent p.a.[18] As the 'qualitative guidance' was re-emphasised,[19] then it is not unfair to say that these were ceilings on some categories of both assets and liabilities.

(vi) The IMF and After, December 1976 — June 1977

During the fourth quarter sterling fell again, reaching a low of 52 in late October (or $1.56). At this point the authorities opened negotiations with the IMF, which as always in such matters was partly the agent of the US and German Treasuries. The negotiations were successfully completed on 14 December. This, and the associated public spending cuts, acted like a Good Housekeeping seal of approval in restoring confidence in both the exchange rate and in domestic monetary management. The exchange rate recovered to $1.70 at the end of the year.

This, and the high level of bond yields (absolutely and relative to short rates), which were 16.40 per cent on 27 October, enabled the authorities to inaugurate the most successful gilts-selling season ever. MLR was cut by ¼ per cent on 19 November and 17 and 24 December. During the quarter, sales of central government debt to the non-bank private sector totalled £2,396m (of which £2,676m was gilts) offset by repayments of other instruments. Lending to the private sector was unchanged (£1,121m) but a fall in the PSBR (to £1,808m) meant that despite a low external adjustment (£220m) M_3 *fell* by 0.1 per cent (£28m). The authorities' new (IMF-inspired) aggregate — sterling M_3 — fell by £56m.[20]

The gilt-edged selling season continued during the first quarter of 1977 despite attempts to restrain it as M_3 and sterling fell below their target growth rates. MLR was reduced on 21 January (by ¾ per cent), 28 January (by 1 per cent), 4 February (by ¼ per cent), 11 March (1 per cent), and 18 March (½ per cent) to end the quarter at 9½ per cent. The extra-large reductions (instead of the usual ¼ per cent) reflected both market pressure and some attempt to slow the sales down. Base rates fell from 14 per cent to 10½ per cent. The twenty-year government bond rate fell from 15.27 per cent on 29 December to 12.50 per cent on 30 March — the speed of the fall gathering momentum as the authorities refrained from selling.

Nevertheless, purchases of public sector debt amounted to £2,274m in the quarter. The PSBR was £2,037m and sterling bank lending to £567m, so DCE (new definition) was £563m. The external influence was heavily positive — £1,013m — so sterling M_3 grew by £104m (0.2 per cent) and M_3 by £417m (0.9 per cent). Thus over the financial year M_3 grew by 9.7 per cent, DCE by £4,808m, sterling M_3 by 7.5 per cent and M_1 by 9.9 per cent. As the IMF limit for DCE was £9,000m and the Chancellor's (July) target for M_3 12 per cent and (December) range for $£M_3$ 9–13 per cent, these were commendable achievements. During the first quarter the banks readjusted their portfolios to bring themselves well within the IBELs ceiling — they were now 2¼ per cent below the 'base level' instead of 6 per cent above it in November — thus they were 5¼ per cent below the ceiling which was abandoned on 12 August.

During the second quarter of 1977 sales of gilt-edged stock continued; during the quarter over £1,200m of central government debt was purchased by the non-bank private sector. However, as bank lending to the private sector was £1,031m in sterling and £156m in other currencies, DCE was £1,527m (new definition) and £1,683m (old definition), comfortably below the 'IMF limit' of £7,700m for the year 1977/8. Sterling M_3 grew by £1,483m (3.7 per cent) and M_3 by £1,724m (3.8 per cent); either a disturbing sign or a necessary correction to the low growth in the two previous quarters. The authorities faced the 're-entry problem' into an era of a positive overseas influence on M_3 and an apparent recovery of the private demand for credit. This would demand both skilled management of the gilt market and a flexible system of control — the views discussed in Chapter 9.

(vii) Some Conclusions

It is clear that the authorities have succeeded in keeping the overall growth of monetary aggregates within bounds and that, following the earlier analysis, this must have contributed significantly to the easing of inflationary pressures. However, there are various issues to be considered before one can decide that the 'new "new approach" ' will solve the UK's problems of monetary management.

(a) Did the authorities crowd out private spending and/or borrowing by running an excessive PSBR?

(b) Was growth in the monetary aggregates too variable? That is, would economic management have been easier with a more stable short-term rate of growth of M_3?

(c) Were the downward movements, and large volatility, of the exchange rate intensified by monetary policy? This must be considered with the related question of whether the UK merely exported its excess monetary growth (and imported cost inflation via the exchange rate instead).

(d) Did the ceilings achieve genuine or cosmetic effects?

From the answers to these, one should be able to answer the fundamental questions arising from the period:

(1) was monetary policy suitable to the circumstances?

(2) were the techniques of control suitable to the objectives of monetary policy?

(3) if they were, was this a short-run or a longer-term phenomenon?

(a) Crowding Out

To some extent the issue of crowding out cannot be separated from the issue of control of public spending, which is considered below. At the same time, the issue of the effects of the level of current spending can be considered independently of whether or not the government intended the actual level or a lower one.

Although discussion of monetary policy in the UK and US in recent years has been largely concerned with the issue of 'crowding out',[21] there are at least seven different meanings attributed to this concept.

All forms of 'crowding out' seem to have as their central idea some form of increased government spending leading to an (undesired) fall in private spending.[22] The first form this may take is crowding out in the goods market at a micro level. The government may, for example, so increase public construction programmes that a shortage of bricks restricts private house-building. This form of crowding out normally seems to occur in the labour market — the government, it is frequently alleged, hires too many of various sorts of skilled labour, e.g. research engineers spending time on Concorde or defence projects, consequently crowding out private research.

Crowding out in the goods market can occur at a macro level. If there is increased public expenditure on goods and services, this may so increase aggregate demand that it exceeds aggregate supply and some demand is thereby rendered ineffective. If the public sector can succeed in fulfilling its plans then private spending must fall in volume terms and this is sometimes termed, reasonably enough, crowding out. However, this effect can be achieved by inflation or by rationing, queueing, etc. As a matter of usage, 'crowding out' is sometimes used to describe the latter but virtually never the former. Nevertheless, logically either might be termed crowding out, making three forms of crowding out in the goods market.

The phenomenon of 'crowding out' in the goods market may have been a problem in the 1950s and 1960s, for example in the UK in 1955, but scarcely in the period 1974–6, given the amount of spare capacity. So attention must be devoted to crowding out when there is spare capacity, due to the behaviour of financial markets. The simplest version of this type of crowding out is when government borrowing (to finance fiscal-expansionary spending) leads to higher interest rates. In models without an accelerator, then an increase in public spending must, *ceteris paribus,* lead to a fall in private investment.[23]

The importance of this form of crowding out depends on the impact of interest rates on the demand for investment and credit. There is virtually no evidence that this is significant.[24] This is reinforced if one notes that real cost of borrowing was significantly negative during the period, if one allows for tax and inflation.

So one must examine those forms of crowding out which depend on imperfections in the credit and/or money market.

One such version draws heavily on the work of Jaffee and the concept of equilibrium rationing.[25] He argues that interest rates are unlikely to clear the market for credit either because of official intervention or because of the constraints imposed by the nature of banking, that is the real and psychological costs of changing interest rates are large. One might add that — as in the UK in 1972–3 — motives other than short-run profit-maximising may also influence bank behaviour, as discussed above. The Jaffee model argues that banks then introduce 'equilibrium rationing', that is they vary the other terms on which credit is granted (collateral, etc.) such that they are in a utility-maximising position subject to the constraint. This model then argues that the effect of increased public sector borrowing from banks is that banks tighten the requirements in which private sector customers can borrow, but do not adjust interest rates. In this case the 'crowding out' is of riskier borrowing, including perhaps smaller loans,[26] and of the expenditure they finance. It is, however, worth emphasising that one might equally expect the opposite response to a larger portfolio with increased holdings of liquid, low-risk public sector assets. Jaffee assumes some form of quantity constraints imposed by the authorities. It is not clear whether the imperfections assumed in the workings of the reserve base/credit multiplier model are consistent with Jaffee's model.[27] Policy-imposed ceilings are considered further below.

In any case one might expect credit rationing to occur in an arbitrary fashion, e.g. first come, first served.[28] This form of arbitrary credit rationing is one of a whole family of forms of crowding out depending on capital market imperfections. Lack of information, oligopoly, inefficiency or a host of other factors may determine who gets credit and therefore what expenditure is crowded out. It is impossible to assess their importance in recent years.

Both the 'Jaffee' and 'imperfection' forms of crowding out depend on an external quantity ceiling. This is provided in 'flow-of-funds' crowding out, which, however, lacks their theoretical rationale.[29] This approach uses official policy/actions to constrain some of the cells in a flow-of-funds matrix and from these deduces consequences for the availability of credit.

For example, using the usual relationships, the public sector borrowing requirement + bank lending to the private sector — non-bank private sector lending to the government = Domestic Credit Expansion (DCE). Given the size of the PSBR and official targets for DCE or (M_3 or sterling M_3), one can then deduce a maximum size of private sector bank borrowing by 'forecasting' the highest or lowest plausible figures for the other items. For example, for 1977—8, someone wishing to predict crowding out might argue as follows (by rearranging the supply side counterpart equation):

− PSBR	£8,500m
+ Non-bank private sector lending to the public sector	£5,000m
− overseas influence on the money supply (overseas sector expected to increase the money supply)	£2,500m
+ Δ Non deposit liabilities	£ 800m
+ M_3 Target (11 per cent)	£5,000m
Implied change in private borrowing from banks	− £ 200m

This 'forecast' would imply that the private sector must *cut* its borrowing from banks in the 1977/8 financial year. As it is implausible to argue that it wants to, then it will be crowded out. It must be stressed that these figures are purely illustrative (they are based on various stockbroking circulars and published forecasts), and that financial forecasting is not a very well developed art so one might vary the figures greatly.[30] This approach assumes an implicit knowledge of the private sector's demand for credit such as to say (either in advance or with hindsight), this point cannot have been/cannot be on it.

Furthermore, no explanation is offered as to how the 'crowding out' (non-satisfaction of demand for credit) affects the economy. However, its operational value is considerable.

In this flow-of-funds form of crowding out, the views of market analysts and the media differ sharply. *The Economist,* for example, seems to have believed that it has been a problem since 1975/6, *Greenwell's Monetary Bulletin* that it became a problem during 1976/7, Phillips and Drew that it will become a problem during 1977/8. A third Gilts Broker, Grieveson Grant, seems to argue that it will not arise until the end of the decade. The Treasury believe that it can be averted by public expenditure cuts and that sectoral guidance can ensure that personal spending, not industrial spending, is crowded out.[31] In my view, one can argue that crowding out has not been a problem as

(1) the banks claim to have had excess funds available for lending to industry throughout the period and no one has challenged this;

(2) the figures in Table 8.1 show that restricting monetary growth has not reduced the availability of funds from the Stock Exchange and financial institutions.

Even allowing for inflation, restricting the rate of monetary expansion has been associated with at least a threefold increase in funds available to industry.

The issue is not strictly related to the longer-term issue of the quality of service provided by financial institutions in the UK,[32] however it is worth stressing that there is no evidence that a general shortage of funds has ever hampered increased investment in the UK, even if it is accepted that such an increase is desirable. A further point is that during the period the 'Treasury View' of the 1920s has been revived, notably in *The Times*,[33] that is that at all times all public spending crowds out private spending, a view which is untenable on any grounds.

One of the (many) propositions to be found in both Keynes' and Friedman's works is the view that in, say, 1931, increased public spending on, say, roads financed by an increase in the money supply would increase output without increasing prices or reducing private spending.

(b) The Variability of Monetary Growth

While the growth rate of money was at a defensible level over the period 1974–7 as a whole, the variations from month to month and quarter to quarter were very large — for example, the rapid acceleration and

Table 8.1

	1972—3	1975—6
M_3 growth	61 per cent	15 per cent
Net domestic issues by UK listed industrial and commercial companies	£475m	£2,850m

Source: *Bank of England Quarterly Bulletin,* Vol. 17, No. 2 (June 1977).

subsequent deceleration in 1976 — see the statistical appendix.

The Bank argues that its variability was not excessive, as Table 8.2 shows.

The variability was partly a consequence of the Bank's gilt-edged 'selling season' — a tender method (see Chapter 9) would have ensured a smoother flow (some new developments in techniques are discussed below), and partly of slow response to developments — in turn the consequence in part of poor statistics. It is difficult to assess the direct economic significance of such variability. However it is clear that it affected market confidence and in this way directly (see Chapter 5, section (i)) contributed to sterling's problems.

(c) Monetary Policy and Exchange Rates

It is not clear what the exchange rate objectives of the authorities should have been (given the cost-inflationary effects of depreciation and the belief that it was necessary to retain competitiveness). Equally it is clear that the execution of the policy was grossly incompetent. However, neither is relevant to the issue here, which is whether monetary policy assisted or hindered the authorities' policy. It seems clear that the (temporary) creation of excess supplies of sterling drove down its international price. One may argue that excess money creation was exported, even if the balance of payments deficit on current account was not affected by monetary developments, as the overseas impact in reducing M_3 was greater than the current deficit (£7,300m against £6,000m between 1974 I and 1976 III). However this effect was not very large.

(d) Were the Ceilings Genuine or Cosmetic?

Any method of rationing automatically imposes costs in terms of inefficiency and misallocation of resources, but these may be worth it in terms of the gains, that is of the extra policy weapon thereby made available to the authorities. More seriously,[34] a system of rationing is bound to be evaded to some extent in a democratic (perhaps in any)

Table 8.2: Variability of Monetary Growth Percentage Changes at Annual Rates

	Standard deviations of:		
	3-month changes[a]	6-month changes[b]	12-month changes
Broadly-defined money stock:			
United States (M_2)	2.8	1.9	1.4
Canada (M_2)	6.1	4.7	3.1
Japan (M_2)	2.7	2.3	1.7
France (M_2)	14.1	6.0	3.6
Western Germany (M_3)	4.2	2.9	1.7
United Kingdom (M_3)	5.7	3.9	1.9
Narrowly-defined money stock (M_1):			
United States	2.8	1.7	0.7
Canada	13.3	8.8	5.8
Japan	6.6	3.5	2.6
France	25.2	8.8	5.8
Western Germany	6.5	4.4	3.0
United Kingdom	7.3	4.1	2.1

a. Calculated as follows:
mid-January — mid-April; mid-February — mid-May, etc. to mid-September — mid-December

b. Calculated as follows:
mid-January — mid-July; mid-February — mid-August, etc. to mid-July — mid-December.

state and this has consequences for policy in that it both makes it harder to enforce and to know what policy is desirable. This was seen above in the case of the UK's old approach which led the authorities to abandon the scheme and in the French case where controls do seem to be effective and, given the authorities' objectives, desirable. Thus the IBELs ceiling must be examined to see how easy it was to evade and by how much it was evaded.

One might expect the ceiling to be evaded in either of two ways, either by the use of parallel markets or by manipulation of their portfolios by banks. In the former case the mechanism would have been as set out below.

The banks were simultaneously turning away deposits (or increasing their margins by cutting the rates paid) and rationing credit, as the whole purpose of the scheme was to avoid rationing credit by price. So both a supply and demand for funds have been created. Normal economic analysis would suggest that these would create a 'free' or 'black' market at some price higher than would have prevailed in a uniform market cleared by price. One might have expected the money brokers etc. to come back into vogue, or more likely, given that they were under a cloud, the corporate money market to grow.

This does not seem to have happened, partly because of the temporary factors of the (largely necessary) ultra-cautious attitude in financial matters induced by the secondary banking crash and partly because the demand for funds was very low anyway. However, in addition there was one factor which permanently reduces the appeal of a parallel market. This is that the authorities are a vigorous bidder for any diverted funds. Thus the non-bank private sector acquired £356m of Treasury Bills in the first quarter of 1977 (and £124m in the third quarter of 1974) following the imposition of IBELs ceilings. These have the same effect of reducing the money supply as any other sales of public sector debt and they thus make the ceiling on bank deposits and (indirectly) on credit effective. They, of course, do not reduce the private sector's liquidity – if anything they increase it, as Treasury Bills are more marketable than wholesale deposits and as marketable as CDs. As above, issues of economic theory are perhaps more relevant in this area than anywhere else in the practical application of monetary policy.

That the banks were able to cut their interest-bearing eligible liabilities in six months in 1976–7 without apparent damage to the economy suggests that some manoeuvring by the banking sector may have taken place. The *Financial Times* suggested that the large increase in the clearing banks' loans on the inter-bank market may have represented loans by the banks to their subsidiaries that were 'earmarked' for on-lending by the subsidiary to particular customers (the subsidiaries being below the ceilings unlike the parents). However this, and similar deals between banks, would only enable individual banks to keep below their ceilings, not the entire banking sector. In fact, by ensuring that all banks were close to their ceilings they would help the authorities – rather as the Federal Funds market assisted in the US by ensuring greater efficiency in the use of reserves.

The Bank suggested that some evasion might have taken place by the use of bills.[35] Most obviously, banks could have encouraged switches to current account by remitting bank charges (for services) or by reducing commitment fees on facilities. Imagine a company had £100,000 on current account, £400,000 in deposit accounts earning 10 per cent interest and was paying £25,000 per annum in bank charges and £5,000 per annum or ½ per cent commitment fee on an overdraft limit of £1m (a 'line of credit' in US or Continental jargon). If it switched £300,000 to current account and had the charges remitted neither it nor the bank would be worse off but the bank would be helped *vis-à-vis* its IBELs ceiling. In the three months following the reintroduction of the ceilings M_1 grew by 0.9 per cent and sterling M_3 fell by 3 per cent, suggesting some such transactions. However, equally it is clear that the ceilings had some effect.

Turning to the fundamental issues.

(1) The Appropriateness of Monetary Policy

It is rather odd to say that any policy was appropriate given the catalogue of disasters which hit the UK economy over the period. However, once the government had decided to let wages 'rip' in 1974, then one must conclude that monetary policy helped to mitigate both the effect of this on unemployment (by helping companies) and also reduced its impact on inflation and helped the 'fight against inflation'.[36] Whether the wages explosion was caused by (Labour) political cowardice in the face of an election or was the result of (Conservative) incompetence in rendering the country ungovernable is an interesting, but here irrelevant, issue.

(2) The Techniques of Monetary Control

It is clear that *in the context of the period* the techniques of monetary control were largely effective. The main problem was the excessive volatility in gilt sales induced by periodic selling seasons. The authorities added, in February 1977, to their armoury the interesting new devices of the 'part-paid stock', whereby sales and payments for stocks are separated. This should enable them to avoid this problem. It also increases the appeal of gilts as a speculative instrument, since the (prospective) capital gain is on the total price of the stock, not that part of it paid-up. This may increase the demand for gilts in total but its advisability is doubtful.

(3) The Long-Run Appropriateness of these Monetary Techniques of Control

It is, however, unfortunately the case that these techniques relied heavily on short-run phenomena and that the UK will need additional weapons — perhaps the US cash base system, as is discussed in Chapter 9.

APPENDIX: HP Statistics 1974–7 and 'IBELS' 1974–7

HP Statistics 1974–7

		New Credit Extended	Changes in Debts Outstanding
1974	I	569	−62
	II	617	−45
	III	652	−22
	IV	679	−26
1975	I	713	− 8
	II	757	12
	III	750	− 5
	IV	772	− 9
1976	I	842	40
	II	873	76
	III	917	105
	IV	978	121
1977	I	1,017	143
	II	1,057	134

'IBELS' 1974–7

1973	Oct.	20,100	1976	Jan.	22,516
1974	Jan.	21,660		Apr.	22,797
	Apr.	21,018		July	23,761
	July	21,831		Oct.	25,215
	Oct.	21,983	1977	Jan.	24,996
1975	Jan.	21,851		Apr.	24,010
	Apr.	22,135		July	24,663
	July	23,156			
	Oct.	22,987			

The Control of Public Spending

The modern history of the control of public expenditure starts with the Plowden Report in 1961.[1] This led to a system of control in constant price terms, known as the PESC system, as the Public Expenditure Survey Committee was supposed to be apex of the system. In fact it virtually never met.[2] This system monitored the volume of spending, e.g. the number of teachers, but ignored the cost of spending, e.g. their salaries.[3]

This was justified in terms of:

(a) Macro-management

In a Keynesian model, the demand on resources ('G') is important, not the money level of spending. The level of public sector wages, for example, affects Personal Disposable Income and so consumer's expenditure (C) which was captured elsewhere in the model. The first round impact of public spending, however, was independent of the cost of goods or services.

(b) Efficiency and Management

It was easier to control public spending in volume terms and long-range public sector planning would be facilitated by ignoring price changes.

The 'relative price effect' measured the difference between the increase in public sector prices and private sector ones. Normally this was positive because of the higher labour input into public sector costs, which meant that input costs rose faster as real wages rose. Public spending measured assuming no change in the price of private sector goods is sometimes termed public spending in cost terms. Thus the ratio of public spending to private spending can be measured in:

(a) constant price terms;
(b) cost terms;
(c) money terms.

The concepts are illustrated by the following example:

	Value
Year 1	
Public Sector	
employs 1 doctor at a salary of £4,000	£4,000
Private Sector	
produces 50,000 loaves of bread (price 10p per loaf)	£5,000
GDP	£9,000
Year 2	
Public Sector	
employs 2 doctors at a salary of £10,000 each	£20,000
Private Sector	
produces 50,000 loaves of bread (price 12½p per loaf)	£ 6,250
	£26,250

Public spending in constant price terms equals £8,000.

The relative price effect is £10,000: private sector prices have risen 25 per cent, public sector ones 150 per cent. The difference (125 per cent) multiplied by the constant price level of spending is £10,000.

In cost terms, public spending in Year 2 has an opportunity cost of 160,000 loaves of bread. Valued at year one's prices, they are worth £16,000. Finally, in money terms public spending is £20,000. Thus at:

(a) constant price terms, public spending has risen 100 per cent and is now 62 per cent of GDP instead of 55 per cent;

(b) cost terms, public spending has risen 300 per cent and is now 76 per cent of GDP;

(c) money terms, public spending has risen 400 per cent and is now 76 per cent of GDP.

There are obvious defects to making decisions in constant price terms.

(a) It assumes that the price elasticity of demand is O both within the public sector and between the public and private sectors.

Thus for example the desirability of building hospitals is not affected by a change in their 'opportunity cost' in terms of schools or washing machines.

(b) It assumes that the substitutability of factors of production is O. Thus, for example, the case for the Open University, a very capital-intensive form of education, has not been affected by the fall in the cost of capital relative to labour and so a reduction in its costs in terms of conventional universities.

(c) As it uses National Income Conventions it measures public inputs and private outputs. This is very misleading when productivity changes, as 'neutrality' involves increasing the public sector.

		Public	*Private*
A:	Output	100	100
	Input	100	100

If productivity doubles (as it did between 1961 and 1975) then the position would be:

B:	Output	200	200 *
	Input	100 *	100

The convention is to define neutrality as equating starred items so the neutral position is

		Public	*Private*
B_2 :	Output	226	134
	Input	133	67

That is public spending is increased by $33\frac{1}{3}$ per cent to achieve neutrality.

This meant that irrespective of the optimal level of public spending the system was understating public spending. This, it must be stressed, does not assume that public sector productivity does not grow, merely that it is not measured. This reinforces the bias described above, whereby in the example public spending was 76 per cent of GDP by measures (2) and (3) and only 62 per cent using the PESC system.

Thus one might object to the PESC system on 'efficiency' (resource allocation) and management grounds. However, the real objections to the system have arisen because of greater emphasis on financial policy and on macroeconomic doctrines which put emphasis on financial (or current price) aggregates, such as the PSBR, DCE or the public sector net acquisition of financial assets. These range from monetarism to the 'New Cambridge School', whose leading spokesman (Wyn Godley) was the chief inventor of the PESC system.

The PESC system as operated by the Treasury seems to have been successful in controlling public spending at constant prices, but this was not what its critics judged necessary.[4] Unfortunately, many critics in the media tended to imply that the Treasury was failing to control public spending rather than succeeding in controlling an inappropriate variable. The emphasis in this criticism was then on incompetence (which was not justified) rather than on an inappropriate control mechanism. 'Cash limits' put money ceilings on public expenditure and have succeeded in controlling what is now judged a more appropriate measure of public spending. However, public spending accounts now have to be kept in three ways — for PESC, for the 'cash limits' and for the supply estimates. This is not an ideal system and further changes have been advocated for this and other reasons by, *inter alia*, Sir John Hunt (the Cabinet Secretary) and Edward Heath.[5] They advocate a Ministry of the Budget, based on the US Office of the Budget and Management. Such change seems unnecessary, as the present system has recently worked well and separate ministries of the budget have not been very successful in Italy or Belgium. In my view, the whole history of dividing Finance Ministries suggests the idea is mistaken, as when the Department of Economic Affairs was established in the UK. However, even if this personal view can be regarded as presumptuous, two facts are undeniable. The first is that there is little evidence to justify the change; the Expenditure Committee rejected it.[5] The other is that administrative reorganisation is always costly and often fails to produce significant benefits, e.g. local government reorganisation.

Notes

1. The scheme is described in 'Credit Control: a supplementary scheme', *Bank of England Quarterly Bulletin*, Vol. 14, No. 1 (March 1974), p. 37. The initial maximum growth rate was 8 per cent between the average of October, November and December 1973 and April, May and June 1974 make-up days. (Banks with less than £3m of IBELs were exempt.) This was laid down in the notice of 17 December. On 30 April 1974 a second notice was issued: 'Credit notice: supplementary deposits', *Bank of England Quarterly Bulletin*, Vol. 14, No. 2 (June 1974), p. 161. This continued the scheme on a three-month moving average basis with growth at 1½ per cent for each month; thus the level for May–July was 9½ per cent above the base line etc.

A further notice ('Credit Control: notice', 28 February 1975, *Bank of England Quarterly Bulletin*, Vol. 15, No. 1 (March 1975), p. 40) suspended the scheme. The scheme was reimposed on 18 November 1976, 'Credit Control: notice', 18 November 1976, *Bank of England Quarterly Bulletin*, Vol. 16, No. 4 (December 1976), p. 434. This time the maximum growth was 3 per cent for February–April 1977 over August–October 1976 and ½ per cent per month thereafter, initially for two months but extended on 12 May 1977, 'Credit Control: notice', 12 May 1977, *Bank of England Quarterly Bulletin*, Vol. 17, No. 2 (June 1977). The scheme was suspended by a further notice 'Credit Control: notice', 11 August 1977, *Bank of England Quarterly Bulletin*, Vol. 17, No. 3 (September 1977), p. 529. The scheme is often inelegantly called 'the corset'.

2. The Special Deposit rate of interest was Treasury Bill rate except between 2 June 1969 and 15 April 1970. Then it was effectively halved as a penalty. Further from October 1973 to November 1974, no interest was paid on Special Deposits representing current accounts to reduce so-called endowment profits. Thus if 50 per cent of a bank's eligible liabilities were current accounts, it received no interest on half its Special Deposits.

3. To operate as a 'tax', overdraft rates would have had to rise to 34 per cent.

4. On 17 December 1973. See *The Times*, 18 December 1973 for details.

5. They were imposed by a White Paper: *Cash Limits on Public Expenditure*, Cmnd. 6767 (HMSO, August 1976). See also *Cash Limits 1977/8*, Cmnd. 6767, and *Cash Limits in 1976–7: Provisional out-turns*, Cmnd. 6902, issued by HMSO in March and August 1977 respectively.

6. *Hansard,* 6 April 1976, col. 237.

7. *Hansard,* 15 December 1976, col. 1534.

8. See, for example, the various publications of Saloman Brothers in the USA and *Greenwell's Monetary Bulletin* in the UK, probably the most respected of financial market analysts in each country; or *The Economist* (virtually any issue).

9. See D. Butler and D. Kavanagh, *The British General Election of February 1974* (Macmillan, 1974); *The British General Election of October 1974* (Macmillan, 1975).

10. See *Bank of England Quarterly Bulletin*, Vol. 7, No. 1 (March 1967), p. 52; *Bank of England Quarterly Bulletin*, Vol. 12, No. 4 (December 1972), p. 407; *Bank of England Quarterly Bulletin*, Vol. 13, No. 3 (September 1973), p. 315.

11. *Bank of England Quarterly Bulletin*, Vol. 13, No. 2 (June 1973), pp. 146–7.

12. This was part of Phase Three of the Heath government's incomes policy. Once the RPI had risen by more than 7 per cent above the October 1973 level, an increase of 40p per week was paid for each further 1 per cent increase. Eleven were 'triggered'.

13. Subsidies were ultimately provided for council house rents, cheese, milk, tea, bread and flour.

14. The period has been analysed, *inter alia*, in D. Morris (ed.), *The U.K. Economy* (Oxford University Press, 1976).

15. See *The Fight against Inflation*, Cmnd. 6071 (HMSO, 1975). For a racy description of the crisis, see J. Haines, *Politics of Power* (Hamish Hamilton, 1976).

16. *Hansard*, 6 April 1976, col. 237, and 22 July 1976, col. 2019.

17. *Bank of England Quarterly Bulletin*, Vol. 16, No. 3 (September 1976), p. 307. In all 'Credit notices' were issued on: 17 December 1973, *BEQB*, Vol. 14, No. 1 (March 1974), p. 40; 12 November 1974, *BEQB*, Vol. 14, No. 4 (December 1974), p. 38; 28 February 1975, *BEQB*, Vol. 15, No. 1 (March 1975), p. 40; 17 December 1975, *BEQB*, Vol. 16, No. 1 (March 1976), p. 35; 18 November 1976, *BEQB*, Vol. 16, No. 4 (December 1976).

18. See footnote 1.

19. See footnote 17.

20. See Appendix A and *Bank of England Quarterly Bulletin*, Vol. 17, No. 1 (March 1977), p. 39.

21. See footnote 8.

22. It may lead to a desired fall in private spending – for example, increased public spending on health care will probably lead to reduced private spending. Friedman has suggested that the Keynesian multiplier may be less than one for this reason. In general, however, public spending is at least as likely to be a complement as a substitute for private spending, e.g. road-building and motoring.

23. See appendix to Chapter I.

24. See *Survey of Applied Economics*, Vol. I (Royal Economic Society, Macmillan, 1973).

25. *Credit Rationing and the Commercial Loan Market* (Wiley, 1975). The concept has also been used by Spencer in 'A Disequilibrium Model of the U.K. Credit Market 1963–74', Treasury Mimeo, 1975.

26. One form of equilibrium rationing might be to cut expenditure on assessing credit risks. In this case one would expect discrimination in favour of larger companies, as it is easier to ascertain their creditworthiness at lower cost.

27. I am grateful to Charles Goodhart, as for so much, for first pointing this out to me in another context.

28. This can be treated as a special case of Jaffee's model by assuming sufficiently high psychological transaction costs. This seems to make Jaffee's model an empty box.

29. See appendix to Chapter I and references therein.

30. See G. E. Hewitt, 'Financial Forecasts in the U.K.', *Bank of England Quarterly Bulletin*, Vol. 17, No. 2 (June 1977).

31. See *Public Expenditure to 1979/80*, Cmnd. 5879 (HMSO, 1975).

32. For this debate see Samuel Groves and Goddard, *Company Finance in Europe* (ICAEW, 1975); *Banking Finance* (Labour Party, 1976); *Banking and Finance: a Reply* (City Capital Markets Committee, 1976); *Finance for Investment* (NEDO, 1975).

33. Especially in editorials and special articles; see a long debate with Michael Posner, former Deputy Chief Economic Adviser to the Treasury, in March 1976.

34. The cost of resource misallocation is generally low, e.g. Whalley has estimated that resource misallocation in the USSR only reduces GDP by 2–3 per cent.
35. *Bank of England Quarterly Bulletin*, Vol. 17, No. 2 (June 1977).
36. Cmnd. 6013 (HMSO, 1975).

Notes to Appendix

1. *Control of Public Expenditure*, Cmnd. 1432 (HMSO, 1961).
2. For an amusing account of its first meeting see R. H. Crossman, *The Diaries of a Cabinet Minister*, Vol. 2 (ed. J. Morgan), p. 90 (Hamish Hamilton, 1976).
3. The system is described more fully in *Public Expenditure White Papers: Handbook on Methodology* (HMSO, 1970); S. Goldman, *Public Expenditure Management and Control*, Civil Service College Study No. 2 (HMSO, 1973).
4. Most of the studies on public spending control are unpublished or of an ephemeral character, stockbrokers' circulars, conference papers or *Times* articles. T. S. Ward, of the Department of Applied Economics, Cambridge, and Special Adviser to the House of Commons Expenditure Committee, has produced the best of these,which, with the House of Commons reports cited below, are the basis of the statements in the text. Some of his work and much other valuable material on the subject can be found in the House of Commons Expenditure Committee reports, especially 'Financing and Public Expenditure', HC 69, December 1975; 'Planning and Control of Public Expenditure', HC 718, November 1976. See also the various Public Expenditure White Papers, the most recent are: Cmnd. 5879 (HMSO, 1975); Cmnd. 6393 (HMSO, 1976); Cmnd. 6721 (HMSO, 1977).
5. House of Commons, 535: 1 (Report), II and III (evidence).

CONCLUSIONS

The ultimate aim of this book is to try to analyse different systems of monetary control in order to draw some conclusions about the appropriate techniques and targets of monetary policy for the future. In particular, the aim is to consider the problems facing an open economy with a sophisticated financial system, such as the UK in the late 1970s and 1980s. Thus this chapter starts by drawing together the various conclusions reached elsewhere in the book and then considers the problems caused by a sophisticated financial system and an open economy. Some consideration is then given to the special considerations that apply to the UK economy, notably the impact of North Sea oil.

The various possible targets, techniques of control and policy options are then analysed and the future and consequences of the choices facing the UK authorities are outlined.

Policy making and control techniques cannot be considered in a vacuum. The ultimate objectives of policy makers are obviously of great relevance to these issues. For example, if price stability is of supreme importance, the case for controls which may stifle initiative and competition is greater than if economic growth takes precedence, yet one cannot assume objectives will be fixed for ever.

However, a control system — using the term to include both instruments and proximate targets — must also take account of those who must operate it. Political sociology is even less advanced than economics but one can safely assume that any policy makers will be fallible and that they will be equipped with less than perfect information. This implies that a control system should be such as to minimise the consequences of errors. One can argue that one of the faults of the 'new approach' was that it demanded a fast response by the authorities to events, whereas both the poor quality of statistics and the nature of official machinery made a slow one inevitable.

Analysis of UK history revealed considerable problems with ceilings on bank assets in the 1960s (though perhaps less so than the authorities thought in 1971) and it became clear that the 'new approach' was probably unworkable in principle and certainly disastrous in practice. Moreover, given the nature of housing finance in the UK and the votes of over 4,000,000 mortgagees, no scheme that demanded such a large volatility of interest rates, and (occasionally) such high levels could be suitable for use in the UK.

The 'new "new approach" ' has worked much better, given the objectives of the government. It might have been better to deflate in 1974, in response to OPEC's oil price increases and the aftermath of the miners' strike, but once it had been decided to delay unemployment and, it was hoped, to minimise it, monetary policy supported the overall stance of policy very well, whereas in 1972–3 it clearly made it much harder for other policies to work. However, it seems that this system of control techniques was dependent on the peculiar circumstances of 1974–6 and is unlikely to work in the long run without reinforcement.

Examination of Germany, France and the USA seems to suggest that virtually any method of control could work given sufficient ruthlessness in enforcing it. On the other hand, any system of control must, to repeat the point once more, fit in with the background and institutions against which it operates.

(i) The Environment (1): A Sophisticated Financial System

The UK is blessed or cursed with what is probably the most sophisticated financial system in the world, sophisticated in that it comprises an enormous array of different types of financial institutions offering slightly different services. As its defenders are fond of pointing out, this may be taken as proof of its flexibility, vitality and ability to serve the nation. Its critics do not agree.[1] This is not the place to consider the issues involved, but one can legitimately argue that the greater diversity of UK institutions compared to US ones reflects a much greater degree of non-price competition in the UK and of price competition in the US. (One might legitimately regard the range of specialised institutions as reflecting similar phenomena to those that induce a department store to provide a Father Christmas for its customers' children.) This non-price competition may be the result of inhibitions on price competition due to official attitudes or the reflection of the underlying natures of the different economies and societies.

Either way, it has serious implications for the conduct of monetary policy. The clear distinction between money and other financial assets becomes ever more blurred as the financial system becomes more complex and sophisticated. One can state this in terms of the problems of defining money. More formally, one can point out that the wider the range of assets (and consequently the narrower the distinctions between them), the closer the substitutes they will provide. Thus one is more likely to be faced with a spectrum of assets with high elasticities of substitutions (as in the Tobin model) rather than the clear break in the liquidity spectrum of the monetarists' model.

This conclusion, though, can be modified somewhat. The first point is that a conventional definition of money dominates any 'liquidity' aggregate, as was seen in Chapter 4 when the problem was examined. The other is that the wide range of sophisticated alternatives are not really open to many individuals in a community where only 50 per cent of adults have even a bank account.[2]

Nevertheless, the structure of UK institutions seems to have various significant implications. The first is that the authorities could never restrict themselves to watching a single target. Supplementary aggregates should be monitored and in the event of any marked divergence between them, the whole stance of policy re-examined. In particular, the possibility of a redefinition of the appropriate variable should be considered. In 1972—3, for example, this type of analysis should have considered the marked divergence between M_1 and M_3. If, as was argued above, the structural changes distorted M_1 in a manner consistent with the rapid growth in M_3 being an accurate representation of 'true' monetary expansion, then the implications would be clear. If other conclusions had been reached, then one might have switched to M_1 as a target variable. This would have been the reaction of a Tobinesque analyst as much a monetarist one. It is argued below how eclecticism on this issue is independent of one's view of how financial flows can be influenced by the authorities and how financial factors influence 'real ones'.

The remaining implication of institutional structures on the UK is the major role of building societies as a provider of short-term assets for the personal sector. If one adds to this the 'stickiness' of building society rates and the political power of mortgagees, the constraint is considerable. In particular the expansionary effect of monetary policy will be felt largely by the housing market, and especially in house prices. Furthermore, the nature of the building society movement offers some justification for 'stickiness' of rates which in turn provides an economic case against using interest rates as a policy weapon. All in all, the authorities are in a cleft stick here. This, incidentally, cannot be a defence of 'Barberism', but strengthens the case against it by suggesting the inappropriateness of high rates of monetary growth. However, structural changes such as the setting up of the JAC may reduce the problem.

(ii) The Environment (2): An Open Economy

The UK is obviously a much more open economy than the US, for
example, imports are equivalent to 30.0 per cent of GDP instead of
9.3 per cent of GDP. It is, however, much less open than, say, the Irish
Republic (51.1 per cent), or the Netherlands (52.2 per cent).
These countries clearly cannot have independent monetary policies
and have the same problems as, say, a municipal authority which sought
to pursue an independent economic policy. (A sovereign state is not
quite as powerless as a town council simply because of the advantages
of sovereignty but is almost so, in these circumstances.)

The UK's economy is in fact no more open than other comparable
middle-sized countries who cannot pursue totally independent policies
if they wished (as the US could; it rarely wishes to) but are not totally
powerless. For example, Germany's import/GDP ratio is 27.4 per
cent.[3]

The effects of an open economy are complex and have been
magnified by the growth of Eurocurrency markets which have given
the world the closest approximation to an international capital market it
has ever had. The problems are listed briefly below.

(a) The dictates of internal and external policy may be in conflict.

This has two, related, aspects. The first is that the two may suggest
opposite policies. For example, to deflate to cure a balance of payments
surplus and to reflate to reduce unemployment. The problem is worse
in its other guise when the implications of success for one policy are to
hamper the other. For example, the expansionary impact of a balance
of payments surplus may conflict with a domestic anti-inflationary
policy.

(b) The ability to use policy instruments for domestic purposes may
be impaired and the effectiveness of policy instruments may be reduced.

For example, capital flows are likely to be interest-sensitive, so that
reducing interest rates will be, *in extremis*, impossible (the authorities
face the equivalent of a highly elastic LM curve.) Similarly, as in Italy in
1969—70, a domestic credit squeeze may be offset by capital inflows.
(Furthermore, the impact of policy measures on the economy is
reduced.)

This is true in all models and represents different manifestations of the same basic problem.

The size of the 'Keynesian multiplier' falls, so the impact of fiscal policy is reduced. An expansion of domestic credit in part leaks overseas; in the monetary theory it all 'leaks'. In a Friedman model, the relationship between 'high powered' money and the money supply is less predictable and the multiplier linking them lower.

The implications of an 'open economy' are:

(i) it is not possible to put so much emphasis on interest rate policy for domestic reasons (as in a closed economy) since it may be necessary to use this instrument for overseas ends, as so often in the UK, especially before 1973. Furthermore the overseas impact of domestic usage may be considerable and unfortunate;

(ii) direct controls are increasingly likely to be evaded with the aid of overseas intermediaries and/or the Eurocurrency market.

In the UK exchange control has been more vigorously supervised than domestic credit control so this has not been much of a problem but is increasingly becoming more important in France. France is more insulated than the UK from international forces, with a less sophisticated financial sector and a much more *dirigiste* (and centralised) system of government.

(iii) the authorities need to reconsider the movement of domestic monetary aggregates in the light of the movement of capital flows.

If the rate of growth of the money supply is being reduced by capital outflows, then the implications for the authorities are very different from those if it is reduced by, say, open market operations. Thus – the IMF uses a DCE target to avoid a balance of payments deficit becoming a proof of financial orthodoxy. Furthermore, the effects may be different, as they are between, say, an expansion of money caused by a budget deficit and an expansion of credit respectively.

(iii) The Environment (3): A Strong Balance of Payments

The UK's balance of payments position has been consistently weak. It has not had a prolonged period of current account surplus this century nor a prolonged trade surplus since 1820; in fact, there have been only eight years with a trade surplus since 1822. The advent of North Sea oil suggests that the UK may be entering a period of chronic surplus. It is possible that this will not arise because of excessive inflation or attempts to reduce unemployment too quickly. Nevertheless, it is quite likely that the UK may become a country with an endemically strong balance of payments and consequently a strong currency. The UK may, in other words, start to have the sort of problems and benefits that have faced German monetary management for many years. One 'textbook' method of avoiding these is to let the currency float upwards sufficiently to balance the balance of payments. It is not clear if this is possible. Certainly, as discussed in Chapter 7, Germany has never found it desirable and her reasons seem sufficient to sway the UK. The additional factor that both UK parties wish to see industry remain competitive will also reinforce this. Thus the UK authorities are likely to be persistently intervening to hold down the exchange rate. It might still be appreciating, if the UK conquered domestic inflation. It would then enter a German-style virtuous circle, wherein lower inflation and a higher exchange rate each led to the other. Nevertheless it is safe to predict consistent net intervention by the UK to keep its exchange rate below the 'market' level.

This in turn implies that the UK will need to keep DCE below the desired rate of monetary growth for the next decade. One might argue that failure to sterilise inflows was one reason why money and credit got out of hand in 1971–2. Repeating this mistake would be highly deleterious to the non-oil sectors of the economy. Thus the UK authorities will need stronger methods of control than they have needed in the past, and these have been used inadequately.

Furthermore, the UK authorities will have to consider two additional policy options. The first is to copy the German battery of controls, especially the Bardepot, designed to keep out at least sudden large capital inflows, if not the endemic inflow induced by the strength of the mark.

In the Governor's speech which inaugurated the new approach he suggested that Special Deposits might be levied against overseas deposits only (or at differential rates.) This is obviously a step towards the Bardepot. It differs in that non-banks are not covered and that interest is paid on Special Deposits.

The other is to consider trying to reduce this endemic inflow by the relaxation of outward exchange control; otherwise there is something paradoxical about having both inward and outward controls. The paradox is not necessarily illogical: the gains from insulation may exceed the costs. The issues here are complex and largely outside the monetary field. It would amount to the quite defensible view that the UK would be better advised to see its citizens own, say, shares in

American industry than to see its capital stock 'regenerated' as politicians desire. It would also probably involve investing short-term loans (the inflows) in longer-term assets. This was, of course, the UK's practice in the period before 1914. It is both dangerous, in that a country is more vulnerable to a loss of confidence as its balance sheet becomes more illiquid[4] and highly profitable. The stronger the UK's balance of payments as a long-term basis, the stronger the case for taking the risk.

From the point of view of monetary policy alone, insulation makes policy-making easier, but like all controls it imposes a cost and if it is not 100 per cent effective then it can be much worse than nothing. Insulation by means other than exchange control is possible. Two-tier exchange rates and two-tier interest rates are possibilities but do not seem either practicable or desirable, for the reasons outlined in the appendix.

Another is the one recommended by Keynes in a *Tract on Monetary Reform*,[5] that is to manipulate the forward rate of exchange to counteract foreign flows. This, however, depends on the applicability of the 'interest parity theory' and does not seem to work sufficiently well to make it more than an auxiliary tool. This is also discussed in the appendix to this chapter.

A strong balance of payments and exchange rate is likely to change the structure of interest rates and in particular to lower short-term rates relative to longer-term ones. This has interesting implications for the sales of government debt. It will clearly reduce sales of short-dated government and local authority bills to the non-bank private sector, that doubled-edged weapon analysed in Chapter 8.

However its effects on gilt sales is less clear. It might switch some private sector funds to the gilt market away from banks and thus help to offset the problems caused by a strong balance of payments. On the other hand, if it is variations in the yield curve, not its absolute level that influences gilt sales (see Chapter 8) then by reducing the authorities' ability to manipulate the term structure, it will reduce the efficiency of the present method of selling, and thus cause the authorities still more problems. It would strengthen the case for 'tender' sales of gilt-edged, discussed below, and increase the doubts already expressed about the desirability of the Bank's ability to sell vast quantities of debt by manipulative techniques that induce quickly falsified expectations.

(iv) Monetary Policy and Monetary Targets

In Chapter 4, it seemed that the appropriate monetary policy for 1972–3 was independent of one's view of the monetarist controversy. Unfortunately, however, this is not always the case. For example, in 1974, the stock market collapse would have suggested to a Tobinesque observer the need to increase the rate of monetary expansion (though in the peculiar circumstances of September 1974 it might have led to a further collapse of share values by reducing business confidence). Thus, the increase in the PSBR in the July 1974 Budget would have seemed a much more logical policy to this observer than to a Friedmanite one. This would also have affected their judgement on whether the Labour government was skilful and/or lucky on the issue of crowding out. Similarly, when monetary growth is reduced by sales of Treasury Bills, the consequences and implications of this depend crucially on one's position on economic theory.

The author's natural tendency is to take an eclectic position, as is no doubt apparent, as this seems essential in view of the indecisive nature of the available evidence. In the world of reality, rather than textbooks, it is clear that any model requires one to observe a variety of financial aggregates. For the monetarist, then, the appropriate definition of money is not too clear at any point and will vary with structural change. From the Tobinesque position, observation of asset prices is not sufficient when elasticities of substitutions can vary so much over time, as can the importance of different assets. Thus the asset flows must be monitored in a world of uncertainty, since prices are no longer an adequate proxy. Thus the Tobinesque position demands the same eclecticism over what to observe. The die-hard 'Keynesian' who believes that credit availability alone matters might look at different aggregates, but his is the one untenable position; clearly financial factors matter. The uncertain area is how they affect ultimate targets.

Thus the information necessary for policy making is clear. The authorities should look at a wide range of financial aggregates, stocks and flows, and on asset prices and in the light of these decide on appropriate policy. However, this might be done as in the basically monetarist style of the 'Fed.' where a range of M_1 is laid down and varied in the light of movements of other variables, notably M_2 and to a lesser extent the Credit Proxy or, more often, the position within the desired range is altered in response to interest rates etc. Or it could be done in the West German method whereby interest rate movements alter the money supply target. Or in fact in an almost infinite variety of ways dependent on which is the principal and which the subsidiary target/indicator. The appropriate one is a question dependent on theory. Furthermore, how the authorities should react is a question of magnitude as well as direction. One could probably reach agreement on direction. Imagine two situations in an economy with, say, 3 per cent inflation and some unemployment with 6–8 per cent growth at annual rate in M_1. In one, the stock market has risen 30 per cent in 3 months, interest rates have fallen and broader aggregates are growing at 20 per cent p.a., in the other all these are stable. All might agree that some contractionary action was necessary in the first but not in the second. However, there is the question of how one expresses the desired proximate target of the new policy in the first economy. However, say one settled this and agreed on M_1; the observers might disagree about the role of M_1, but agreement could still be reached. The neo-monetarist would probably be content to reduce M_1 growth to 4–5 per cent, the Tobinesque one would probably be happy to see 0 per cent for 6–9 months to cut back the growth in broader aggregates to 10 per cent p.a. or less and to, at least, restrain any further growth in share prices. This is obviously only illustrative of how different analysts might react, but is probably a reasonable example of how the different schools would react. It is possible that central bankers relying on 'judgemental feel' and City analysts would be less willing to use quantitative measures of their views, preferring 'significantly slower' to '10 per cent not 20 per cent', but the distinction is unimportant. In reality, no figures are so precise as to be more than steps towards clear, vigorous thinking and illustrations of orders of magnitude, to paraphrase Keynes's argument for compiling national income statistics.

In a world of uncertainty about where one is and how one can move elsewhere, an intermediate position is appealing, as it seems to minimise possible damage, thus compromise has its intellectual rationale. Virtually all results either in conventional economic theory or game theory suggest that in fact the optimal solution is some sort of compromise in a model where one is unclear about the structure of the system and about the values of the current position.[6]

One can challenge this position on the grounds that it would justify navigation based on uncertainty as to whether the world is flat or round. However, this is unfair as in fact one has rejected quite a lot of conceivable models and in a navigational analogy has a choice of two routes, where forecasters differ as to where the risk of hitting icebergs are higher. To suggest assuming that both may be correct and so being cautious is not silly. Economic policy-making has the advantage that gradualism is possible, normally at any rate — there are very few theories that suggest disaster once some variable exceeds x per cent but no problems at all if it is below it.

The case for targets on quantities rather than prices is strengthened by uncertainty. As changing a credit flow would be the objective of changing interest rates, then a policy with a measurable quantitative impact (ceilings or a reserve base) becomes more desirable *vis-à-vis* one using a more indirect route.

Thus it seems reasonable for the UK authorities to set a target for a broad monetary aggregate, probably sterling M_3, but to have supplementary targets for alternative definitions and to reappraise policy whenever these are breached or there are sharp movements in equity prices, or other movements in 'confidence'. The response to a loss of confidence is logically to expand but the dangers of this are obvious and were noted by Keynes in this context.

However, an eclectic position carries its own dangers as were illustrated by the new approach. The loss of clarity and direction that comes from belief that more than one variable matters must be offset by a greater willingness to act, not a lesser one.

To summarise various ideas expressed elsewhere in this book. Monetary policy is ultimately the study of, and reaction to, movements in various indicators and proximate targets. Monetary policy consists of manipulating discount rates, open market operations, some direct controls, etc., to try to achieve (or help achieve) some desired combination of inflation, unemployment, growth, capital flows and exchange rates. Why have a money supply (or DCE, credit, liquidity or interest rate target) at all? Why not, say, have a rule that if unemployment is above target then open market operations must relax the monetary situation and vice versa. As has been pointed out,[7] if one is uncertain about the effect of, say, open market operations on money and money on activity, then one must reduce the risk of error by looking only at open market operations and money (unless some pattern of negative covariances produces compensating errors.) However, one would justify proximate targets, or indicators, as:

(i) attempts to capture transmission mechanisms;
(ii) that in view of the variable time lags and the intricacies of the transmission mechanisms, one may better monitor the impact of policy at some point other than instrument or ultimate target. This, of course, takes a wider view of the implications of uncertainty than does

Waud's model.

Money targets and indicators should not be a be-all-and-end-all of economic policy but observance of them may be the best available policy. Less strongly, the setting of explicit targets may be necessary to ensure consistency between different aspects of policy, e.g. the implications of a monetary target for the PSBR. Further, if targets are only breached as a conscious decision for articulated reasons, then the risk of a recurrence of 1971—3 is averted.

(v) Policy Options

Thus far it has been argued that the UK must monitor and seek to control a variety of financial aggregates in the light of the constraints imposed by the UK's structure of the economy and the favourable balance of payments conjuncture. Further, the authorities should seek a system of control adequate for this purpose and should not hesitate to use it as vigorously as is necessary. In the choice of the system and of the techniques which comprise it, they should be guided by past history and the experiences of other countries. This section reviews possible policy options and seeks to point out their costs and benefits; they are grouped under the headings used in the appendix to Chapter 7, indicated by the bracketed letters.

(a) Altering the Size of the PSBR (a)

In 1975—6, this became one of the principal tools of monetary policy. Nevertheless, it should be a strategic rather than a tactical weapon since the costs of very frequent changes in public spending and taxation are very high both for the public and private sector. North Sea oil revenues and a higher level of demand will reduce the very high level of PSBR that the government has, deliberately, run in the middle of the 1970s, so a return to a level that would not impose strain on the financial system in the absence of the depression is likely.[8]

The level of the PSBR can and probably should be varied to offset developments in the private and overseas sector, but it is clear that while such variations can be excessive, the indictment of 'fine tuning' is convincing. Without going to the extreme of a budgetary rule, then it is possible to try to ascertain what should be the normal level of the PSBR. The constant employment Budget deficit concept more widely used in the US than the UK can be used to define a 'neutral' fiscal policy stance. The calculations done on this basis in the UK suggest that a PSBR of £2,000m (at full employment) would be a desirable level.

It is possible to try to construct a similar total from a monetary approach, if the authorities have a (long-run) view of the desirable growth in M_3. If 8 per cent is a reasonable target for M_3 then this implies that M_3 should grow by about £3,500m (using 1977 as a base level). In the late 1970s and 1980s the overseas influence on the money supply is likely to be about £1,500m, so DCE growth should be about £2,750m, assuming non-deposit liabilities grow at about £750m p.a. The private sector's natural (full-employment) appetite for public sector debt is estimated by the leading gilts brokers at about £3,500m (including National Savings, etc.). The private sector's demand for bank credit is harder to estimate. If £4,000m p.a. is taken as a plausible estimate, then the implied neutral PSBR is about £2,250m, rather but not significantly higher than the fiscal policy neutral one.

Thus one can argue that this approximate level of the PSBR would be a suitable base level for the authorities. In the event of a world depression, or collapse of private sector confidence, they would be well advised to increase it (and vice versa) to provide a strategic background against which monetary and financial policy could operate.

It should be borne in mind that just as the impact of fiscal policy is not fully measured by the PSBR nor is its monetary impact. If it is reduced by the sale of financial assets (as with BP shares in 1977–8), then the effect is equivalent to sales of government securities rather than to an expenditure change and in particular, *ceteris paribus*, should reduce the non-bank private sector's demand for gilt-edged to some extent, and similarly with government lending or acquisition of financial assets likely to reduce private sector borrowing from the banks. Hence public sector transactions in financial assets are partially offset in their effects on the monetary aggregates by the effects on the private sector's desired holdings which they generate.

(b) Quantity Controls on Private Sector lending to the Government (f)

There seems little to justify such controls *per se*. Forced loans, which is what they amount to, have a very long history of heading the list of royal crimes in the UK: they were partially responsible for Richard III and Charles I losing their thrones, and provoked a rebellion against Edward II. Under their modern guise of, say, trustee legislation they are equally indefensible, being both inequitable and inefficient.

It is, however, arguable that any portfolio constraint on banks amounts to a forced loan to the government, e.g. in the USA the compulsion to hold Federal Reserve Deposits, and that fairness demands extending such ratios to non-bank financial intermediaries, especially as the distinction between banks and non-banks is not very clear-cut. Monetary policy would be helped by such measures.

There are arguments against this. The banking sector cannot refuse to provide residual finances to the sector; legal tender laws compel it to provide its liabilities in exchange for public sector ones. A bank is legally defined and the distinction is becoming more clear, with greater supervision (see Chapter 7). Banks earn monopoly rent from control of the money transmissions mechanism so the constraint is a fair *quid pro quo*, one might argue.

The issue is really concerned, however, more with monetary policy than equity. A non-bank financial intermediary can provide credit and liquid assets, if not money. Thus any decision to control these implies a control on the non-bank financial intermediaries (OFI). If a decision is made in favour of non-price controls for banks, then it should be extended to OFIs, as is argued below. Public sector lending ratios (like other portfolio constraints) are one such device.

(c) By Price Effects on Non-Bank Private Sector Lending to the Public Sector (g)

The question of how the authorities can induce the private sector to hold public sector debt is crucial to monetary control. The 'cashiers'' and 'economists'' theories and the methods used since 1974 were discussed above. Some doubts were expressed about the durability of the present method (Chapter 8).

The most widely canvassed alternative is a 'tender method' of selling public sector debt, or at least the bond element of this. The authorities would auction a fixed quantity of debt and allow the market to determine the price, as is sometimes done in the US.

One argument for this is incontrovertible. It would be possible to use it to reduce the month-to-month variability of monetary growth, since this 'offset' to the PSBR and private sector bank borrowing could be set at any level, so as to adjust M_3 (or sterling M_3) to a desired level. In practice, given data lags, it would mean that this month's target reflected last month's PSBR and bank credit (not the current one) so the total elimination of variations in month-to-month growth could not be achieved. It would also require rather more accurate seasonal adjustment of the PSBR and bank credit than has yet been achieved. Nevertheless, variability would be reduced if not eliminated. The gilt-edged 'selling season' may have some merits for institutional managers, though these are difficult to see, but any 'lumpiness' in demand could be accommodated by variation in maturities offered, etc., or even by the

Bank varying the quantities offered in accordance with its market judgement. In this way, the authorities would achieve only that degree on monetary variability made desirable by the preferences of bond-holders, not that part of it induced by the Bank's own actions.

On the other hand, such stability might mean greater variability of interest rates, which is not costless. Nevertheless, the present method involves some considerable instability in rates as the authorities hoist rates preparatory to letting them fall slowly. So this objection is not crucial.

A more basic problem is what is the effect on the average cost of the public sector debt (and on the average level of interest rates) for any given path of monetary growth. Obviously debt service charges are not unimportant, even if they should not override the dictates of monetary policy. *The Economist*, which has frequently advocated such a scheme, has argued that it will reduce the average cost of the public sector debt.[9] Their argument is that most of the sales occur near the bottom of the upswing induced by the Bank's actions and are therefore at above the average interest rate. This is unverifiable and in any case ignores the fact that the pattern of interest rates is changed. The counter-argument is that bonds are sold on both the level and change of rates (as a proxy for expectations). If the tender scheme was adopted, then the gilts market should become an 'efficient', 'rational' one, and the expectations element would be eliminated. Therefore a higher level of rates would be necessary to sell any given quantity of bonds (so long as the interest elasticity of bonds sales were independent of the expectation elasticity, this separability seems plausible).

Thus, one would argue that the present selling season has merits — so long as it works — but there seems no reason not to use tender methods when necessary. In particular, this was shown in the autumn of 1976, when the authorities did not know how high rates had to rise before the market believed them to be at their peak. In fact the autumn of 1976 seems a classic case when the authorities would have found 'tender' gilts a useful method of controlling the situation, and would have averted the monetary explosion described above.

The authorities might also extend their armoury by offering index-linked securities. The authorities have in fact issued a limited quantity of index-linked SAYE securities,[10] but have objected to index-linked because they might lead to indexation of most lending and borrowing. Accepting this for the moment, the case for full indexation will be considered. The case for this is firstly that as interest rates do adjust (at least partially) to inflation, it would be more efficient if the adjustment were automatic and accurate. More important, it would reduce uncertainty. The Chicago-Manchester argument against index-linking has always been that it would be unnecessary because some nominal rate would achieve the same end.[11] This ignores the problem that interest is taxed whether it is genuine income or capital-protecting, and that even Fisher expected that it would take forty years for interest rates to adjust to inflation. More fundamentally, if part of the interest rate is a premium against inflation, then unless all expectations of inflation are identical, correct and held with certainty, then the higher nominal rate is inferior to the indexed contract.

Borrowers are often unwilling to pay 'high rates', while lenders regard these same rates as being very unsatisfactory. Both are right! This paradox is because the lender fears that he may lose because of inflation, while the borrower fears that if inflation abates then he will be encumbered with a crushing obligation. To be technical, both parties are not solely interested in expected returns/costs; variance matters, so a relationship in nominal terms does not lie on the contract curve. Therefore both will gain by a switch to index-linking. Thus as both sides are risk-averse, then if the uncertainty were removed, then either real rates would be lower or the volume of funds borrowed higher.

Another advantage — closely related to the previous one — is that high nominal rates as a 'protection' against inflation in effect compel the repayment of capital. If (ignoring or after tax), inflation and interest rates are both 10 per cent p.a., then every year the borrower's interest payment is just sufficient to keep the lender's capital intact. Nevertheless (unless he borrows further funds) the borrower has had to repay (in real terms) 9 per cent if his outstanding debt at the end of each year. This causes cash flow problems for mortgagees and, from the point of view of debt management, it means that companies could borrow at a lower service cost.

The public sector is similarly affected. The real value of the National Debt falls with inflation and this 'inflation tax' is frequently incorporated into economists' analysis. The effect of higher nominal rates on the PSBR is not treated as debt repayment though it legitimately might be. Gordon Pepper, in particular, has argued that it should be in *Greenwell's Monetary Bulletin*.

The contrary argument on debt service charges is basically that money illusion enables the authorities to sell bonds. This seems ludicrous.

A more sophisticated variant is that if inflation accelerates then debt service charges rise. However, this is only in money terms (and may be less than the higher nominal rates anyway) and can be financed out of the higher tax yields. If inflation falls, high nominal rates impose a higher real debt burden. In any case the argument should be relative to expectations. '

Indexed bonds could be sold when confidence fell, unlike conventional issues, and would thus greatly facilitate monetary control.

Index-linked securities would appeal to all those looking for a hedge against inflation (pension funds, small savers). The success of property bonds shows the appeal of indirect hedges while unit trust investment, indeed the whole 'cult of the equity' shows the latent appeal of index-linked bonds. Further, if index-linked securities were available, then the appeal of property, farm land, antiques, etc. would lessen. If index-linked bonds had been available in 1972 then instead of bidding up property, land and antique prices, the hedge money would have financed the huge Budget deficit in a non-inflationary way.

Increases in interest rates have been — and are likely to be — frequently necessary for reasons of economic management as a result of accelerations in the rate of inflation. Yet such rises are both inhibited by political constraints and unpopular when they occur. Index-linking would avoid this problem.

Most important of all, index-linking would protect many of those most vulnerable to inflation. If one fears (as the Chancellor of the Exchequer does) for the effect of inflation on 'the fabric of democratic society', then this protection of the weak is both desirable and necessary. Otherwise, those losing by inflation (*rentier* groups and savers generally) may either provide the raw material for a right-wing authoritarian government or elect a right-wing union government which will provoke a 'revolutionary confrontation' . . .

Justice is probably the strongest argument in favour of index-linking. Inflation is the most vindictive and cruel of all taxes and the most arbitrary and unfair method of redistributing wealth. Thus to protect the weak and ill-advised investor seems very desirable and essential. To me, it seems to be a denial of a basic civil right that people cannot plan for the future or save for retirement.

The arguments against indexation are weak. It is argued that the government would lose control of interest rates. The corollary of this argument is that in a world of price stability, the government could not change interest rates, an obvious fallacy. In this context, it is clear that the government can change real rates by offering different terms on bonds, open market operations, etc.

It is also argued that it causes losses for existing holders of gilt-edged.

These holders lose by inflation or higher nominal rates in any case.
If the holders hold to maturity, they are no worse-off if others can hold
index-linked securities. So if they switch, they cannot be worse off.
There would be little effect on the inflationary spiral. This would be
small as interest is only 2 per cent of total costs, so a self-perpetuating
spiral is unlikely. This is why the case for indexed bonds is stronger
than for indexed wages. The most usual argument is that 'the Government would be abandoning the fight against inflation.' The argument
that by mitigating the effects of something, one condones it, is
incredible. No one would claim that the existence of unemployment
pay, sickness benefit and criminal injuries compensation means that the
government condones unemployment, sickness or crime, or that it
would combat them more if these were abolished.

It has been accepted in the above discussion that sales of index-
linked bonds by the authorities would lead to a cross-the-board
indexation. This is almost certainly ill-founded as indexed and un-
indexed bonds have been traded simultaneously in Brazil, Finland and
Israel.

It is true that the authorities would be well advised to operate only
in either real or nominal bonds, but not both. Even so, if it operated in,
say, real bonds, nominal ones could be sold by tender (as in the USA).

(d) Price Effects on Bank Lending to the Private Sector (e)

Obviously the effect of interest rates on the demand for credit cannot
be ignored but the constraints on the use of this as a principal instrument of policy seem considerable. Certainly the authorities would never
be sufficiently convinced of the need to adjust interest rates sufficiently
in time. Equally, more information is needed about the demand for
credit before it can be the basis of a control system.

(e) Quantity Controls on Bank and Other Credit (d)

The above argument implies that some consideration should be given to
the question of direct controls on credit. The question of whether this
should be done is really a political question. Some cost is imposed in
terms of efficiency and misallocation of resources but the authorities
can control the sectoral allocation of credit (this could be done by
explicit taxes and subsidies and seems to me a better way of achieving
this than direct controls).

However, the issue is really one of the authorities' control against the
restrictions on freedom imposed and the administrative costs incurred.

In particular the case for controlling consumer credit is very strong as this is easier to control and might still be used (in the spirit of Radcliffe) as an *emergency* weapon if comprehensive controls were rejected. Here the benefit of a quicker response would be held to outweigh the fact that the controls were discriminatory and unlikely to work for very long.

The case for some form of direct control of credit falls into two halves — demand management and financial policy. With the problems facing the authorities at any time in demand management, some form of short-term, quick-acting method of curbing consumer credit may be essential. On the one hand, it is the only way of curbing aggregate demand without increasing the Retail Price Index, either directly or indirectly, and on the other, front-loading of the impact of credit policy seems highly desirable. Furthermore, whether justifiably or not, consumer credit is usually regarded as interest-insensitive. Thus direct controls may be necessary to reduce its growth rate. Given that, unfortunately, short-term demand management problems, like the poor, will always be with us, this should be a permanent feature of the armoury available to UK policy makers.

The selective aspects of consumer credit controls obviously raise some problems for industrial strategy, but the gains here from ensuring a more even growth in the demand for consumer durables over the longer term would outweigh any costs arising from their impact on a few industries. Further, that industry should benefit from selective credit controls as a bias in favour of industry is, of course, one of the justifications for their existence.[12] Finally, the balance of payments case for selective credit controls seems decisive, even with a chronic surplus.[13]

Next, the financial policy case for controls is considered, deliberately avoiding specifying whether one should seek to control money, credit, liquidity, DCE or any other aggregate, since broadly most indicators move together and similar problems arise in seeking to control any of them.

There seem to be four separate reasons why one might need some form of direct control on non-bank consumer credit (and will if direct controls were imposed on banks).

(1) It might be necessary to make any form of financial policy work, given the problems of leakages, squeezing balloons, etc. There is little point in controlling only one element of credit rather than making some attempt to have a more comprehensive system of controls, unless price is the only weapon used.

(2) Even if it were possible to control total credit, liquidity, etc. satisfactorily by controlling the banking system only, it would probably not be a practicable policy because of the growing reluctance of the banking system to participate in such an obviously discriminatory system. In that case the additional legislation, etc. needed to control banks would probably raise more problems and be more open to the charge of *dirigisme* than some comprehensive system of credit control.

(3) In any case, a partial system of controls is both unfair and tends to lead to a misallocation of resources.

(4) Finally, but by no means the least important reasons for direct controls of personal credit, is that selectivity is desirable in itself. It seems a perfectly proper aim for the authorities to seek to direct credit if they are prepared to pay the cost. To put it another way, if someone has to be crowded out, then the authorities should be the best judge of who should be crowded out.

Thus, given the strong *prima facie* case for a system of direct control on non-bank personal credit, two further questions arise. The first is, can one devise a workable system of achieving this control? Second, do the costs of this system outweigh the benefits outlined above?

There do seem to be some other considerations that should be taken into account in one's deliberations, however. One is the transitional problems that will arise as hire purchase controls disappear. At the risk of being accused of being a paternalist, there are considerable dangers that a switch to liberalism may lead to some people acquiring excessive indebtedness. This, besides being socially undesirable, is likely to lead to additional burdens upon the social security system and, perhaps most seriously of all, it may lead to a short-run, import-fed boom in consumer durables at a point when demand will be extremely high in this sector anyway. Thus it is necessary to slow down the effects of the abolition of the present system of the direct control of consumer credit, even if it were felt that in the long run no such controls were either possible or desirable.

To consider some of the loopholes that may arise.

(1) Loans to employers to their employees for the purchase of, particularly, cars and to a lesser extent other consumer durables do seem to be a potential loophole which might seriously damage the system devised. Obviously if a company can borrow from a bank and then on-lend to its employees, then any system of selective credit control has almost totally broken down. There are other problems

associated with these low-interest loans which were partially dealt with in the 1976 Budget,[14] but purely within the area of credit control it seems that something needs to be done. This is especially so if some form of restraint on pay increases is to remain for the next few years, since the combination of credit rationing and pay restraint suggests an obvious disguised pay increase in the form of access to credit.

(2) The legal position concerning consumer credit unions is unclear and they are of growing significance even though still very small. If individuals can lend to each other outside the ambit of the authorities' control then a potentially serious loophole seems to have developed.

(3) The problem of second mortgages may be of some importance in this context. Even though building societies etc. may restrict their lending to those undertaking house improvements etc., the effect of the loan may be increased spending in other areas.

(4) Asset ratios for insurance companies' etc. lending to persons could be considered.

(5) The possibility of margin requirements on Stock Exchange transactions should be considered. These would, on the one hand, restrict one of the uses of personal credit which is a potential destabilising economic influence, and on the other hand by restricting the total borrowing of some individuals, would probably reduce their expenditure on consumer durables and houses.

(6) It may be possible to control non-bank credit institutions via the banking system as is done in France. There, for example, banks impose their own credit ceilings on retailers as a condition of the retailers getting any credit from the bank. The possibility of such controls depends upon both the banks' knowledge of their customers' activities and upon their willingness to use this in the interests of official policy. I am personally extremely dubious as to the practicability of any such scheme, but it may be worth some investigation as it offers some advantages to the banks in exchange for their co-operation — collectively banks would gain from curbing their competitors even though the individual bank would lose business.

If enforcement problems were not too large, a system of incremental ratios (on the lines of supplementary Special Deposits) might be the best way of enforcing ceilings without introducing too many rigidities into the system. For example, assuming it was desired to restrict the overall growth of personal credit to 5 per cent, one could have some progressive system of deposits, say as follows:

3– 5 per cent growth: 20 per cent Special Deposit
5– 7 per cent growth: 30 per cent Special Deposit
7–10 per cent growth: 50 per cent Special Deposit
10 per cent growth: 100 per cent Special Deposit

These would obviously combine some of the features of a ceiling with some of the features of a tax on the extension of credit, since, for example, 100 per cent deposit would be equivalent to doubling the effective cost of funds to the lending institution.

Any system of control would probably have to be based on the licensing system introduced under the Consumer Credit Act of 1974. Yet this is not designed to be used for this purpose and, in fact, during the debates on the Bill this purpose was disclaimed. One hopes the authorities will face the issue squarely and either accept a comprehensive system of control or cease to try to direct credit.

This, it is hoped, gives some idea of the implications of, and the case for and against effective ceilings. Unlike, say, 'tender gilts', it is largely an all-or-nothing issue. The exception is the use of restrictions on personal credit as a one-shot quick-acting weapon in an emergency. This is discriminatory, in that the less well informed citizens get hurt, but is defensible.

(f) Quantity Controls on Bank Liabilities (a)

The IBELs ceiling discussed in Chapter 8 has one great advantage over other direct controls in that the authorities can ensure that the would-be evasive funds do not destroy the control completely. If the public sector bids sufficiently vigorously for short-term funds diverted from the banking sector then the 'credit' and (in a very narrow sense) 'money' effects of the control remain even though the private sector's portfolio is at least as liquid.

The control has the disadvantage that the banking sector seems to have a reasonable amount of flexibility to manoeuvre round it and so the problem that a control may reduce the value of statistics as indicators is acute. The control has also been defended *because* it may be 'cosmetic' in its effects, that is, it may reassure nervous monetarists without affecting economic reality. The reasoning behind this is ingenious but, for obvious reasons, unacceptable.

The IBELs ceiling on the whole does not seem to have a role in monetary control in the long run, despite its value in 1974–6.

(g) Price Effects on Bank Deposits (b)

Given the quantity of bank deposits that pay interest then the overall interest elasticity of the demand for money will be very low.[15] This 'monetarist' result intensifies the likely magnitude of the effects of monetary control but means that interest rate manipulations must be very large to *cause* a change in the money supply.

(h) Portfolio Constraints (h)

There are two well established competitors here: a reserve base system of the US or German type and the public sector lending ratio suggested by Sir John Hicks and revived by Tony Courakis.[16]

The difference between them is relatively small. A reserve ratio scheme without payment of interest on the assets (as in the US) acts as a tax on banking, to a limited extent; a 10 per cent ratio is equivalent to a tax of 0.5–1 per cent of a bank's deposits, and 1/10 of its gross receipts. Furthermore the authorities can conduct open market operations between the reserve and non-reserve asset portions of their debt held by banks.

The case for the public sector lending ratio scheme is that 'it supports the market in government bonds',[17] that is it does not cause banks to 'dump gilts' when their reserve ratios are under pressure. However, the merits of these are dubious, if the authorities are not committed to 'leaning into the wind' and to interest rate stability (as both Hicks and Courakis assumed). If they are, then of course the authorities' *de facto* open market operations (to maintain the price of bonds) undo the effect of the attempt to constrict banks. If they do not, then the rise in interest rates will perhaps induce private sector purchases of bonds or inhibit borrowing and thus reinforce the squeeze. Thus the US-type scheme seems the more desirable.[18]

A reserve ratio scheme does not avert the necessity that an increase in interest rates will accompany a reduction in the rate of monetary growth, but it minimises it in an uncertain world, as discussed above.

However, if it does not apply to all those acting as banks, then it is open to evasion in the same way as any ceiling on deposits or loans — it merely combines the two into one.

Hence the problem with non-member banks in the USA. Furthermore anyone can act as a financial intermediary merely by borrowing and lending. So evasion is potentially enormous. Nevertheless reserve base schemes have two saving graces.

The first is that the banking sector can be defined so as to include all institutions which provide cheque facilities and/or have access to clearing facilities; a crucial distinction from a behavioural aspect. The other is that if a short-term claim is held on an obscure financial intermediary then it will be regarded as less liquid than one on the Chase Manhattan or Midland Bank. This does apply so much to large companies issuing Bills (although the major US pioneer of disinter-mediation was Penn Central, hardly an encouraging precedent). Even without entering into the debate on how the credit multiplier operates with 'non-bank' financial intermediaries, and even with 'do-it-yourself' intermediation,[19] one might conclude that a ratio had merits.

If a large company started to use inter-corporate loan markets on a large scale, would it start to 'take positions' and to act as an intermediary by both borrowing and lending? There seems little reason to doubt that it might as this is a natural extension of their activities. A company needing money in two months' time will borrow now and lend for two months if there is a favourable opportunity, so why not 'intermediate'? This argument is persuasive but nevertheless the distinction between those engaged in banking and others seems clear-cut in Germany and the USA (ignoring the state-chartered banks). Despite these theoretical problems, a reserve base system can work. It does, however, involve a belief in 'money', 'liquidity' and 'portfolio balance' transmission mechanisms rather than credit ones. Further-more, the distinction between 'banks' and 'non-banks' is more blurred in the UK, as was discussed above. On balance, a reserve asset scheme seems workable in the UK if only because the new supervisory control scheme outlined in Chapter 6 will give more precision to the term 'bank'. If a 'bank' is relatively free of supervision, then the incentive this creates may make the monetary policy distinction viable. (However undesirable the weakness of control is from a supervisory viewpoint, it may be desirable from a policy one.)

(i) Interest Rate Ceilings (k)

The case for interest rate ceilings – i.e. Regulation Q – seems very weak. At best it is a device to subsidise mortgage borrowers at the expense of small savers. The arguments above seem decisive, though the economic problems can be small, as with the IBELs ceiling, if the public sector bids for any funds that stray from the protected group of SLAs or building societies.

(vi) The UK's Choice

The UK is likely to have to face a choice of which techniques of monetary control to use, especially if management of the gilt-edged market ceases to work smoothly. Lower public-sector deficits may help but a positive overseas influence on the money supply will work the other way. They might use any of the three UK schemes analysed above, but would probably be better advised to copy the more intellectually coherent and successful models abroad. Which to adopt depends on the objectives selected and the costs and benefits ascribed to, say, sectoral control of credit flows or economic efficiency. Some control of non-bank financial intermediaries and, possibly, of corporate and retail lending must be considered by the authorities. Again, there are costs and benefits to such controls but ineffective controls are the worst of all worlds.

The Bardepot and occasional (but not exclusive) use of 'tender' gilt-edged selling should almost certainly be added to the authorities' armoury in any case. A reserve base system of the American type would be useful even if the authorities use a basically *dirigiste* system of control. Nevertheless the authorities must accept the implication of the need for an effective monetary policy — an effective system of control and a willingness to use the system chosen.

APPENDIX: Two-tier Exchange and Interest Rates

Two-tier exchange and interest rates are both devices to try to insulate the domestic economy from overseas influences. Two-tier interest rates try to segregate domestic and overseas holders of assets in a currency so as to pay different interest rates to them. Normally the argument is that they permit a lower level of domestic interest rate and a higher capital inflow than otherwise but in the UK North Sea oil scenario or Germany's consistent problem they could be used in reverse. Two-tier exchange rates have normally been used by those with strong currencies to allow a 'financial franc' to appreciate above the level of the 'trading franc'. Thus again two markets are created. The object is to avoid a loss of competitiveness caused by an appreciating exchange rate.

The desire to separate the rate of interest paid by domestic borrowers from that received by overseas holders of sterling has appealed to economists since, at least, Keynes (in 'Tract on Monetary Reform'). His solution, however, was not to issue a special security for non-residents, but for the authorities to manage the forward exchange rate so as to change the covered interest rate. A special case of the

Keynesian solution is for the authorities to guarantee some or all overseas holdings of sterling securities against a depreciation (as for example, the Basle guarantees). Another policy option is for the government to issue foreign-currency denominated securities, as, of course, the nationalised industries have done in the UK since 1973.

The most relevant points are listed below.

(1) Two-tier interest rates would attract or repel uncovered arbitrage funds as well as covered. However, the latter have never been very large (perhaps £20–30m for each 1 per cent) and it seems almost inconceivable that anyone would ignore exchange rate risks in the 1970s and 1980s.

(2) Interest rates are not a very effective way of inducing movements of capital even in the most favourable of circumstances. Both econometric and institutional estimates are of about £50–£100m for each 1 per cent change in covered interest rates.[1]

(3) The cost of two-tier interest rates to attract funds is very large since, presumably, the higher rate would have to be paid on all non-resident, or at least all official non-resident, holdings. Given the size of these, the extra cost in terms of interest payments even within one year would almost certainly be greater than the extra funds. Of course when funds are being repelled this is a bonus. This cost-saving effect could also be achieved by the Bardepot or by a special tax on overseas holdings of UK assets. Special taxes have been used to repel borrowers, notably the Interest Equalisation Tax in the US, and could deter lenders instead.

(4) Two-tier interest rates as a defensive measure seem to have two unfortunate political/presentational effects:

(a) It is unfair to pay a higher rate of interest to, say, Arab sheikhs than to (especially small) domestic savers;

(b) the extra cost would appear as part of published public expenditure figures, alternatives need (and probably would) not.

(5) It seems unlikely that it would be possible to insulate the markets for very long anyway, the crucial objection. Arbitrage operations, possibly via the subsidiaries of multinational companies, would circumvent the aim of the policy.

(6) Forward market operations are, in theory, costless, so long as the authorities are prepared to operate on an infinite scale (and thus succeed in pegging the present and future spot rate). However, this is unrealistic, so one must take note of two disadvantages of forward market operations. Firstly their open-ended nature. Second, the

extreme unwillingness of the executors of policy to be involved in them after the débâcle of 1967, with its £356m cost. Unlimited forward commitments to hold down a currency are obviously easier but one cannot roll them over for ever.

(7) Forward market operations could be used for other purposes. For example, a large (forward) discount on sterling could assist exports without increasing import prices if, as seems to be the case, a larger proportion of exports than imports are covered by sales in the forward market.[2]

(8) Guarantees, like forward market operations and non-sterling denominated securities, have the advantage of reducing, or even eliminating, the lender's uncertainty. This is likely to mean they are cost-effective (as well as economically efficient).

Thus, to summarise, the two-tier interest rate seems a poor weapon at times of balance of payments weakness and inferior to the Bardepot at times of strength.

Two-tier exchange rates have been used by both France and Italy, but usually as a prelude to a formal appreciation. Segregation of the markets is impossible in the long run. Even if not, the case for the Bardepot and sterilisation operations seem conclusive. The former protects the exchange rate against any short-term inflows and the latter against longer-term ones.

Notes

1. See Chapter 8, footnote 32, for references to this debate.
2. Press reports, September 1977, of various surveys.
3. See the annual article in the *Bank of England Quarterly Bulletin*, usually in the June issue, for the UK's overall balance sheet of assets and liabilities.
4. See footnote 3.
5. Reprinted in *The Collected Writings of J. M. Keynes* (Macmillan for the RES, 1971), vol. V.
6. The 'economics of uncertainty' in this context is surveyed in C. A. E. Goodhart, *Money, Information and Uncertainty* (Macmillan, 1975), Chapter 12.
7. R. Waud, 'Proximate Targets and Monetary Policy', *Economic Journal* (1973).
8. Congdon has made one analysis of this effect in Messell's *Monthly Gilt Review* for October 1977. He suggests a level in 1980 of perhaps £1½ bn.
9. *The Economist* contained various articles on this theme in the second half of 1976.
10. A maximum of £20 per month can be subscribed unless one is over 65, when the limit is £500.
11. Friedman, of course, supports indexation.
12. The UK's controls have usually been justified on the grounds that industry's

interest sensitivity is greater, so price rationing discriminates against them.

13. The import content of consumer durables is so high, and seems to be growing, that demand management cannot ignore this.

14. Finance Act, 1976.

15. See Goodhart, ibid., Chapter 3 B.

16. In a paper presented to the Money Study Group in October 1972.

17. Quoted from the paper.

18. See the author's 'Techniques of Monetary Control: The U.K.'s Choice', EPAG Discussion Paper, No. I.

19. For this see Goodhart, ibid., Chapter 5 and Chapter 6, and J. Gurley and E. Shaw, *Money in a Theory of Finance* (Brookings Institute, 1960).

Notes to Appendix

1. J. P. Hutton, 'A model of capital flows, exchange rates and official intervention 1963–70', *Review of Economic Studies* (June 1977).

2. This seems to be one of the preliminary conclusions of a study carried out under the supervision of Professor John Williamson and G. E. Wood, financed by the Ford Foundation. However, less than half of either exports and imports are covered in forward markets. Most trade is invoiced in the currency of the exporting country.

APPENDIX A: A CHRONOLOGY OF EVENTS IN MONETARY POLICY, 1951–JUNE 1977

1951

8 November — Bank Rate revised from 2 per cent to 2½ per cent, the first post-war increase.

1952

29 January — Hire purchase restrictions imposed.

12 March — Bank Rate raised to 4 per cent.

1953

17 September — Bank Rate lowered to 3½ per cent.

1954

13 May — Bank Rate lowered to 3 per cent.

July — Hire purchase controls.

1955

27 January — Bank Rate raised to 3½ per cent.

24 February — Bank Rate raised to 4½ per cent.

25 February — Hire purchase controls reintroduced. The Bank of England announced that it was going to support the market for transferable sterling.

19 April — In the Budget the Chancellor said that he would rely on 'the resources of a flexible monetary policy to counter . . . an over-rapid expansion of demand'.

26 July — Further hire purchase restrictions were introduced.

27 October — Budget-tax increases.

1956

16 February — Bank Rate raised to 5½ per cent.
Hire purchase controls tightened.

24 July — The Chancellor told clearing banks to reduce the rate of increase in bank advances.

11 December — £200 million drawn on the IMF and standby credit of £440 million arranged.

1957

7 February	Bank Rate was lowered to 5 per cent.
9 April	The Chancellor, Mr Thorneycroft, in his Budget speech told banks to keep credit 'within bounds'. Banks were not to give a loan unless they were sure it was 'strictly temporary' and that such a loan was the appropriate form of finance for the purpose in question.
April	Radcliffe Committee established.
19 September	Bank Rate raised to 7 per cent, 'firstly to help control the growth of the domestic money supply and secondly as a measure to help stop the speculation against sterling'. Ceiling on bank advances (£2,000m).
8 October	The Chancellor stated that it was the policy of the government to stop the increase in the money supply.
29 October	The banks were told that certain advances guaranteed by the Export Credits Guarantee Department need not be included when calculating their total level of advances.

1958

20 March	Bank Rate was lowered to 6 per cent.
15 April	In his budget speech the Chancellor restated the need for restraint in bank lending.
22 May	Bank Rate lowered to 5½ per cent.
19 June	The Chancellor announced that a system of 'Special Deposits' was to be introduced, and the existing limitations on the aggregate of bank advances were to end from the beginning of August.
14 August	Bank Rate lowered to 4½ per cent.
5 September	Chancellor stated that the competition for consumer credit resulting from the introduction of banks of new loan schemes was in line with the government's policy.
29 October	After a gradual relaxation of credit controls, starting in July, the remaining hire purchase controls were removed.
20 November	Bank Rate lowered to 4 per cent.
27 December	Convertibility of sterling announced.

1959

5 February	The control of capital issues was ended.
8 April	An expansionary Budget with substantial tax cuts.
20 August	The report of the Radcliffe Committee on the working of the monetary system was published (Cmnd. 827).
12 November	The Chancellor of the Exchequer warned that credit expansion would need watching if it continued at such a fast pace.
26 November	The Chancellor announced that new arrangements were to be introduced for co-ordinating Treasury and Bank of England policy.

1960

21 January	Bank Rate was raised to 5 per cent. This was the first change in Bank Rate since November 1958.
4 April	In his Budget speech the Chancellor warned that there should be caution about the further extension of credit.
28 April	The first call for Special Deposits was made by the Bank of England of 1 per cent of the gross deposits of the clearing banks and ½ per cent for the Scottish banks, to be lodged on 15 June. The Chancellor announced the immediate reimposition of hire purchase controls.
23 June	Bank Rate was raised to 6 per cent. A further 1 per cent Special Deposits was called, to be paid in two stages, 20 July and 17 August.
27 October	Bank Rate was lowered to 5½ per cent.
8 December	Bank Rate was lowered to 5 per cent.

1961

12 January	The first issue of the *Bank of England Quarterly Bulletin* was published.
19 January	Hire purchase restrictions were eased.
17 April	In his Budget speech the Chancellor, Mr Selwyn Lloyd, announced two new 'economic regulators' designed to reduce the dependence on monetary and credit restrictions.
1 July	Lord Cromer becomes the new Governor of the Bank of England.

25 July	A crisis resulting from a sustained outflow of funds from Britain brought about the introduction of a package of restrictive measures which included an increase in the Bank Rate of 2 per cent to 7 per cent and a call for Special Deposits of a further 1 per cent. Bank of England requested all banks to reduce rate of growth of advances and to discriminate in favour of exporters.
4 August	The UK was granted IMF credit of £714 million.
10 August	The finance houses were asked by the Bank of England to seek finance for expansion only from the banks.
5 October	Bank Rate lowered to 6½ per cent.
2 November	Bank Rate lowered to 6 per cent.

1962

8 March	Bank Rate lowered to 5½ per cent.
22 March	Bank Rate lowered to 5 per cent.
26 April	Bank Rate lowered to 4½ per cent.
31 May	The Bank of England made a repayment of Special Deposits to the clearing banks of 1 per cent to be paid in two stages. Relaxation of advances request of 25 July 1961, but discrimination remained.
4 June	Hire purchase controls relaxed.
27 September	It was announced that a further 1 per cent Special Deposits was to be repaid to the clearing banks in October.
3 October	Selective restrictions on lending by banks and other financial institutions were withdrawn.
23 October	Minor relaxation of hire purchase regulations.
29 November	The remaining Special Deposits of 1 per cent were repaid to the clearing banks.

1963

3 January	Bank Rate was lowered to 4 per cent.
3 April	The Chancellor announced a very expansionary budget with government expenditure expected to rise by 7½ per cent over the previous year. Also, for the first time in many years a deficit was planned. The public sector borrowing requirement was to be £690 million for the coming year.

16 October	Minimum liquid assets ratio of the London clearing banks reduced from 30 to 28 per cent.

1964

27 February	Bank Rate was raised to 5 per cent.
14 April	The Budget proposed that last year's deficit would in the present year be turned into a small surplus by means of increased taxation. Government expenditure however was to go up by £570 million, an increase of 8½ per cent. The public sector borrowing requirement was also to go up to £790 million.
July	Hire purchase controls relaxed.
28 July	IMF renews the $100 million of standby credit to the UK for a further twelve months.
8 November	The Paris Club placed $400 million with the IMF for Britain to draw.
11 November	Mr Callaghan's first Budget tries to alleviate the balance of payments situation.
23 November	Bank Rate was raised by 2 per cent to 7 per cent.
25 November	The UK gets $3,000 million credits from central banks.
8 December	Banks, building societies, insurance companies and pension funds to reduce their lending and to give preference to export finance and investment.

1965

6 April	The Chancellor announced in his Budget that for the coming year government expenditure was to increase by 10 per cent over the previous year. The public sector borrowing requirement was also to rise.
29 April	The Bank of England called for 1 per cent Special Deposits.
5 May	Banks and financial institutions ordered to restrict their lending to the private sector in the coming year to 105 per cent of March 1965 level.
12 May	The IMF approves a further drawing by the UK of $1,400 million.
3 June	Hire purchase restrictions were increased. Bank Rate was lowered by 1 per cent to 6 per cent.
27 July	Measures were taken to improve the balance of payments situation. Hire purchase controls were

tightened with a reduction in the pay-back period.
Government expenditure was to be cut and less
finance for imports was to be provided by the banks.

1966

1 February	The Bank of England told the banks and financial institutions to continue the lending ceiling announced in May 1965 until further notice.
7 February	Hire purchase controls were tightened.
3 May	In the Budget it was announced that government expenditure for the coming financial year would rise by 8.5 per cent. The public sector borrowing requirement was estimated at £287 million.
12 July	The Chancellor announced that the limit on bank advances would remain at least until March of the following year.
14 July	Bank Rate was raised to 7 per cent and 1 per cent Special Deposits called.
20 July	Hire purchase controls were further tightened, and it was announced that government spending was to be cut.
10 August	Banks told to try harder to provide 'essential' finance within the 105 per cent ceiling.
1 November	Banks reminded of official priorities.

1967

26 January	Bank Rate was lowered to 6½ per cent.
6 February	It was announced by the Chancellor that finance for house-building was to be a priority category for bank lending.
13 March	Basle credits of $1,000 million agreed for the year.
16 March	Bank Rate was lowered to 6 per cent.
11 April	In the Budget the Chancellor announced a number of changes in monetary policy. First, hire purchase controls were eased. Second, the ceilings were removed on advances but sectoral guidance re-emphasised. Government expenditure in the coming year was to rise by 14 per cent and the public sector borrowing requirement was estimated at £943 million.
4 May	Bank Rate was lowered to 5½ per cent.

7 June	Hire purchase controls relaxed.
29 August	Further hire purchase relaxation on consumer durables.
11 September	The IMF announces agreement on 'Special Drawing Rights'.

1967

19 October	Bank Rate was raised to 6 per cent.
9 November	Bank Rate was raised to 6½ per cent.
12 November	Britain negotiates $250 million credit to help finance debts to the IMF due in December.
18 November	Sterling was devalued from $2.80 to $2.40, a devaluation of 14.3 per cent. Banks were asked to show restraint on lending to the private sector and Bank Rate was raised by 1½ per cent to 8 per cent. Hire purchase controls were tightened.
21 November	Overnight inter-bank rate 1256 per cent.
12 December	All institutions providing hire purchase finance were asked to show restraint in making such loans.

1968

16 January	Large curbs in public expenditure were announced.
8 February	The government approved the Monopolies Commission verdict that the proposed merger between Lloyds and Barclays banks would be against the national interest.
19 March	In the Budget it was estimated that government expenditure for the coming year would rise by 5.6 per cent and that the public sector borrowing requirement would be £358 million.
21 March	Bank Rate was lowered to 7½ per cent.
23 May	Banks ordered to restrict private sector lending to 104 per cent of the November 1967 level.
14 June	The Bank of England announced details of a 'Cash Deposit' scheme.
30 August	Reduction in bank lending to non-exporters is ordered.
9 September	Chancellor announced the arrangement of $2,000 million standby credit.
19 September	Bank Rate was lowered to 7 per cent.
17 October	The Bank of England's Governor announced that

more attention should be given to the control of the money supply.

18 October	National Giro opened for business.
1 November	Hire purchase controls were tightened.
22 November	Banks told to reduce advances to the private sector to 98 per cent of the November 1967 level by March 1969.

1969

31 January	Banks reminded of qualitative and quantitative directives.
27 February	Bank Rate was raised to 8 per cent. Banks again reminded of official priorities.
15 April	The Budget was expected to reduce demand by between £200 million and £250 million.
22 May	The Bank of England announced that there was to be a limit on domestic credit expansion of £400 million for 1969/70.
31 May	As a penalty for non-compliance with the advances ceiling, the rate of interest paid on Special Deposits was halved.
11 September	The Chancellor made it clear to the banks and other financial institutions that there would be no relaxation of the credit squeeze.
1 October	The clearing banks cut their base rate by ½ per cent without a change in Bank Rate.

1970

1 January	The first $3,500 million allocation Special Drawings Rights.
5 March	Bank Rate was lowered to 7½ per cent.
26 March	Britain makes the final drawing from the IMF of the standby credit arranged in 1969. At the same time repayment of the 1965 drawing was advanced from May.
14 April	In his Budget the Chancellor announced a reduction in Bank Rate by ½ per cent to 7 per cent. An increase of 5 per cent for bank lending was to be permitted for the coming year, however the banks were asked to give priority to lending for export purposes. Special Deposits were to be raised by

	½ per cent to 2½ per cent. The full rate of interest on Special Deposits was restored.
29 May	The Select Committee recommends the publication of the Bank of England accounts.
28 July	Clearing banks requested to slow down growth of advances.
1 September	The finance houses introduced a 'base rate' instead of having to rely on the Bank Rate.
27 October	The Chancellor announced cuts in public expenditure.
29 October	Special Deposits were further raised by 1 per cent to 3½ per cent for the clearing banks.
1971	
12 January	Exchange control measures were to be tightened. From now on application had to be made for all foreign currency borrowing.
15 February	Decimal currency was introduced.
24 March	The Crowther Committee report on consumer credit was published. Its major recommendation was the abolition of control over consumer credit.
30 March	In his Budget the Chancellor relaxed the restrictions on bank lending to restricted catogories.
1 April	Bank Rate was lowered to 6 per cent.
14 April	The Bank of England document, *Competition and Credit Control*, was published.
15 April	The Access credit card was introduced by Lloyds, National Westminster and Midland banks.
19 July	Hire purchase restrictions were removed as part of a reflationary package announced by the Chancellor.
21 July	New arrangements for discount houses announced, see Chapter 2, section (v).
16 August	The United States government announced that official convertibility of the dollar into gold had been suspended. Following this news the London foreign exchange markets were closed. The market was re-opened on 23 August when sterling was permitted to float.
31 August	New measures introduced to discourage the inflow of funds from abroad.
2 September	Bank Rate was lowered to 5 per cent.

10 September   The Bank of England paper 'Reserve Ratios and Special Deposits', published (see Chapter 2). From 15 September banks were to abandon their interest rate agreements and from 1 October rates were to be related to a base rate set by each individual bank.

15 September   Base rate for the London clearing banks set at 5 per cent.

16 October   Base rate was lowered to 4½ per cent by Barclays.

26 November   Other clearing banks reduce base rates to 4½ per cent.

17 and 18 December   A Ministerial meeting of the 'Group of Ten' countries and Switzerland was held in Washington where a general realignment of the major exchange rates was agreed, usually known as the Smithsonian Agreement. A new middle rate for sterling against the dollar of $2.6057 was established, re-valuing sterling against the dollar just over 8½ per cent from the previous rate of $2.40. The effective exchange rate for sterling appreciated by 1–2 per cent, depending on the method of calculation. At the conclusion of the meeting the UK authorities removed the exchange control restrictions against inflows from abroad which had been imposed the previous August and October. The margin on either side of parity within which an IMF member's currency could fluctuate was widened from 1 to 2¼ per cent.

1972
21 March   In the Budget the rules regarding the financing of extended transactions were modified so that UK companies controlled by residents of the EEC, together with Denmark and Norway, could now borrow for client investment in the UK without limit. The limit on borrowing in the UK for direct investment in developing regions was also removed for other foreign-owned companies.

    The Budget was designed to increase the rate of growth in output to 5 per cent between the second half of 1971 and the first half of 1973. The Chancellor announced that this rate of growth would necessitate a growth in the money stock that

	was 'high by the standards of past years . . . in order to ensure that adequate finance is available for the extra output'.
28 April	The UK repays all short- and medium-term official overseas borrowing for the first time since May 1964.
1 May	The UK decides to join the scheme for narrower currency bands introduced in April by the EEC countries, 'the Snake'. Currency fluctuations were to be reduced to 2½ per cent from 4½ per cent.
9 and 13 June	The clearing banks' base rates raised to 5 per cent.
22 June	Sterling was floated 'as a temporary measure'. Bank Rate was raised to 6 per cent.
28 June	The Bank of England 'exceptionally' made available to the clearing banks temporary sale and re-purchase facilities in short-dated gilt-edged stock at an interest rate of 6½ per cent.
30 June	Base rates raised to 6 per cent.
21 July	Some clearing banks' base rates raised to 7 per cent. Others followed on 25 July and 12 September.
7 August	The Governor of the Bank of England sent a letter to members of the banking system asking them to try to meet the growing demand from industry for bank finance and that they should 'as necessary, make credit less readily available to property companies and for non-industrial purposes'.
9 October	Bank Rate was replaced by minimum lending rate (MLR) (see page 51).
13 October	MLR raised.
27 October	MLR raised.
9 November	The Bank of England makes a 1 per cent call for Special Deposits (£220 million), which was the first call for Special Deposits since the introduction of the new system of credit control.
1 December	MLR raised to 7¾ per cent.
8 December	MLR raised to 8 per cent.
12 and 13 December	Clearing banks' base rates raised to 7½ per cent.
19 December	White Paper on Public Expenditure published, estimates growth in government expenditure for the coming year at 2½ per cent (Cmnd. 5178).
21 December	Bank of England calls 2 per cent Special Deposits

(£450 million).

1973

1 January	Britain became a member of the EEC.
3 and 4 January	Some clearing banks' base rates raised to 8½ per cent. Others followed on 9 and 25 January.
19 January	MLR lowered down to 8¾ per cent. Call for another 1 per cent Special Deposits.
12 February	The London foreign exchange market was closed for one day following very heavy pressure on the US dollar which was subsequently devalued by 10 per cent against gold.
15 February	Clearing banks' base rates raised to 9½ per cent.
6 March	Pressure on the US dollar was only slightly alleviated by the devaluation of 10 per cent, and consequently the London foreign exchange market was formally closed 'until further notice'. The Budget: National Savings were made more attractive. The pound would continue to float independently of the EEC common float, as it was not practicable under the circumstances to join the common float on the basis of the conditions embodied in the Community's scheme. A further development announced in the Budget was that capital gains on new Certificates of Deposit would no longer be tax-free.
12 March	A European float against the dollar was agreed, but sterling was to continue to float independently.
19 March	London foreign exchange markets were re-opened.
23 March	MLR lowered to 8½ per cent.
27 March	Meeting of the IMF 'Group of Twenty' in Washington which agreed an abortive new international monetary system based on 'fixed and adjustable' parities.
3/4 and 5 April	Clearing banks' base rates lowered to 9 per cent.
13 April	MLR lowered to 8 per cent.
11 May	MLR lowered to 8 per cent.
18 May	MLR lowered to 7¾ per cent.
21 May	The Chancellor announced proposed public spending cuts expected to total £500 million in 1974/75.
22 and 23 May	Clearing banks' base rates lowered to 8½ per cent.
15 and 16 June	Clearing banks' base rates lowered to 8 per cent.
22 June	MLR lowered to 7½ per cent.

19 July	Arrangements for control of discount houses changed (see Chapter 2, section (v)).
20 July	MLR raised to 9 per cent.
27 July	Officially induced rise in MLR to 11½ per cent, the sharpest rise since 1914.
2 August	Clearing banks' base rates raised to 10 per cent.
22 and 23 August	Clearing banks' base rates raised to 11 per cent.
6 September	An extension of the Basle agreement for another six months in a modified form was announced by the Treasury, the expiry date having been 24 September.
11 September	The new governor of the Bank of England, Mr Gordon Richardson, ordered banks and finance houses to exercise 'significant restraint' on the provision of credit for persons, other than for house purchase. Banks were also ordered to limit interest rates on deposits under £10,000 to 9½ per cent.
19 October	MLR lowered to 11¼ per cent.
13 November	MLR was raised from 11¼ per cent to 13 per cent. The formula for establishing the MLR was temporarily suspended. A further call was made for 2 per cent Special Deposits, making 6 per cent in all.
14 and 15 November	Clearing banks' base rates raised to 13 per cent.
17 December	Supplementary Special Deposits scheme introduced (see Chapter 8). The outstanding 1 per cent Special Deposits revoked. Controls on HP transactions and other non-bank credit were also re-introduced. The Bank of England ordered Barclays Bank (for Barclaycard) and the Joint Credit Card Company (for Access) to raise the minimum monthly payment to £6 or 15 per cent of the outstanding balance.
19 December	A modification was announced to the scheme for export finance provided by clearing banks for periods of over two years. From the beginning of 1974 the single fixed rate of 6 per cent which had been operative since March 1972 was abandoned. Business done on credit for two to five years carried a new rate of 7 per cent, whilst for business done on credit over a period longer than this there was to be a range of rates from 6 per cent to 8½ per cent.

1974

4 January	MLR was lowered to 13¾ per cent.
31 January	A replacement of ½ per cent of Special Deposits was made.
1 February	MLR was lowered to 12½ per cent.
4 February	½ per cent of Special Deposits repaid.
5 February	Details of 'Lifeboat' announced (see Chapter 6).
13 March	The Bank of England agreed that from this date all local authority bonds should be issued in the same form and quoted on the Stock Exchange.
26 March	The Chancellor in the Budget estimated that public spending would increase in the coming year by £700 million and that the public sector borrowing requirement would be £2,700 million; a reduction of £700 million. It was also announced that the Bank of England, in conjunction with the clearing banks, was to borrow for the government $2.5 billion in the Eurodollar market, the largest loan ever raised in the international capital market.
4 April	Bank of England repaid 1 per cent Special Deposits.
5 April	MLR lowered to 12¼ per cent.
11 April	MLR lowered to 12 per cent, and clearing banks' base rates lowered to 12½ per cent.
18 April	A further ½ per cent of Special Deposits was released.
19 April	The Building Societies Association passed on to its members an offer of a loan amounting to £100 million from the government who also undertook to offer a further £100 million a month for the following four months at 10½ per cent interest, provided that the rate of interest societies paid to ordinary investors on 9 April was not increased, together with the proviso that mortgage rates should not be increased before 19 May.
30 April	The Bank of England announced that in the six-month period after April/June, the three-monthly average of banks' interest-bearing eligible liabilities would be permitted to rise above the previous 8 per cent by 1½ per cent a month before 'supplementary Special Deposits' had to be lodged.
13 May	Some clearing banks' base rates stood lowered to 12 per cent. Others followed on 23 and 24 May.

24 May	MLR lowered to 11¾ per cent. Clearing banks' base rates stood at 12 per cent.
22 July	The Chancellor announced a mini-Budget designed to stimulate demand. The increase in the public sector borrowing requirement for the year was estimated at £340 million.
6 August	The government announced its intention of introducing two new index-linked national savings schemes.
20 August	The Bank of England decided that the monthly and quarterly statistical data supplied to them by the clearing banks was inadequate. Supplementary returns were to be completed at least quarterly from 30 September.
20 September	MLR lowered to 11½ per cent.
October	The government draw $250 million tranche of the $2.5 billion loan announced in the March Budget.
12 November	In the third Budget of the year the Chancellor announced that the guarantee of certain official overseas holdings of sterling (Basle Agreement) which had first been made available in September 1968 would be discontinued when the present arrangements expired at the end of the year. It was announced that the supplementary Special Deposits scheme would continue for another six months. A credit control notice was issued to banks ordering them to restrict lending to personal and financial sector. The Bank of England and the clearing banks, together with other financial institutions, made arrangements with 'Finance for Industry' to expand this company's capacity to provide medium-term finance for investment. As a result of the Budget measures the public sector borrowing requirement for the year now stood at £5,500 million.

1975

17 January	MLR lowered to 11¼ per cent.
20 January	Clearing banks' base rate lowered to 11½ per cent.
24 January	MLR lowered to 11 per cent.
7 February	MLR lowered to 10¾ per cent.
14 February	MLR lowered to 10½ per cent.
28 February	The supplementary Special Deposits scheme was

	suspended. Credit control notice issued to banks reinforcing qualitative guidance.
4 and 6 March	Clearing banks' base rates lowered to 10¾ per cent and 11 per cent.
7 March	MLR lowered to 10¼ per cent.
21 March	MLR lowered to 10 per cent.
25 March	Clearing banks' base rates lowered to 10¼ per cent and 10½ per cent.
15 April	In the Budget the Chancellor announced cuts in public expenditure of £900 million at 1974 prices. The estimated public sector borrowing requirement 1975/6 was roughly 10 per cent of GDP, some £7,800 million, which was still larger than the preceding year.
18 April	MLR lowered to 9¾ per cent.
22 April	Clearing banks' base rate lowered to 9½ per cent.
2 May	MLR raised to 10 per cent.
2 June	The first index-linked National Savings bonds on sale.
17 June	The pound sterling reaches an all-time low at 26.7 per cent below its December 1971 level.
1 July	New government inflation policy announced in the White Paper, *The Attack on Inflation.* Cash limits on public expenditure were proposed (Cmnd. 6151).
25 July	MLR raised by 1 per cent to 11 per cent.
5 August	Clearing banks' base rate raised to 10 per cent.
24 September	The government make available another £80 million for investment in industry in an attempt to help create more jobs.
3 October	MLR raised to 12 per cent.
6, 7 and 8 October	Clearing banks' base rate raised to 11 per cent.
7 November	The Chancellor announced plans to apply to the IMF for a £975 million loan.
14 November	MLR lowered to 11¾ per cent.
21 November	The government told the local authorities that a cash limit would be placed on general grants paid by the government, which finance roughly two-thirds of their current expenditure.
28 November	MLR lowered to 11½ per cent.
18 December	Some relaxation in the minimum terms for hire purchase announced. However, cars were excluded.

	Credit control notice issued to banks reaffirming qualitative guidance.
24 December	MLR lowered to 11¼ per cent.
31 December	In his *Financial Times* message the Chancellor repeated his pledge 'to prevent any significant increase in public expenditure programmes after this year'.

1976

2 January	MLR lowered to 11 per cent.
12 January	Clearing banks' base rate lowered to 10½ per cent.
15 January	The Bank of England announced that 1 per cent of Special Deposits would be temporarily released on 19 January.
16 January	MLR lowered to 10¾ per cent.
23 January	MLR lowered to 10½ per cent.
30 January	MLR lowered to 10 per cent.
30 January	Clearing banks' base rate lowered to 10 per cent.
6 February	MLR and the clearing banks' base rate lowered to 9½ per cent.
10 February	The pound fell to its worst ever level against foreign currencies at 69.6.
10 February	The temporary release of Special Deposits redeposited with the Bank of England (see 15 January).
19 February	White Paper (Cmnd. 6393) on public expenditure to 1979/80. Cuts of £3,000 million to be made.
27 February	MLR lowered to 9¼ per cent.
5 March	MLR lowered to 9 per cent.
6 April	In the Budget the Chancellor announced the restrictions on hire purchase for motor caravans was to be abolished but was to continue on cars so as not to 'stimulate imports'. The public sector borrowing requirement for the year 1976/7 was estimated at £10,425 million or 12 per cent GDP.
6 April	White Paper on cash limits published (Cmnd. 6440).
23 April	MLR raised to 10½ per cent.
17 May	The Bank of England took the unusual step of making a standby credit facility available to cover the deposits of the British merchant bank, Edward Bates.
21 May	The pound fell to $1.7807, a record low of trade-weighted depreciation of 38.8 per cent. MLR raised to 11½ per cent.

25 May	Clearing banks' base rate raised to 10½ per cent.
7 June	The 'Group of Ten' plus Switzerland and the Bank for International Settlements provided \$5.3 billion in standby credits to support the pound.
22 July	Cuts in public spending of £1,000 million were announced, designed to bring the public sector borrowing requirement down to £9 billion for the financial year 1977/8. The Chancellor set a target of about 12 per cent for the growth of M_3 in the coming year. Credit control notice issued to banks tightening qualitative controls.
3 August	White Paper published, *The Licensing and Supervision of Deposit Taking Institutions* (Cmnd. 6584) (see Chapter 6).
16 August	A call for Special Deposits of £350 million was made.
10 September	MLR raised by 1½ per cent to 13 per cent, its highest level since 1973.
13 September	Clearing banks' base rate raised to 12 per cent.
29 September	The Bank of England announced that it was applying to the IMF for the remaining credit tranches.
7 October	MLR raised to a record 15 per cent, as a result of the Bank of England suspending the MLR formula. A further 2 per cent of Special Deposits were called.
27 October	The pound fell to a new low against the dollar of \$1.5726.
29 October	Clearing banks' base rate raised to 14 per cent.
5 November	The Bank of England deferred 1 per cent of Special Deposits for one month.
18 November	The supplementary Special Deposits scheme was reintroduced. Credit control notice to banks re-emphasised qualitative controls.
19 November	MLR lowered to 14 per cent.
10 December	Payment of Special Deposits was again postponed for a month.
15 December	The Chancellor announced a new package of economic measures, including a £1 billion cut in public spending for 1977/8.
21 December	Negotiations completed with IMF for a standby arrangement enabling UK to draw SDR 3,360 million in stages over a two-year period.

1977

10 January	First drawing of IMF facility SDR 1,000 million ($676 million).
10 January	Bank for International Settlements, with the support of banks from eleven countries, provided UK with a $3 billion medium-term facility ('Safety Net').
13 January	Special Deposits of 2 per cent were repaid and an outstanding call for 1 per cent was cancelled.
17 January	2 per cent of Special Deposits were repaid to clearing banks.
21 January	MLR lowered to 13¼ per cent.
25 January	UK and foreign banks raised a medium-term loan of $1.5 billion on behalf of the UK government, of which $250 million was drawn in February.
25 January	Clearing banks' base rate lowered to 13 per cent.
27 January	First part of White Paper on public expenditure published (Cmnd. 6761). Two per cent (£360 million) of Special Deposits repaid.
28 January	MLR lowered to 12¼ per cent.
31 January	1 per cent Special Deposits repaid by Bank of England.
3 February	MLR lowered to 12 per cent.
3 February	Clearing banks' base rate lowered to 12½ per cent.
17 February	Clearing banks' base rate lowered to 11½ per cent.
25 February	The second part of the Public Expenditure White Paper published.
10 March	MLR lowered to 11 per cent, after suspension of formula.
10 March	Clearing banks' base rate lowered to 10½ per cent.
18 March	MLR lowered to 10½ per cent.
25 March	Clearing banks' base rate lowered to 9½ per cent.
29 March	In the Budget the Chancellor announced that the expected public sector borrowing requirement for the year would be £8.7 billion.
31 March	MLR lowered to 9½ per cent.
7 April	MLR lowered to 9¼ per cent.
15 April	MLR lowered to 9 per cent.
22 April	MLR lowered to 8¾ per cent.
29 April	MLR lowered to 8½ per cent.
29 April	Clearing banks' base rate lowered to 9 per cent.
6 May	Clearing banks' base rate lowered to 8½ per cent.

| 12 May | The Bank of England announced that the supplementary Special Deposits scheme was to be extended for a further six months. Growth in banks' interest-bearing liabilities in the coming year to be no higher than 3 per cent. |
| 13 May | MLR lowered to 8 per cent where it remained until August 1977. |

APPENDIX B: DEFINITION OF THE MONEY SUPPLY

Considerable confusion arises from the fact that there are at least five different definitions of the money supply used in discussions of UK monetary policy. Two of these are alternative definitions of the 'narrower' money supply. One is the M_1 series published by the Bank of England, the other is the definition used by the Federal Reserve system in the US. This definition is used by the IMF and by the OECD in their reports on the UK economy. The chief difference between them is that the UK definition includes various interest-bearing sight deposits (currently about £2,500m). Over the financial year 1976/7 these grew by 19.9 per cent so that the Bank of England definition of M_1 rose by 9.9 per cent and the US definition showed an increase of only 8.6 per cent.

The confusion is even greater with the broader monetary aggregate. Here there used to be two alternative definitions, the M_3 series produced by the Bank of England, and the other US M_2 definition used by the OECD. Since December 1976 the IMF have used a third series — sterling M_3 — which is now the aggregate used in defining UK money supply targets. Thus whereas for the financial year 1976/7 the target was for 12 per cent growth in M_3; for 1977/8 the target is for between 9 per cent and 13 per cent growth in sterling M_3. The difference between the two concepts is principally that sterling M_3 excludes foreign currency deposits by UK residents. This is obviously of most importance at a time of lack of confidence in sterling, when one would expect these deposits to grow. Thus the old definition of M_3 is likely to grow faster than sterling M_3 whenever there is a lack of confidence in sterling, for example in 1976/7, when the increase in sterling M_3 was 7.7 per cent, in total M_3 9.8 per cent. Table B.1 shows how the definitions vary in their treatment of different assets.

Table B.1: Alternative Definitions of the Money Supply

	UK M$_1$	US M$_1$	US M$_2$	UK M$_3$ (US Credit Proxy)	£M$_3$
Notes and Coin	Yes	Yes	Yes	Yes	Yes
Private sector demand deposits in native currency*	Yes	Yes	Yes	Yes	Yes
Private sector interest-bearing sight deposits in native currency	Yes	No	Yes	Yes	Yes
Public sector deposit in native currency	No	No	No	Yes	Yes
Public sector deposit in foreign currency	No	No	No	Yes	No
Private sector interest-bearing 'retail' deposit in native currency (time deposit less than $50,000)	No	No	Yes	Yes	Yes
Private sector interest-bearing wholesale deposit, in native currency Certificate of Deposit in native currency	No	No	No	Yes	Yes
Private sector deposit with native bank in foreign currency	No	No	No	Yes	No
Non-resident deposit in native currency	No	No	Yes	No	No

* i.e. sterling for the UK
  dollars for the US

Fuller definitions of M$_1$ and M$_3$ can be found in the June 1970 issue of the *Bank of England Quarterly Bulletin*, the full definition of sterling M$_3$ in the Treasury's *Economic Progress Report* for January 1977.

APPENDIX C: STATISTICAL BACKGROUND

This appendix aims to provide the background figures necessary to understanding monetary management in the UK. It is in five sections:

A. the UK economy 1964–77;
B. the growth of monetary aggregates;
C. an analysis of monetary growth 1963–77;
D. additional monetary statistics;
E. selected interest rates;
F. the PSBR, actual and forecast 1971–7.

All figures are taken from *Economic Trends*, the *Bank of England Quarterly Bulletin, Statistical Abstract* (Bank of England, Vol. I, 1970, Vol. II, 1975) or *Financial Statistics*.

The most recently revised figure is always given, although sometimes the original published figure is also included. Thus as some figures have been more recently revised than others, the figures are not on a consistent basis. For example in Table C.3, Bank lending to the private sector is divided into sterling and foreign currency. For some periods, the components have been revised more recently than the total so they are given as published and the consequent total included. For other periods, the total but not the components have been revised so all three totals are the latest available but clearly are inconsistent.

TABLE C.1: The UK Economy 1964—77

		Real GDP (per cent change 1 year earlier	Price Level (per cent change 1 year earlier	Earnings (per cent change 1 year earlier	Unemployment (per cent)	Balance of Payments (Current Account £m)
1964		5.9	3.3	7.7	1.7	−355
1965		2.8	4.8	7.1	1.4	− 27
1966		1.8	3.9	6.6	1.5	100
1967		2.7	2.5	3.6	2.3	−301
1968		3.7	4.7	7.8	2.4	−275
1969		1.7	5.4	7.8	2.4	462
1970		2.2	6.4	12.1	2.6	735
1971	I	1.5	8.6	13.0	2.9	141
	II	0.8	9.8	11.6	3.3	278
	III	1.5	10.1	11.1	3.6	392
	IV	1.5	9.2	9.5	3.8	237
1972	I	1.4	8.0	NA	4.0	120
	II	3.1	6.2	11.6	3.8	121
	III	2.1	6.5	12.1	3.7	−105
	IV	4.1	7.7	15.5	3.4	− 5
1973	I	8.6	8.0	NA	3.0	138
	II	4.6	9.3	14.9	2.7	− 32
	III	4.9	9.2	14.5	2.5	−235
	IV	2.3	10.3	12.5	2.2	−347
1974	I	−3.5	12.9	9.2	2.5	−877
	II	0.6	15.9	14.9	2.5	−887
	III	2.3	17.0	19.8	2.6	−772
	IV	1.7	18.2	25.3	NA	−844
1975	I	3.6	20.3	32.9	3.1	−541
	II	−2.5	24.3	27.6	3.6	−309
	III	−4.8	26.5	26.4	4.2	−579
	IV	−3.3	25.3	21.7	4.8	−221
1976	I	−0.4	22.5	19.7	5.2	− 90
	II	0.7	16.0	17.5	5.3	−390
	III	1.6	13.7	13.5	5.5	−511
	IV	2.4	15.0	12.3	NA	−414
1977	I	−1.3	16.5	11.7	5.6	−461
	II	0.2	17.4		5.6	−204

Note: Some earnings figures and unemployment figures were not collected because of industrial disputes.

Table C.2: The Growth of Monetary Aggregates 1963—77

(i) *Annually* (financial years)

	M_1	$£M_3$	M_3
1963/4	6.8		7.3
1964/5	3.1		5.9
1965/6	5.8		9.3
1966/7	0.6		3.6
1967/8	6.5		9.3
1968/9	2.4		7.6
1969/70	1.7		2.4
1970/1	13.7		12.3
1971/2	9.3		14.4
1972/3	10.0		27.3
1973/4	3.3		25.2
1974/5	16.7	8.5	10.7
1975/6	15.9	7.0	8.2
1976/7	9.9	7.6	9.7

(ii) *Quarterly*

		M_1	$£M_3$	M_3
1971	I	4.0		3.2
	II	1.3		1.6
	III	3.3		2.7
	IV	2.0		5.3
1972	I	3.3		4.7
	II	4.3		7.1
	III	1.5		4.6
	IV	4.0		7.2
1973	I	−0.3		5.7
	II	6.7		4.7
	III	−2.6		8.1
	IV	2.1		6.9
1974	I	−2.7		3.1
	II	2.9		1.8
	III	3.9		3.7
	IV	7.3		3.1
1975	I	2.7	0.8	1.1
	II	2.7	2.0	1.4
	III	5.1	3.6	4.6
	IV	2.0	0.2	0.6
1976	I	4.9	0.9	1.3
	II	3.8	3.2	4.0
	III	3.8	4.6	5.4
	IV	0.0	0.1	−0.1
1977	I	3.3	0.3	0.9
	II	4.0	3.7	3.8

(iii) *Monthly* (banking month ending between 13 and 21 of month given)

				M_3
1971	July			0.5
	Aug.			1.0
	Sep.			0.7

Table C.2: The Growth of Monetary Aggregates 1963—77 *(continued)*

		M_1	£M_3	M_3
1971	Oct.			1.2
	Nov.	1.2		1.3
	Dec.	1.7		1.1
1972	Jan.	0.2		2.5
	Feb.	0.8		0.3
	Mar.	3.2		2.5
	Apr.	1.5		2.8
	May	1.3		2.0
	June	2.1		3.3
	July	−0.6		1.5
	Aug.	0.3		1.2
	Sep.	0.9		1.8
	Oct.	1.6		1.2
	Nov.	−0.1		1.0
	Dec.	1.8		2.8
1973	Jan.	0.2		2.3
	Feb.	1.0		3.7
	Mar.	0.9		1.5
	Apr.	2.3		1.6
	May	0.2		0.9
	June	0.3		1.9
	July	2.8		3.2
	Aug.	−0.4		2.6
	Sep.	−1.7		2.3
	Oct.	−1.3		2.4
	Nov.	0.5		1.2
	Dec.	−0.5		1.9
1974	Jan.	1.4		2.3
	Feb.	−0.8		2.2
	Mar.	—		0.4
	Apr.	2.6		0.3
	May	−0.6		0.9
	June	−1.3		−0.2
	July	2.3		2.8
	Aug.	0.7		1.6
	Sep.	0.4		−0.2
	Oct.	2.0		0.4
	Nov.	−0.1		1.0
	Dec.	1.6		—
1975	Jan.	3.4		1.1
	Feb.	−0.3		1.0
	Mar.	2.0		0.9
	Apr.	2.3		0.2
	May	0.7		1.5
	June	0.2		−0.3
	July	2.2		0.7
	Aug.	2.4		1.6
	Sep.	1.5		0.5
	Oct.	0.5		1.2
	Nov.	—		−0.6

Table C.2: The Growth of Monetary Aggregates 1963—77 *(continued)*

		M_1	$£M_3$	M_3
1975	Dec.	1.4		
1976	Jan.	−0.3		—
	Feb.	3.8		1.1
	Mar.	0.8		1.5
	Apr.	2.0		0.4
	May	−0.7		1.3
	June	0.1		0.5
	July	3.6		1.2
A	Aug.	0.8		1.9
	Sep.	2.5		1.6
	Oct.	−1.6		2.1
	Nov.	0.8		1.5
	Dec.	1.9		0.9
1977	Jan.	−1.9		−0.6
	Feb.	0.9		−1.5
	Mar.	—		−0.6
	Apr.	3.5		0.1
	May	0.4		3.0
	June	1.9		0.7
	July	2.2		0.9
				1.0

TABLE C.3: An Analysis of Monetary Growth (£m). Public-Sector Borrowing Requirement.

+ Bank Lending the Non-bank Private Sector
− Private Sector Lending to the Public Sector

		Central Government Borrowing Requirements	Other Public Sector Borrowing Requirement	Total	In Sterling	In Foreign Currency	Total	Central Government	
1963	I	5	135	140	NA	NA	194	− 97	
	II	17	189	206	221	− 1	220	109	
	III	53	189	242	197	6	203	− 79	
	IV	78	176	256	68	− 4	64	70	
1964	I	152	151	303	208	5	224	− 82	
	II	23	191	215	190	11	201	18	
	III	98	135	233	293	11	304	− 90	
	IV	161	78	239	266	4	270	33	
1965	I	86	142	228	260	40	300	0	
	II	300	69	369	115	3	118	36	
	III	134	174	308	39	0	39	12	
	IV	90	210	300	41	33	74	− 45	
1966	I	109	21	120	146	12	158	215	
	II	246	107	353	− 20	7	− 13	6	
	III	206	64	270	36	− 7	29	51	
	IV	− 18	226	208	−140	+ 6	−134	− 155	
1967	I	374	55	429	64	14	78	− 263	
	II	281	203	484	− 51	33	− 18	57	
	III	288	216	504	327	11	338	− 22	
	IV	212	234	446	170	65	235	− 78	
1968	I	484	− 10	474	126	45	171	13	
	II	301	135	436	239	32	271	175	
	III	58	227	285	54	26	80	− 74	
	IV	− 84	170	86	109	84	193	201	
1969	I	−409	200	−209	277	34	311	238	
	II	−356	110	−246	−112	25	− 87	− 12	
	III	− 12	− 75	− 87	252	71	323	− 146	
	IV	−120	195	75	12	38	50	− 170	
1970	I	−309	148	−161	311	25	336	− 302	
	II	−295	210	− 85	378	77	455	143	
	III	8	− 26	− 18	165	133	298	188	
	IV	− 74	320	−246	− 25	251	226	− 80	
1971	I	269	306	575	222	87	309	− 825	
	II	−111	193	82	107	95	202	− 250	
	III	303	52	355	559	45	604	− 629	
	IV	173	186	359	584	4	588	− 605	
1972	I	137	23	160	1,456	154	1,610	− 236	
	II	223	255	478	1,632	243	1,875	− 226	
	III	605 (294)	20	625	926	182	1,108 (1,076)	− 119	
	IV	631 (691)	144	775	1,484	344	1,828 (1,945)	− 195 (− 168)	(−183)
1973	I	574 (516)	79	653	1,202	289	1,464 (1,456)	− 136	
	II	860 (717)	211	871	1,032	51	1,163 (984)	− 534	(−14)
	III	325 (676)	867	1,192	1,835	410	2,115 (1,679)	− 344	(−559)
	IV	562 (692)	684	1,246	1,768	407	2,252 (1,889)	− 386	(−403)
1974	I	524 (253)	554	1,076	939	322	1,267 (1,432)	− 108 (−83)	(−190)
	II	717 (797)	859	1,576	1,365	225	1,590 (1,503)	− 639 (−668)	
	III	901 (777)	610	1,511	1,250	148	1,398 (1,447)	− 483 (−521)	
	IV	1,349 (1,727)	820	2,169	175	241	416 (332)	378 (373)	
1975	I	1,458 (1,782)	1,060	2,518	136	− 41	95 (23)	−1,659 (−1,630)	
	II	2,298 (2,192)	522	2,820	1	+ 239	240 (613)	− 556 (−435)	
	III	2,717 (2,515)	−129	2,588	−454	314	−141 (−82)	−1,234 (−1,221)	
	IV	1,903 (1,910)	686	2,589	− 69	13	− 56 (−14)	−1,897 (−1,955)	
1976	I	1,890 (2,213)	596	2,486	196	− 23	− 173 (308)	−1,435 (1,434)	
	II	2,189 (2,168)	673	3,862	844	− 38	806 (1,022)	−1,118 (1,078)	
	III	2,030 (1,791)	326	2,356	982	211	1,193 (967)	− 668 (−665)	
	IV	677 (825)	1,131 (973)	1,808 (1,798)	893 (892)	228 (286)	1,121 (1,178)	−2,396 (2,376)	
1977	I	1,562 (1,207)	469 (444)	2,037 (1,651)	577 (567)	560 (662)	1,137 (1,229)	−2,274 (2,182)	
	II	1,676	− 18	1,658	1,073	156	1,229	−1,216	

		= DCE						
Issue Department	Other Public Sector Borrowing Requirement	Total	New Definition	Old Definition	± Overseas Adjustment	− Change in Non-Deposit Liabilities of Banks	= Money Sterling M_3	Supply M_3
0	−194	− 293		102	− 35	31		39
0	−149	− 40		399	− 25	− 86		275
0	−126	− 205		239	− 8	− 39		193
0	−128	− 58		307	− 62	5		203
0	−161	− 243		326	− 164	− 13		107
0	− 67	− 49		411	− 153	− 15		198
0	4	− 86		415	− 137	− 87		227
0	−159	− 126		411	− 290	+ 28		121
0	−140	− 140		327	− 219	− 38		131
0	−162	− 126		345	42	− 64		339
0	−154	− 142		187	− 24	− 37		192
0	− 33	− 78		309	− 9	+ 12		299
0	−114	101		363	− 111	15		293
0	− 65	− 59		287	− 187	− 11		83
0	− 98	− 47		207	− 32	−112		172
0	−102	− 257		− 155	− 110	− 8		− 81
0	− 14	− 277		248	− 75	− 6		299
0	−197	− 140		323	− 2	− 1		327
0	− 65	− 77		714	− 261	− 63		431
0	− 83	− 161		516	− 278	45		287
0	− 31	18		656	− 455	46		218
0	−144	31		797	− 265	− 23		450
0	− 34	− 108		213	69	− 99		227
0	− 95	106		325	− 224	− 86		247
0	− 89	149		208	− 3	33		
0	− 8	− 20		− 325	267	− 50		
0	−101	− 247		40	34	+ 110		133
0	− 65	− 235		− 70	416	− 35		271
0	16	− 286		− 163	347	−143		93
0	− 47	− 4		436	172	19		657
0	67	255		538	− 131	− 26		378
0	− 86	− 166		230	212	− 60		458
6	114	− 605		141	+ 794	− 1		519
1	18	231	58	33	456	−111	403	421
0	49	− 580	372	357	388		442	399
5	24	− 576	508	457	348	−318	442	447
								470
						62	918	826
								1,100
− 1	− 42	− 279	1,254	1,223 (1,090)	− 308	−104	842	941 (980)
58	− 34	− 202	2,037	2,110 (2,250)	− 427	− 35	1,575	1,658 (1,660)
− 58	− 22	− 199	1,398	1,385 (1,220)	− 118	−328	952	991 (950)
0	−130	− 325	1,978	2,147 (2,412)	− 248	−185	1,545	1,696 (1,778)
226	−155	− 65	1,639	1,755 (1,557)	211	−342	1,508	1,705 (1,355)
− 88	−311	− 933	1,340	1,320 (1,329)	− 114	84	1,310	1,283 (1,179)
− 41	−183	− 468	2,497	2,771 (2,759)	− 418	− 77	2,002	2,250 (2,345)
204	−238	− 420	2,726	2,936 (2,912)	− 528	−150	2,048	2,160 (2,187)
118	−596	− 586	1,585	1,593 (1,517)	− 260	−327	873	1,214 (1,000)
− 339	−701	−1,679	1,237	1,459 (1,357)	− 878	−198	278	685 (611)
− 54	−433	− 970	1,896	2,014 (1,952)	− 622	−361	895	1,215 (1,099)
− 24	−581	− 227	2,177	2,523 (2,527)	−1,198	204	1,209	1,107 (1,372)
268	−304	−1,659	835		− 396	−168	271	392 (290)
− 259	−113	− 928	2,041		−1,138	−213	690	522 (631)
4	269	− 961	1,175		246	−115	1,306	1,743 (1,622)
− 11	−108	−2,016	413		− 86	−264	63	245 (314)
3	−168	−1,600	1,427		− 847	−244	336	508 (436)
6	−150	−1,262	2,710		−1,314	−178	1,218	1,633 (1,390)
8	13	− 647	2,892		− 786	−307	1,799 (1,390)	2,276 (2,122)
309	−167	−2,254	285 (325)		− 168	− 95	22 (−17)	− 56
− 234	−571	−3,079	−563 (−830)		782	−115	104 (90)	417 (405)
− 84	− 87	−1,387	1,527		495	−539	1,483	1,724

NOTE TO TABLE C.3

A Note on Signs

All items appear with the sign indicating the effect on the money supply. Thus, for example a negative in the debt sales columns indicates that the authorities sold debt, thus reducing the growth of M_3.

The table represents an identity (except that one component of DCE, sterling lending to the overseas sector, is omitted; it is not clear why this is included in DCE anyway). It can also take on causal significance in that if, say, central government debt sales rise then, *ceteris paribus*, M_3 will be lower than it otherwise would be. It is never clear when *ceteris* is *paribus* but some items clearly react to others — e.g. issue department purchases of Commercial Bills are a Bank reaction to other developments or are mutually determined, or are substitutes/complements.

Initially published figures.

The figures in brackets give the initially published figures for the major aggregates.

Table C.4: Some Additional Monetary Statistics, 1970–5 (£m)

		Purchases of Gilt-Edged Securities by Non-Bank Private Sector	Bank Lending to Public Sector
1970	I	349	102
	II	− 99	177
	III	− 182	173
	IV	17	555
1971	I	726	229
	II	197	302
	III	513	503
	IV	410	691
1972	I	109	−359
	II	99	−809
	III	69	98
	IV	145	57
1973	I	202	448
	II	494	57
	III	317	173
	IV	449	290
1974	I	214	−133
	II	679	−606
	III	341	−52
	IV	−405	435
1975	I	1,652	49
	II	386	1,313
	III	722	1,774
	IV	1,643	−55
1976	I	1,092	80
	II	829	−75
	III	599	809
	IV	2,676	−775
1977	I	1,658	−26
	II	550	428

Table C.5: Selected Interest Rates, 1970—7 (per cent, per annum)

		Bank Rate/ MLR	Base Rate	3-Month Interbank Rate*	20-Year Bond Rate	FT-Actuaries 500 Share Index
1970	I	7.5		8.75	8.72	152.7
	II	7.0		7.88	9.42	132.9
	III	7.0	Equal to	7.25	9.16	145.0
	IV	7.0	Bank Rate	7.19	9.70	141.7
1971	I	7.0		7.38	8.9	145.1
	II	6.0		7.84	8.95	172.2
	III	5.0	4.75	7.50	8.5	184.7
	IV	5.0	4.5	4.69	8.1	196.3
1972	I	5.0	4.5	4.87	8.38	214.7
	II	6.0	6.0	7.75	9.27	206.1
	III	6.0	7.0	7.56	9.42	199.7
	IV	9.0	7.5	8.94	9.75	216.9
1973	I	8.5	9.5	9.94	10.00	190.6
	II	7.5	8.0	8.06	10.22	193.1
	III	11.5	11.0	13.34	11.49	181.5
	IV	13.0	13.0	16.19	12.37	150.0
1974	I	12.5	13.0	15.75	14.48	120.4
	II	11.75	12.0	13.32	15.29	107.8
	III	11.5	12.0	11.97	14.89	78.7
	IV	11.5	13.25	12.97	17.39	68.4
1975	I	10.0	10.5	15.50	13.44	119.6
	II	10.0	9.5	13.44	14.74	131.1
	III	11.0	10.0	10.62	14.23	148.8
	IV	11.25	11.0	10.72	14.82	165.1
1976	I	9.0	9.5	8.50	13.75	175.1
	II	11.5	10.5	11.22	13.68	166.4
	III	13.00	12.0	12.81	15.32	144.5
	IV	14.25	14.0	14.37	15.2	163.4
1977	I	10.5	10.5	9.12	12.53	190.2

*Local Authority Rate until 1971 III.

Table C.6: The PSBR, Forecast and Actual 1971–7 (£m)

	PSBR Post Budget Forecast	Actual	Net Acquisition of Financial Assets – Post Budget Forecast	Actual
1971–2	1,209	1,326	378	677
1972–3	+3,358	2,855	2,441	2,055
1973–4	4,423	4,276	2,853	3,106
1974–5	2,733	7,602	1,170	5,914
1975–6	9,055	10,773	7,571	8,226
1976–7	11,962	8,820	10,586	7,666
1977–8	8,471		7,577	

Table C.2: The Growth of Monetary Aggregates 1963–77 (continued)

	M_1	$£M_3$	M_3
1971 Oct.			1.2
Nov.	1.2		1.3
Dec.	1.7		1.1
1972 Jan.	0.2		2.5
Feb.	0.8		0.3
Mar.	3.2		2.5
Apr.	1.5		2.8
May	1.3		2.0
June	2.1		3.3
July	–0.6		1.5
Aug.	0.3		1.2
Sep.	0.9		1.8
Oct.	1.6		1.2
Nov.	–0.1		1.0
Dec.	1.8		2.8
1973 Jan.	0.2		2.3
Feb.	1.0		3.7
Mar.	0.9		1.5
Apr.	2.3		1.6
May	0.2		0.9
June	0.3		1.9
July	2.8		3.2
Aug.	–0.4		2.6
Sep.	–1.1		2.3
Oct.	–1.3		2.4
Nov.	0.5		1.2
Dec.	–0.5		1.9
1974 Jan.	1.4		2.3
Feb.	–0.8		2.2
Mar.	—		0.4
Apr.	2.6		0.3
May	–0.6		0.9
June	–1.3		–0.2
July	2.3		2.8
Aug.	0.7		1.6
Sep.	0.4		–0.2
Oct.	2.0		0.4
Nov.	–0.1		1.0
Dec.	1.6		—
1975 Jan.	3.4		1.1
Feb.	–0.3		1.0
Mar.	2.0		0.9
Apr.	2.3		0.2
May	0.7		1.5
June	0.2		–0.3
July	2.2		0.7
Aug.	2.4		1.6
Sep.	1.5		0.5
Oct.	0.5		1.2
Nov.	—		–0.6

Table C.2: The Growth of Monetary Aggregates 1963—77

(i) *Annually* (financial years)

	M₁	£M₃	M₃
1963/4	6.8		7.3
1964/5	3.1		5.9
1965/6	5.8		9.3
1966/7	0.6		3.6
1967/8	6.5		9.3
1968/9	2.4		7.6
1969/70	1.7		2.4
1970/1	13.7		12.3
1971/2	9.3		14.4
1972/3	10.0		27.3
1973/4	3.3		25.2
1974/5	16.7	8.5	10.7
1975/6	15.9	7.0	8.2
1976/7	9.9	7.6	9.7

(ii) *Quarterly*

		M₁	£M₃	M₃
1971	I	4.0		3.2
	II	1.3		1.6
	III	3.3		2.7
	IV	2.0		5.3
1972	I	3.3		4.7
	II	4.3		7.1
	III	1.5		4.6
	IV	4.0		7.2
1973	I	−0.3		5.7
	II	6.7		4.7
	III	−2.6		8.1
	IV	2.1		6.9
1974	I	−2.7		3.1
	II	2.9		1.8
	III	3.9		3.7
	IV	7.3		3.1
1975	I	2.7	0.8	1.1
	II			
	III			
	IV			
1976	I			
	II			
	III			
	IV			
1977	I			
	II			

(iii) *Monthly* (banking r

1971	July	
	Aug.	
	Sep.	

POSTSCRIPT

Since I delivered the manuscript of this book in October 1977, a number of developments have occurred, none of which changes the basic argument of the text. A very few factual statements are no longer correct, e.g. Mr Miller is now chairman of the 'Fed'. Of more importance, the Bank of England has now suspended the MLR formula and fixes and announces the rate overtly. Previously it had the power to override the formula but normally determined the rate indirectly by signals to the Discount Market; in the text this was compared to a 'fig-leaf'.

Regrettably, the fears expressed in Chapter 8 that the money supply was in danger of getting out of control have been realised. Growth of £M₃ in 1977-8 was over 16 per cent compared to the 9-13 per cent target. All too reminiscent of 1971-2, the summer and autumn of 1977 were a crucial turning point in monetary mismanagement. The authorities compounded their errors by complacency in spring 1978. This experience clearly strengthens the case for a new system of control. Two minor theses of the book have also been reinforced. Once more successful operation of the control system required earlier reactions than the authorities were capable of. Secondly, the poor quality of UK monetary statistics was re-emphasised by the official error in seasonal adjustment, which meant that growth in £M₃ was underestimated for most of the year (by about 2 per cent). This period also strengthens the case for multiple targets. Every other aggregate signalled the change much earlier than the published £M₃ figures. Thus, concentration on one target helped to conceal the dangers inherent in the official policy stance. The new target for 1978-9 is 8-12 per cent growth in £M₃ on a rolling basis' — this seems to mean that the target will be reassessed regularly rather than in the US sense of having a target to meet every month.

Finally the Bank of England evidence on the secondary banking crash to the Wilson Committee has confirmed all the author's criticisms of the Bank and has suggested that his scepticism concerning the skill used in launching the lifeboat was more justified than eulogies recorded elsewhere. The authorities are trying to regain control of the situation; whether they will succeed is not clear.

INDEX